The

ROUND

of My Life

COMPILED BY DALE CONCANNON

HEADLINE

To Robert Aziz

Your golfing efforts I welcome

Your knowledge of sporting trivia I envy

Your topspin forehand I would gladly buy

But, above all, your friendship I value

First published in 1998
by HEADLINE BOOK PUBLISHING

10 9 8 7 6 5 4 3 2 1

British Library Cataloguing in Publication Data
Concannon, Dale
The round of my life
1.Golf
I.Title
796.3'52

ISBN 0 7472 1994 X

Typeset in Great Britain by
Letterpart Limited
Reigate, Surrey

Designed by Grahame Dudley

Printed and bound in Italy by Lego S.p.A.

HEADLINE BOOK PUBLISHING
A division of Hodder Headline PLC
338 Euston Road
London NW1 3BH

Acknowledgements
The author would like to extend his grateful thanks to the following people:
David Begg; Jim Elkins, Benson and Hedges; Guy Whittings, IMG; Sergio Gomez; Andrew Chandler, ISM; Gordon Simpson; Sylvonne Bailey, Hodder and Stoughton; Scott Tolley, Golden Bear Inc.; Mark Garrod, Golf Writers Association; Roddy Carr, Amen Corner; Alistair Johnson, IMG (USA); Maria Acasia, Amen Corner; Ken Brown, Sky Sports; Matthew Harris, Golf Picture Library; John Simpson; Steve Beddow; Peter Oosterhuis; Richard Dodd; Renton Laidlaw; John Hopkins; Phil Pilley; The Emirates Golf Club, Dubai; Bob Warters, Editor *Golf Weekly*; Colin Callander, Editor *Golf Monthly*; Pete Masters, Editorial Director *Golf World*; Jock Howard, *Golf World*; Ken Schofield, Executive Director PGA European Tour; Valerie Steele and Julie Medlock, PGA European Tour; Mitchell Platts, PGA European Tour; Liz Kahn; Gaston Barras, Canon European Masters; David Clarke, Editor *Golf World*; Colin Snape, The Warwickshire; Herbert Warren Wind; Percy Huggins; Christina Steinmann; Max Faulkner; Lauren St John; Guy Faulkner; Rosemary Anstey; Linda Milton, *Golf Weekly*; Ian Marshall, Headline Books; Tim McNulty and Kathy Widick, United States LPGA; John Paramour, PGA European Tour; Walter Mechilli; Phil, Gill and Jan, Sheldon Golf Picture Library.

Select Bibliography
My Greatest Day in Golf by Darsie L Darsie. Alvin Redman Publishers.
Seve: The Biography by Lauren St John. Corgi Books.
Golfing Greats by Gordon Simpson. Sportsprint, Edinburgh.
Jack Nicklaus: My Story with Ken Bowden. Ebury Press. Imprint of Random House UK Ltd.
Great Opens by Michael Hobbs. David & Charles Ltd.
Golf's Greatest by Ross Goodner. Simon & Schuster.
Life with Lyle by David Musgrove and John Hopkins. Heinemann Kingswood.

Photographs
All photographs in this book are from the Phil Sheldon Golf Picture Library and the archive photographs are from the Dale Concannon Golf History Collection at the Phil Sheldon Golf Picture Library.

Contents

F o r e w o r d

If someone came up to me and asked, 'What was the round of your life?', I would struggle. Like most amateur golfers I've had my occasional moments of brilliance but picking out one particular round is a tough one. After all, how do you decide? Would it be your best ever score, or the round that won you the monthly medal? How difficult must it be then if you are a top professional with a string of major titles to your name. One can only imagine the choices involved. Perhaps that is why this is such a fascinating idea for a book.

When pressed, I have to reluctantly admit my greatest round came almost three decades ago at Alloa Golf Club in Scotland. Playing my home course, I had just turned 15 and was holding down a 6 handicap. Par was a stiff 70 and I managed to shoot this particular day a one-under par score of 69. Imagine my delight as a young teenager managing to break par for the very first time. Everything just clicked. I can still recall many of the individual strokes and despite starting with a bogey, finishing with a bogey and even going out-of-bounds at the 12th, the memory of that round remains as pleasurable today as it did then. In fact, the only thing that detracts from it is the sobering realisation that the best score I've had at Alloa in all the years since is a 71!

Having been born and bred in Scotland, it is probably not surprising that golf has always played an important part in my life. Indeed, I remember picking up my first club about the same time I kicked my first football. Yet in many ways golf was always my first love. Like most boys I thought nothing of playing three rounds a day in the summer months and not always on the same course. I even remember giving up football twice because it interfered with my golf practice!

I was also a great follower of the game. In July, I would sit glued to the television whenever the Open came around enjoying everything about it. The spectacle, the drama, the cut and thrust of tournament play, and like many Scottish youngsters I longed to be part of it. For me, this was a glamorous and exciting world and despite the success I would later enjoy in my chosen career, I have often wondered how different things would have been if I had decided to ply my trade at St Andrews instead of Anfield. Yet one brief look at some of the great rounds outlined in the pages of this book has cured me of that fantasy forever.

Almost without exception, every round was put together under the most severe pressure imaginable. And while playing in a Cup final at Wembley in front of a full house of screaming fans has its own pressures, at least there are another ten players around to dig you out of a hole if

things are going badly. Reading through some of the greatest rounds in major championship history, it soon becomes obvious that the players themselves were very much alone.

While I have witnessed many of the rounds described from the comfort of my armchair, I count myself privileged to have been there at Turnberry in 1977 to watch perhaps the greatest round of all – the so-called 'Duel in the Sun' between Jack Nicklaus and Tom Watson. I had just signed for Liverpool from Partick Thistle and it was my second ever visit to the Open Championship – the first had come at St Andrews in 1970. I was there to watch my long-time hero, Jack Nicklaus. For me the 'Golden Bear' was always the greatest and, while I knew about his clashes with the legendary Arnold Palmer in the early sixties, he seemed to symbolise everything that was wonderful about the game.

I followed him on the opening day when he shot 68 and was rooting for him in the last round. Living every stroke he played that day, I thrilled to his early birdies and felt concern when Watson came back to take the lead with just a few holes remaining. On the final green, I remember feeling heartbroken when the younger man tapped in his winning putt after Jack had rolled one in from 30 feet for a birdie. In some odd way, it is quite comforting to know that Tom Watson has chosen that round as the round of his life.

I am sure that many of you will have similar memories as you read through the pages of this wonderful book. Whether it is Seve or Woosie, or Nick Faldo, as you select your own favourites and relive their greatest round with them, I am sure that all the drama and excitement of each tournament will come flooding back. I, for one, certainly remember feeling absolutely elated when Big Jack came through on the final day to win the Masters in 1986.

This book has everything for the golf fan. Many of the selections will surprise and in some cases astound the reader. But what I find especially interesting is how none of the professionals picked a Ryder Cup round. Considering all the drama which surrounds the biennial event it came as a real surprise. Then again, it just seems what most golfers knew all along. That golf, unlike soccer, is an individual game after all.

Finally, I am delighted that the Alder Hey Rocking Horse Appeal will benefit from sales of this book. It remains a charity close to my heart from my old Liverpool days.

Enjoy the book.

ALAN HANSEN

Introduction

The best ideas for a book are often the simplest ones. So, when I was asked to contact thirty of the world's top golfers to find out which had been their most memorable round, I naturally jumped at the chance. Then the doubts set in. Having interviewed many of the players in the past it struck me how hard it would be nailing them down to one year, one tournament and ultimately one choice. After all, how do you approach legendary professionals like Jack Nicklaus or Arnold Palmer and ask them to select one round from all the great ones they have played throughout their careers?

In the end I need not have worried. The straightforward nature of the question brought nothing but a positive response from the players I spoke to. Instead of reacting to my journalistic enquiry 'What is the round of your life?' with the expected answer 'the next one', they found the question intriguing and in many cases gave their time most generously. Perhaps inevitably, some asked for time to consider an appropriate answer. But, to my constant surprise, the next time I approached them they actually *had* thought about it and often in some detail. I began to wonder why no one had asked this most simple of questions before.

In a year-long journey which took in Dubai, Washington DC, Wentworth and Troon, the 'rounds' themselves also offered a revealing insight into the golfers concerned. While the occasional player would change his mind from one meeting to the next, it surprised me just how few selected their lowest tournament score. Indeed, many of the rounds selected for this book were not even the best score that particular week! I found that, unlike most amateurs who would sell their favourite putter for the chance to shoot 62 around Wentworth, like Tony Jacklin did in the World Matchplay one year, top professionals *expect* to make low scores every week.

It soon became obvious that finishing in the top thirty of a tournament by making a 63 instead of a 69 actually meant very little in terms of that one special round. It was soon obvious that, in golf, the particular tournament you win counts a great deal more than the number of minor titles you end up with. By far the most important are the four majors, and without doubt the final selections reflect this to a greater or lesser degree. But what other vital elements made each round special? The answer to that question is what made this such a fascinating book to research.

For many of the great players featured in this book it was often the circumstances in which the round was played which made it so memorable. In most cases the choice represents a pivotal moment in the golfer's career – even a crisis in some cases – and it was often this which gave the round its drama and importance. That is why I have taken such pains to outline the golfer's life up to that point and in some cases beyond. Only then does the relevance of the round become clear. As one European Ryder Cup player told me, 'You really have to know what I went through to know how much that round meant to me.'

Compiling this book also offered me the unique opportunity to delve into some rounds which I had witnessed first hand. While too young to remember Max Faulkner's Open win at Royal Portrush in 1951, I was privileged to be at Turnberry in 1977 to watch the youthful Tom Watson go head-to-head with the mighty Jack Nicklaus. It was my first Open Championship and one which would go down as one of the greatest in the event's long history. For me it was a time of wonder and, even though accommodation consisted of a leaking tent in a nearby farmer's field, nothing can dim the memory of that wonderful final round.

For those following the action that day had everything. Set against the scenic backdrop of a sun-baked Ailsa course, the 'Duel in the Sun' had all the ingredients for a classic encounter from the start. Having battled away for three scorching days two of the greatest professionals of all time were matched together in the final round of the Open with the title up for grabs. They were clear of the field and both were playing at their absolute peak, so it was always going to be something special.

The record books show that Watson came out on top with a magnificent 65 to Nicklaus' 66. But I was still curious whether or not it would be his choice for this book. Of course there were other possibilities. Only three months earlier Watson had defeated his closest rival in similar circumstances to win the Masters at Augusta. The same circumstances applied to the United States Open at Pebble Beach in 1982 when he chipped in so dramatically from off the 17th green during the final round to secure victory. So perhaps Watson's decision was not an easy one after all.

Having arranged to meet the eight-times major winner during one of the practice days for the 1997 Open at Royal Troon I became filled with a sudden anxiety. While there was absolutely no doubt in my mind that Turnberry represented his finest golfing hour, perhaps there was in his. Mulling over the likely possibilities, I asked myself, was it really possible that after sharing that emotional roller coaster with him two decades before that he would choose another round? The answer when it came was a definite no. For someone who values the traditions of the game so highly, there was never going to be any other choice. For Watson, beating the 'greatest golfer who ever lived' to win the Open Championship in the country of golf's birth was never going to be second best to anything. In fact he seemed quite irritated when I suggested there might be some other possibilities.

Not long after that experience I was asked to write a magazine article entitled 'The greatest round ever played?' In it I attempted to set out the reasons why I believe that no other round has ever come close to the brilliance displayed that day at Turnberry. Not surprisingly that great round won hands-down in the readers' poll conducted by the magazine a few weeks later. Thanks for the memory Tom.

I took a similar pleasure in all the rounds featured in this book. Each one had its own story to tell and the detail behind some of the great championship-winning rounds made them even more fascinating. As each player described the various twists, turns and moments of good fortune encountered along the way I began to realise how much there was to the experience of being a top-class golfer.

Take Davis Love III, for example. When first approached about his most memorable round, this amiable American struggled to better his 62 during the Kapalua Invitational in Hawaii in 1996. Sounding a little embarrassed he asked that I contact him again later in the year. A few weeks later I did – straight after he won the 1997 United States PGA Championship at Winged Foot! There was certainly no problem getting him to choose a round that day.

Of course there was the odd surprise along the way. For some, like Colin Montgomerie and José-María Olazábal, it was not a major championship which inspired their final choice. There were also no Ryder Cup rounds selected which perhaps confirms what most of us knew all along – that while team golf may be dramatic and exciting, golf is an individual sport at heart. In some cases the player's recall was sketchy but, whatever the round, the fascination lies in the selection itself and the reasons behind it.

Without doubt, each of the chapters taught me something new about the player concerned. Being able to reminisce about some of the greatest rounds ever played with the golfers themselves is a privilege I shall not forget. Yet this book is not only a tribute to the players concerned, but to the game in general. Like most golf writers I am a fan at heart, and while I interviewed enough top professionals to fill this book twice over, I wanted the thirty players finally featured to reflect golf as a whole. But whatever the final choice – European or American, past or present, male or female – they are all wonderful golfers. And no matter who your personal favourite is, I hope you enjoy reading about golf at its very best.

DALE CONCANNON

AUGSBURG
GERMANY
1998

Severiano

Ballesteros

65 in the final round of the Open
Championship at Royal Lytham & St Annes,
Lancashire, 14–17 July 1988.

Without a major win since the 1984 Open Championship at St Andrews, Seve Ballesteros returned to Royal Lytham & St Annes, the scene of his first Open triumph in 1979. Back then he was named the 'car park' champion after his amazing ability to make birdies from seemingly impossible positions. In 1988, he returned slightly older and wiser, and certainly more in control of his flamboyant golf game. Going into the final round trailing tournament leader Nick Price by two, Seve produced possibly the most disciplined display of his career. In a wonderful exhibition of shot making, his 65 finally eased the Zimbabwean into second place, despite Price having shot a highly creditable 69. A compelling contest throughout, it remains among the most talked about final rounds in Open Championship history.

No golfer has come closer in modern times to attaining mythical status than Seve Ballesteros.

Having made the impossible seem possible so often throughout his career his fans actually came to believe that nothing was beyond him. In the 1997 Ryder Cup at Valderrama, his desire for glory was no less evident as he prowled about the Spanish course driving his team on to victory against the United States. That was as captain but the charismatic Spaniard will best be remembered for his playing feats. As the winner of five major championships, including three Opens and two US Masters, his impact on the European game is incalculable. The first professional after Tony Jacklin to break the American stranglehold on the game's top prizes, Seve paved the way for others like Faldo, Lyle, Woosnam, Langer and Olazábal to follow.

For all the lows of recent years, Seve Ballesteros remains the most naturally gifted golfer of his generation. Brilliant yet often controversial, his unique brand of swashbuckling golf inspired millions to take up the game in the eighties. At his peak Seve probably had the greatest following of any golfer since Arnold Palmer twenty years before. Popular wherever he played, fans identified with the great passion he exhibited for the game, for he was never one to hide his emotions. His fans pulled for him when he was in contention, celebrated when he won, and felt real sadness when he lost out.

Yet even at his imperious best he probably hit more poor shots in one tournament than Jack Nicklaus did in an entire season. And while his best days now seem behind him, Seve remains as fiercely competitive as he was when he finished joint runner-up to Johnny Miller in the 1976 Open at Royal Birkdale. Back then he was a fresh-faced teenager with a captivating smile and fearless golf game. Today problems with his back have taken their toll, but the effect he has on his fellow players is still quite revealing.

'No matter how bad he's playing,' said Tom Lehman after their singles match in the 1995 Ryder Cup at Oak Hill, 'or how much you think you have him nailed down, you just can't take your eyes off him. He sort of looks over and mentally says, "You better watch this next shot – it could be the greatest shot you will ever see." '

For the past two decades, overcoming the odds has been Seve's stock-in-trade. Often wild off the tee but an acknowledged genius around the greens, he would often come through to win in the most unlikely circumstances. At Royal Lytham in 1979, he won his first Open Championship after hitting a drive into a car park on the final day. Yet that was always a large part of his appeal. Dashing and unpredictable, Ballesteros won countless tournaments because 'three of those and one of them counts four' and he knew it.

After making his European Tour debut back in 1976 Ballesteros has racked up an impressive list of 'firsts'. These include being the first European to win the Masters; the first European to reach number one in the world rankings; the first Spaniard to win the Open Championship; the first player to win six European Order of Merit titles; the first European to win over 72 events worldwide. The list goes on. So which round out of all the great ones he has played does Seve Ballesteros select as the round of his life?

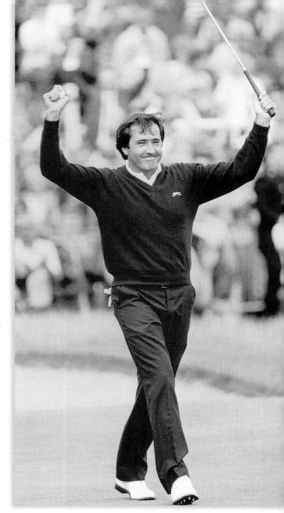

A triumphant Seve Ballesteros on the final green at Royal Lytham in 1988.

Choosing one round out of my career and saying that round was better than this one is very difficult. Each one is special for different reasons. At the Open in '76 I finished second with Jack Nicklaus and it was a very proud moment for me sitting next to such a great player at the prize giving. Winning my first Open at Royal Lytham was also very special not only for me but my family as well. It was the same for my two Masters. My brother Manuel was there when I became the youngest player ever to win in 1980. Then when I won again three years later, my father was there to see me win. He had seen me play in Spain many times but it was the first time he ever watched me play in America.

But I think any time you win a major it is very satisfying. If I was to pick one tournament it would probably be St Andrews in '84. Holing that putt on 18 to win the Open with Tom Watson playing his best behind me is something I will never forget. It is funny, but every time I watch the video at home, it looks like my putt will stop on the lip, so I always make a little nudge with my shoulders and finally it goes in. But there my final round was very good but not fantastic. No, if I choose one it would be my last round against Nick Price at Royal Lytham in 1988. To win two Opens on the same course is not very usual. Also I played such a great round to win [65], and that is why it will always be special to me.

Severiano Ballesteros Sota was born on 9 April 1957 in Pedrena, northern Spain. The youngest of four brothers, he picked up his first club at the age of seven – a rusting 3-iron head with a stick for a shaft. Part of a close-knit family who lived close by the Royal Pedrena Golf Club, the young Seve spent much of his free time hitting stones along the beach at nearby Santander Bay. When the shaft broke he would seek out another, cut it to the right length and continue on. It was in this way that he developed the baffling array of shots for which he would become famous.

'The biggest influence on my life, my career,' he said, 'was the atmosphere where I grew up. The family home was close to the golf course in Pedrena. My father (Baldomero) was caddying, my uncle, Ramon Sota, was playing professional golf and so were all my brothers.'

Following the example of Baldomero Jnr, Manuel and Vincente, the raw but enthusiastic teenager embarked on his own professional career in early 1974. Despite having no amateur record to speak of, he competed in the Portuguese, Spanish, Madrid and French Opens backed with a $1000 sponsorship from Madrid radiologist, Cesar Campuzano. Yet his first professional round outside Spain was not all that promising. Playing at Estoril in the Portuguese Open, he shot a heart-breaking first round score of 89 – and this on his 17th birthday!

Somewhat daunted by missing the cut in each of his first four events, Ballesteros returned home to win the Spanish under-25 championship over his home course at Pedrena. Confidence restored, he used the £500 first prize to fund another assault on the European Tour. This time he had more success, finishing a highly creditable third behind Peter Oosterhuis in the Italian Open in Venice. After ending his first year in 118th place in the Order of Merit with £2,915, he looked to widen his horizons the following season.

Seve's British debut came in the 1975 PGA Championship at Royal St George's, and in typically windswept conditions he missed the cut after rounds of 79 and 84. While he would get over his first bitter taste of links golf to win three Open Championships, his record at Sandwich in the two decades which followed shows what little affection he has retained for the Kent course. Yet it was his first experience of a big European event and he was determined to take full advantage of some of the benefits it offered to a rising young golfer.

I remember there was a guy from Dunlop who was giving out free balls on the practice ground. I didn't speak English so I say to my brother Manuel, 'You know this is a very difficult course and I need plenty golf balls.' So he introduced me to this man and tells him I am a very good golfer, so he will give me some to play with during the week. So he takes out a dozen and gives me a box of three balls. I say to Manuel, 'This is good. That will be enough for six holes; what about the rest of the tournament?' So he ask the man again and he says to me real serious, 'If you make the cut on Saturday I will give three more, OK?' That shows how much things have changed on tour. These days I get six dozen per week!

By that stage, Seve was still relatively unknown outside his native Spain, despite doubling his previous year's prize money on his way to 26th position in the Order of Merit in 1975. Within twelve months all that changed in spectacular fashion after his wonderful performance at the Open Championship at Royal Birkdale. In a top-class field which included players like Jack Nicklaus, Johnny Miller, Gary Player and the holder, Tom Watson, Seve went into the final round leading the tournament.

Playing in the swashbuckling style which would later become his trademark, the slim, dark-haired Spaniard, with his matinée idol looks, captured the hearts of the British golfing public that week. On the final day, huge crowds flocked around him as he threatened to break the American stranglehold on the tournament. With no home player in contention, the anticipation and pressure was enormous. Yet as far as the 19-year-old Severiano Ballesteros was concerned, the chance to compete against the very best players in the world was just what he had dreamed of.

Paired in the last match with Johnny Miller, the latest golden boy of US golf, Ballesteros had no other game plan than to go for broke. They had already played together the day before, with the more experienced Miller getting the better of

their first encounter, though he was still two strokes behind going into the final day. The Californian was asked what he thought of his young opponent's game. Perhaps a little frustrated at his inability to shake-off the bold and determined young Spaniard, he commented, 'You need patience over here. You cannot throw everything at the pin.'

Delight as Seve's chip from the side of the 18th green in the final round slips by the hole leaving him a winning putt from no more than a few inches.

With Manuel translating throughout the week because of his brother's broken English, Seve gave his own answer to the waiting reporters, 'I am still young. When I am older there will be time to be careful.'

On the final day, Seve played well but lacked the Houdini-like touch he had employed to get himself out of trouble earlier in the week. He was still launching himself at each drive with absolute abandon, but the outrageous luck which Miller accused him of having in the third round finally ran out. A double-bogey at the tough 468-yard par-4 6th, followed by a disastrous treble-bogey at the par-4 11th effectively ended his chances.

Having watched his young opponent fall out of contention in the opening nine holes, Miller to his credit had put an arm round Seve's shoulder and encouraged him to keep trying since second place was still within his reach. As they walked towards the 13th tee, the black cloud which had pervaded the Spaniard's world suddenly lifted. 'I was feeling bad because he was struggling,' said the American. 'He's such a pusher, you know, he's so competitive. And I was basically just saying, "Why don't you regroup and get it together?" '

For Ballesteros, those words of encouragement made all the difference. He was now six strokes behind Miller, but runner-up in the Open was something worth fighting for. So just as the golfing pundits were writing him off, Seve came back strongly with three birdies and an eagle in the last six holes for joint second with Jack Nicklaus. And, perhaps typically, Seve saved the best for last. Pin-high on the par-5 18th in two, he was left with an impossible chip over sand to a green hardened by the July sun. With seemingly little option other than floating a shot onto the middle of the green then hoping to hole an impossibly long putt for the birdie he needed, he squeezed the ball between two greenside bunkers with a low running chip that skilfully used the natural contours of the green to bring it no more than four feet away from the pin. It was a stroke of sheer brilliance that Seve still describes as among the finest shots he has ever made.

Seve acknowledged the lasting applause of the Birkdale crowds with the widest of smiles. He had finally arrived in the big time and the plaudits were not long in coming. Top coach John Jacobs, who was watching the action on television, commented afterwards, 'This boy is a genius. If he ever learns to play, he will be unbeatable.' As the dust settled on the famous links the Open may have had a new champion in Johnny Miller, but perhaps more significantly European golf now had a potential world beater in Severiano Ballesteros.

Building on his performance at Royal Birkdale, Ballesteros recorded his first Tour victory in the Dutch Open only weeks later. Another win at the Trophée Lancôme in Paris later in the season went some way to making him number one in Europe for 1976. It was an incredible feat and even being conscripted into the Spanish army in early 1977 failed to halt his progress. Holding on to top spot in the European Order of Merit for the next two years he spent much of his time giving lessons to high-ranking officers at a small 9-hole course outside Madrid, and was even given extended leave to compete both in Europe and in the US Masters. It was probably among the happiest periods of his life – and almost certainly his fittest.

The next few years confirmed his stature as a world-class player with tournament victories in Japan, New Zealand and Australia. In 1978, he made his all-important United States PGA Tour breakthrough by winning the Greater Greensboro Open at a stroll.

As number one, Ballesteros was expected to be a key figure in the first European Ryder Cup team to play the Americans at the Greenbrier in September 1979. Having won the Open Championship at Royal Lytham only eight weeks before, much was expected of the young Spaniard. Perhaps too much as things turned out. Partnered in the foursomes and fourball matches with fellow countryman Antonio Garrido, Seve did not find the overall experience a pleasant one. As a war of words threatened to rage between European team captain John Jacobs, and team members Ken Brown and Mark James, the Spanish pair contributed only a single point from the six available. The media was quick to criticise them both, with the brunt falling on the hapless Ballesteros.

Two years later with the biennial event switching to Walton Heath in Surrey, Seve once again had his troubles with the Ryder Cup. Having added the US Masters to his growing list of majors in 1980, he seemingly had the credentials for selection but amazingly had not been picked even though he was available to play. Understandably, this controversial decision made headlines on both sides of the Atlantic. The problem, it seemed, was the thorny subject of appearance money, an issue which was to haunt Ballesteros throughout a large part of his career.

In the early eighties many European tournaments depended on attracting big-name Americans to boost the quality of the field. Sponsors insisted on it and were often prepared to pay financial inducements to players like Tom Weiskopf, Lee Trevino and Johnny Miller to guarantee their appearance. Ballesteros, who spent most of his time beating such players on their home turf, understandably thought that, if they were worth the money, so was he. Unfortunately, the embryonic European Tour and its secretary, Ken Schofield, believed otherwise. Yet so strong were Seve's convictions that he competed in only seven European Tour events that season. It even reached the point where Seve refused to pay his Tour membership fee of £50.

John Jacobs, who was Ryder Cup captain once again, had even rung Seve in America just weeks before the team selection was due and asked him to reconsider. Desperate to have his best player available Jacobs tried time and again to settle the affair. Stubborn to the last, Seve failed to meet him even halfway. He was asked to compete in the last two selection tournaments, the Carrolls Irish Open at Portmarnock and the Benson and Hedges at Fulford, but remained in the United States without further explanation. A few days later the decision was made. Seve was out.

With accusations of greed in the golfing press, and the suggestion that he had not supported the European Tour as well as he might, Ballesteros' reputation had been tarnished for the first time in his career. He would return to the Ryder Cup fold at PGA National in 1983, an older and, perhaps, wiser man.

Thankfully, the break in 1981 did not dull his lasting passion for the event. Indeed, in recent years Seve has been the Ryder Cup's greatest supporter and, along with Tony Jacklin, has breathed life into an event which had looked in terminal decline. From his legendary playing partnership with fellow Spaniard, José-María Olazábal, to his triumph as winning Ryder Cup captain at Valderrama, no name has been written larger in the match's long history than that of Severiano Ballesteros.

Away from team events, Seve's individual career blossomed in the eighties. Between 1976 and 1986 he won 52 tournaments, was second 20 times, third 18 times, and missed only four cuts. Dominating the Order of Merit, he was the first professional to break through the £1 million prize money barrier, with year end positions from 1976 to 1988 that included five firsts, two seconds and two thirds.

After he won his second US Masters in 1983, and second Open Championship at St Andrews in 1984, Seve sat proudly at the top of the world rankings. The following year would be equally successful with five European wins, including his fourth World Matchplay title in four years. Seemingly set to dominate the rest of the decade, confidence for Seve Ballesteros was at a career high. Yet one small lapse in concentration in the final stages of the 1986 Masters was to have repercussions for years to come.

After finishing joint runner-up to Ben Crenshaw in 1985, Ballesteros had been in prime position to win his third Masters in '86. Playing the par-5 15th on the final day, he was leading by two strokes and strolling to victory. Having hit the perfect drive, he seemed in good shape to birdie the hole and gain another shot on his nearest challenger, Jack Nicklaus. Perhaps scenting his third Masters victory, he had shaken hands with his brother and caddie, Vincente, after making eagle on the par-5 13th only minutes before. 'I thought when I eagled the 13th, I was the champion,' he said afterwards.

Standing in the middle of the 15th fairway, both Seve and his playing partner Tom Watson had been forced to wait while Nicklaus stalked a putt for his own eagle. In typical fashion, the Golden Bear had refused to play until the noise around the green had quietened down to a respectful hush. Minutes passed away before he eventually missed. Tapping in for the birdie which halved the margin between himself and Ballesteros, he strode confidently off to the next.

Like Watson, Ballesteros is a quick player by nature and the delay obviously had its effect. Lining up his 4-iron approach from 210 yards out, his swing looked a little uncommitted and the result was disaster. Pulled a few yards left, the ball danced briefly across the surface of the lake guarding the front of the green, before finally sinking out of sight. Minutes later Seve walked off the green with a bogey six. Still numb with disbelief, he three-putted the 17th for another bogey and it was all over.

Ballesteros had lost tournaments before but this was somehow different. Like all the best players he had the ability to raise his game a notch when the pressure was really on. Confidence was his life blood and the air of invincibility which he carried onto the golf course like a shield had rarely been dented. But at Augusta that year, not only did he fail to put pressure on his closest rivals, but had even, dare we say it, choked.

For the temperamental Spaniard, it was inconceivable that such a thing had happened. For the remainder of the 1986 season, he continued in normal fashion eventually finishing top of the Order of Merit with earnings of £259,275. His slip at Augusta apparently forgotten, his wins in the British Masters, Irish Open, Monte Carlo Open, French Open, Dutch Open and Trophée Lancôme, gave him his best ever season in Europe.

'I don't want to take anything away from Jack,' Seve said about the US Masters result, 'he played fantastic golf. But I think for me not to win was almost a miracle under all the circumstances. Eight out of ten times I would have won. It was *destino*.'

This had been a favourite expression of Ballesteros' throughout his great days in the eighties, but this time it glossed over what had been a deeply upsetting moment in his career. Like acid burning slowly through metal, the damage had been done and the following year would see not only a massive change in his golf, but his personality as well.

'For a while we all felt that Seve, under the severest pressure, would always pull off the magical shot,' said John Jacobs some years later. 'I think something of that left him when he dumped it in the water at Augusta.'

Something that did leave him throughout the '87 season was his ability to win golf tournaments. In an inexplicable year-long drought, Seve's only victory came in the Suze Open at Cannes-Mougins. Seve had been forced to play more tournaments in Europe because of his long-standing wrangle with the United States PGA Tour over the number of appearances he was required to make and he began to struggle badly. Worse still, tournaments began to slip away where before they would have certainly been added to his collection of titles.

Sadly for Ballesteros this included the 1987 Masters, where missing a short putt on the 10th green took him out of a three-man play-off with Larry Mize, the eventual winner, and Greg Norman. Driven back to the clubhouse by Ken Schofield, the Spaniard had sobbed uncontrollably. The experience brought back memories of the previous year, and proved the catalyst that exposed his previously hidden torment. Apart from in his golfing difficulties, Seve had continued to suffer greatly from the loss of his beloved father, Baldomero, who had succumbed to cancer in March 1986. The Masters had meant a lot to both of them and for Seve this was one heartbreak too far.

Still too proud to request any special treatment from the United States PGA Tour, who restricted him to playing only in the Masters and US Open, Seve cut a solitary figure for the remainder of 1987. In the months that followed, the pressure began to take its toll and by the Open Championship at Muirfield, where Nick Faldo emerged triumphant, things had changed for the worse. Gone was the smiling, charismatic and youthful figure so beloved by the public. In his place, was a morose, brooding individual, who stalked the fairways with little apparent interest in anything. Yet despite this he would eventually finish the season in a highly creditable sixth place in the European Money List with earnings of £172,711.

Even before the 1988 season began, there was some speculation about Seve being past his best. Four years had passed since he had won a major championship and despite his coming close to winning the Masters, the US Open and US PGA on more than one occasion, the knives were out. Still fourth in the world rankings, Seve's brilliance over the past few years had made a rod for his own back. People expected more from him and, while no one really doubted his competitive spirit, there were those who questioned whether or not he had the nerve to win again.

That summer at the Open Championship at Royal Lytham & St Annes, Seve Ballesteros would finally give them the answer.

Returning to the scene of his greatest triumph had an immediate and revitalising effect on Seve. Almost like returning home he felt something good would happen if only he could stay in contention. This was his course and long before arriving at Royal Lytham he had spent hours back in Pedrena looking at videos of his 1979 Open victory and searching for inspiration. On Monday 18 July, a day not even scheduled to be part of the tournament, he finally found it – a round so special, that he would later select it as the 'Round of his Life'.

Even before the Open got underway there had been a number of changes in Seve's outlook. In March, he had won his first tournament for eleven months in the Mallorcan Open at Santa Ponsa, beating his countryman José-María Olazábal into second place by six strokes. Exactly a month later he beat Greg Norman, among others, at the first extra hole of a four-way play-off for the Buick Classic, his first victory in the United States for three years. Another important change was his choice of new caddie for the season, Ian Wright.

Wright had been employed since the PGA Championship at Wentworth in May and his calm, down-to-earth attitude appeared to have rubbed off on Seve in the two months they had been together. Far more relaxed than he had been in previous months, Seve's decision to employ someone other than one of his brothers was seen as a positive step. Only the year before Seve and Vincente had rowed during the final round of the United States PGA – a tournament Seve was leading at the time!

Lytham on the Lancashire coast had been cold and miserably wet in the run-up to the championship. Yet Seve had already outlined to Wright his plan for tackling the course in minute detail. Wright, who had only caddied for journeyman players like Brian Marchbank and Carl Mason in the past, must have listened in absolute wonder as his boss explained with absolute certainty how he was going to win the Open. When the tournament opened on Thursday 14 July 1988, Seve set about putting his plan into action.

Playing under a leaden sky, Ballesteros began with a birdie on the opening par-3, and went to the turn in just 30 shots to grab the early lead. Finishing with a 67, including two penalty strokes for unplayable lies, Ballesteros sat proudly at the top of the first round leader board. On a cold, breezy day, only two other players had managed to break 70, the American Brad Faxon and the Australian Wayne Grady.

'This is my best start in a major since the 1980 Masters,' said a happy Seve at the post-match press interview. 'Last year at Muirfield, I had to wait 28 holes before I get my first birdie. This time it took one.'

Relaxed and more approachable than he had been for any major championship in years, Seve added a second round 71 for a halfway total of four under par, one stroke behind Zimbabwean, Nick Price. Seve was asked what score would win the Open, 'The course is very difficult. Right now, I would settle for a couple of 71s over the last two rounds. I think four under par will be good enough to win.'

In the third round, scheduled for the Saturday, the rain which had threatened for most of the week finally arrived. With holes around the turn having lakes instead of greens, the day's play was abandoned just after midday. Even though some of the early players had completed large parts of their round, all scores were deemed void – which was devastating news for American Hubert Green, who started the day at five over par and had recovered to level before being called off the course.

After long deliberation by the R&A Championship Committee, it was decided that play would be extended to 36 holes on the Sunday. Then, as more rain sleeted down in the afternoon, it was announced that, for the first time in its long history, the Open would be carried over to a Monday finish. So, with the course still bearing the marks of the previous day's flooding, play began in earnest on Sunday morning. The day was still dank and dismal, and the entire atmosphere was strangely muted. It was usually a day of high drama but for the thousands who turned up to watch the third round action it was difficult to get excited if you were unsure about seeing it to a finish.

Yet finish they did with Nick Faldo moving firmly into contention with 68, as did Sandy Lyle with a best-of-the-day score of 67. Ballesteros, partnered by Nick Price and Craig Stadler, had his adventures on the way to 68, including one shot where he hit the ball six inches with the back of his sand-wedge! Seve finished level with Faldo on 206, with both former champions remaining two strokes adrift of Price going into the last round. Still confident about his chances for the following day Seve said, 'It will be tough in the final round, and the winner will be the man who can best take the pressure. I have coped with it before, I don't see why I can't do it again.' Then maybe thinking back to his most recent disappointments he added, 'But you never know.'

Wearing the same lucky blue sweater and white shirt that he had worn in both 1979 and 1984, Ballesteros set about making his dream come true. Paired with the two Nicks, Faldo and Price, he felt confident that this would be his day. The early pressure was firmly on Price with three former Open champions, Ballesteros, Faldo and Lyle, breathing down his neck. After all had made par figures to the 6th, Price's lead was halved to one stroke when both Ballesteros and Faldo made birdie.

At the 7th, a long par-5, Price made a birdie only to find he had lost ground to the rampant Spaniard who made a glorious eagle. In fact, if Seve's arrow-straight long iron from over 210 yards had been a few inches left, he might have bagged himself an albatross. Then, in what would later be seen as a turning point in his fortunes, Faldo struck what seemed to be an equally good second to the 7th only to find a large bank between his ball and the hole. Three putts later he had lost the initiative. And with Ballesteros and Price playing quite supremely throughout the rest of the round, there was little opportunity for Faldo to break into what increasingly seemed like a two-man show.

'It became almost a matchplay situation then,' said Price afterwards. 'Although I tried to stick to the game plan that had got me there, he [Ballesteros] has the wonderful ability, like all great players, to elevate his game one notch.'

Holing his eagle putt on the 7th seemed to inspire Ballesteros. Grabbing his opportunity like a man whose life depended on it, he birdied the 8th, the 10th and

11th to draw ahead of Price for the first time. Then a bogey on the 12th dropped him back into a share of the lead and the roller-coaster ride which had begun back at the 6th was now truly under-way.

In what proved a wonderful exhibition of iron play over the remaining half dozen holes, the affable Nick Price more than held his own. After almost holing his second to the 13th, he had tapped in for birdie only to find Seve holing a 20-foot putt to match him. Like two sharp and agile middleweight boxers, each man looked to gain some advantage over the other, but without any success at first. In the punch and counter punch of the final round, the most telling blow did not come until the par-4 16th.

It was on this hole back in 1979 that the Ballesteros legend had really begun. Lashing the ball off the tee, his wildly sliced drive had finished among some parked cars to the right of the fairway. From this seemingly unknown part of the Lan-cashire links, he had pitched back on the green and holed his putt for an outrageous birdie. In 1988 Seve played the hole in far more disciplined fashion; a 1-iron 227 yards to the right edge of the fairway, followed by a precise short-iron approach to three inches from the pin. Price, who made a regulation par on the hole, stood and watched in awe as the Spanish wizard weaved a bit of magic.

'He struck a perfect 9-iron, I mean absolutely perfect,' Price said later. 'I looked at a replay about three weeks later and I don't know how it didn't go in because it actually came into the pin on the left and finished behind the hole on the right. So it must have lipped the cup or something. It didn't put the trophy in his hands right then and there. There were still two tough holes to go. But it sure helped his cause.'

After losing out to Tom Watson in the 1982 Open at Royal Troon, Price, like Ballesteros, was fighting his own demons about losing majors in the final round. Down by a single stroke to the Spaniard, Price stepped on to the tough par-4 17th and made the mistake of hitting his drive onto some broken ground caused by the bad weather. Somewhat relieved to obtain a free drop, he eventually recovered well to match par with Ballesteros, but it was never going to be enough and the Zimbab-wean knew it.

Coming to the final hole four under par for the round, Seve knew that a par would probably give him the title. Before the final round had even begun, Sandy Lyle predicted that level par would not be good enough to win with a score of 68 or

69 needed. While Lyle's score of 74 would ultimately give him a share of joint 7th, Price had obviously taken him at his word. Coming to the final hole needing par for 68 he knew that it would not be good enough unless Seve had some sort of disaster. But having come this far, Seve was not going to throw it away now.

Like most finishing holes in the Open Championship, the par-4 18th at Royal Lytham is a severe test. Over 430 yards long, it requires a long accurate drive into a narrow landing area surrounded by a sea of sand. Lengthened since Tony Jacklin boomed his tee-shot down the middle to win the 1969 Open, the main hazard for the drive was a small pot bunker 260 yards from the tee down the right hand side that was an almost certain dropped shot for a player who caught it – and it was exactly there Ballesteros looked to have hit his drive. The highly agitated Spaniard demanded to know if his ball had found the bunker. 'Is it past the bunker?' he asked Wright more than once. Trying to look calm, Wright told Seve what he wanted to hear, yes it had slipped past the bunker. Starting the long walk down the final hole, Seve again turned to his caddie, 'Are you sure it's past the bunker?'

Minutes later the crisis was over. Price later admitted his shock at seeing his opponent's ball had carried the bunker. Yet only moments later another chance presented itself. Playing out of scrubby rough, Seve pulled his second shot left of the green and into further heavy grass. Price knew the chances of the short-game magician taking more than two to get down were slim, but if he could just make a birdie, perhaps the pressure would tell.

In such moments, major championships are won and lost. Looking to push Ballesteros into a mistake, Price could put his second no closer than 40 feet from the flag. No longer really worried that his opponent would make birdie, Seve knew one last chip and putt would give him the title. He pushed his hands slightly ahead of the ball for the shot and it came out of its tangly lie low and fast, skidded its way up the green, and spun to a halt only inches away from the pin. There were nostalgic shades of his chip to the final green at Royal Birkdale in 1976. It was a vintage piece of Ballesteros brilliance that had the large crowd around the final green cheering for minutes after.

Moments later the tournament was all over. Nick Price finished with a disappointing three putts for 69 and Seve tapped in his putt for a magnificent round of 65, among the lowest final rounds in Open Championship history. Nick Faldo finished third after an uninspired round of 71, with Fred Couples and Gary Koch in joint fourth.

Having written his name on the famous Open trophy for the third time, Seve Ballesteros knows the importance of his win. 'I had begun to think I was finished. My confidence was down after I hit the ball into the water to lose the Masters in 1986. I was worried. But I decided all I could do was try and wait for my chance and momentum to come back. It was my turn to win.'

Some years later the Spanish maestro looked back on his 1988 Open victory in slightly more reflective mood. In an excellent biography by Lauren St John he was quoted as saying:

> Only once or twice does a man get to play so well. I knew at the time that I had reached some sort of peak, that it was a round of golf I would think fondly of for the rest of my life. I remember saying that I hoped there would be another as good, but there hasn't been. Now I think it will probably remain the best round I play.

Thomas

Björn

70 in the final round of the Loch Lomond
World Invitational at Loch Lomond Golf
Club, 19–22 September 1996.

After graduating from the PGA Challenge Tour only the year before, Thomas Björn went into the final round at the Loch Lomond World Invitational searching for his first victory in a major European event. Having been in contention since the second round, he ended the third day tied for the lead at six under par with Frenchman Jean Van de Velde. Then, showing some of the form which would later see him proclaimed Rookie of the Year for 1996, his one under par score of 70 in the final round proved just good enough for victory. His win by a single stroke over a top-class international field proved to be a breakthrough victory in the widest possible sense. Not only did he become the first Dane to win on the European Tour, but the £125,000 first prize went a long way to securing his place on the European Ryder Cup team which defeated the United States at Valderrama the following year.

As a rainsoaked Thomas Björn held the Ryder Cup aloft on the clubhouse steps of Valderrama in 1997, he could have been forgiven for thinking he had finally arrived. Having contributed to Europe's glorious final day triumph with an invaluable half in the singles against Open champion Justin Leonard, the grin he bore throughout the presentation ceremony revealed just how much it meant to him personally. Practically unknown only a year before, he had risen through the ranks of European golf to become one of the most highly rated young professionals in the world game.

At first sight the gangling 6 feet 2½ inches Danish professional looks an unlikely candidate for golfing stardom. A two-time European Tour school failure, his unorthodox cross-handed putting method, employed since his early teenage years, looked certain to break down under pressure. Even four victories on the Challenge Tour in 1995, en route to qualifying for the main circuit, had failed to convince many of his critics. Indeed, any doubts they had about his ability to win under pressure were borne out in the Scandinavian Masters in 1996 when he lost a three shot lead going into the last day. Despite finishing tied for seventh it was not the type of thing you expected from a rising European star.

Björn was clearly hugely talented, but the question still remained, how well would he perform down the final stretch of an important tournament? He was often touted as a future Ryder Cup player, but no one knew just how well his fragile putting method would stand up in such a cauldron of tension and high expectation. But the answer to those questions would be given in the final round of the inaugural Loch Lomond World Invitational in 1996. Björn's performance in holding on to beat a top-class field and record his first win on the European Tour added up to a round which he would later select as the 'Round of My Life'. As Björn himself says,

> I have no doubt which is the round of my life. The Ryder Cup at Valderrama was very special but for me personally it has to be my final round at Loch Lomond in 1996. It wasn't the first time I had competed under such pressure but it was the first time I lasted under it.

Thomas Björn arrived at Loch Lomond that Sunday morning knowing he had a great opportunity to win the tournament. Playing wonderfully controlled golf around one of the toughest courses on the European Tour, his six under par three-round total had shattered the widely held belief that no one would break par for the event. Frenchman Jean Van de Velde shared the lead and they were both four shots ahead of Australian Robert Allenby in third and home favourite Colin Montgomerie in fourth. The title looked destined for one of the two young professionals – but which one?

On taking his place in the players' changing room, Björn found a handwritten note taped to his locker from Glasgow Rangers and Denmark football international, Brian Laudrup. Looking to encourage his fellow countryman in this, the most important round of his career so far, it simply read, 'Good luck, I hope you win.' It was just the inspirational start Björn wanted.

'It really made me feel good,' said the affable Dane who later admitted that it was Brian's brother, ex-Barcelona star Michael, who was really his hero. Yet despite this, the note had the desired effect.

> I went out there and felt like a winner. I'd already learned a lot of lessons from leading the Scandinavian Masters after three rounds and then losing it on the last day. I said that if I got into the same position, I'd make sure I would not let it slip again. But I've got to admit that even though I thought I could win, I expected it to be in a smaller event. This is big and I beat some of the best players in the world.

In European terms, the Loch Lomond World Invitational event was big. The first playing of what promised to be a top-class tournament was also the first big event for the Tom Weiskopf-designed golf course that had received rave reviews since its opening only a few years earlier. Situated on the shores of the loch itself and stretching to over 7,000 yards, it had recently been voted best new course in the world by a panel of American golf writers. In one article it had even been described as the 'Augusta National of Scotland' and, while the cold weather which greeted the opening three days made it seem a million miles from sunny Georgia, there were certainly touches of the US Masters for the inaugural event.

The tempting combination of playing for a large prize fund over one of the best prepared courses in Europe had attracted a quality field, including Nick Faldo, Ian Woosnam and Colin Montgomerie. Yet while all three would mount solid challenges throughout the week, the £125,000 first prize seemed destined from early on to be fought for by some of European golf's lesser lights.

Jean Van de Velde had begun his challenge with a modest 75 but moved into contention with a superb six under par 65 on day two. An experienced campaigner, he followed this up with an equally impressive 67 early in the third day and looked to have taken control of the tournament. But after sitting at the top of the leader board for most of the day, he was joined on six under par by the relatively unknown Danish professional, Thomas Björn. Björn had led the tournament at the halfway stage at three under par after opening rounds of 70 and 69, which had prompted a mad scramble as journalists hunted through their media guides looking for information on the rookie pro from Denmark.

Inevitably most comment would focus on his rise to golfing prominence through the back door route of the PGA Challenge Tour, which up to this point had produced few potential champions of note. But whatever the story printed that Saturday, Björn would be grabbing most of the headlines come Sunday evening.

Thomas Björn showing typical style with a long iron in the final round of the 1996 Loch Lomond World Invitational.

Born in Silkeborg on 18 February 1971, Björn had picked up his first golf club at 11 years of age. He won the Danish Amateur title twice in the early nineties while also representing his country in both the European and World Team Amateur Championships. Then, despite having missed out in the PGA Tour Qualifying School in 1992, he turned pro less than a year later. Surprisingly for one so physically gifted and highly skilled, his early years in the pro game were spent struggling to earn a living.

Failure to earn his player's card for the European Tour in 1993 inevitably led to a rapid reappraisal of his situation. Having missed out twice, he now looked for some regular tournament play and turned to the newly established PGA Challenge Tour in the hope of earning an exemption to the senior Tour by finishing in the top fifteen of the Money List. It proved a good decision. The invaluable experience gained in his first season on the Challenge Tour led to four victories in his second including two in Denmark and one each in England and Switzerland.

Finishing the 1995 season as number one with earnings of £47,000 not only qualified him for the main Tour, but had marked him out as a possible star of the future. 'I knew what it took to be a winner, having done it on the Challenge Tour,' he said. 'The only thing that changed for the 1996 season was the fact I had to adapt my game to playing at a higher level.'

Building on his success, Björn approached his first full year on the main Tour in a confident frame of mind. Even before Loch Lomond, he had already achieved a measure of success after finishing tied seventh in both the Dubai Desert Classic in February and the Canon European Masters in early September. That along with his 'disappointing' seventh place in the Scandinavian Masters meant he had already earned enough to be sure of his Tour card for the following season. It was an important consideration for the Dane as he battled it out with Van de Velde, Allenby and Montgomerie in the tense final round. Any financial pressure he may have felt earlier in the season to keep his card had been removed and now he could concentrate on winning the title.

The leaders were paired together on the final day as usual, and any thoughts their more experienced pursuers might have had that Björn and Van de Velde would crumble under the weight of expectation were quickly dismissed. Reaching the turn in level par 36, they both maintained their four-stroke advantage with neither Allenby (36) or Montgomerie (35) mounting any sort of credible challenge. Both were unable to improve further, finishing third and fourth respectively with rounds of 70. Indeed the only real threat came in the unexpected shape of Jonathan Lomas,

Björn watching the action with his Ryder Cup team-mates behind the 17th green at Valderrama on the final day of the 1997 match.

whose six-birdie round of 68 would close the gap to just two strokes at one point.

Moving into the final nine holes, it was obvious that the title would go to one of the two leaders. Both were playing well, yet it was the less experienced Björn who took the upper hand. Birdies at the 13th and 14th opened up a three stroke cushion but a nervy three putt on the next green cut the lead back to two. The last three holes would be a very tense affair for the young Dane. Three pars would probably be good enough, but could he make them?

I think when you are looking to win your first tournament, it's almost the worst position to be in, needing just pars to win. I was leading by a lot going into the last few holes and knew I just had to keep hitting the fairways, hitting the greens and taking two putts. It sounds simple, but when you are out there I can tell you it's pretty damn tough.

Björn was looking red-faced with the tension and, if there was a time to crack, it would come on the 16th or 17th. Having steered his approach shot wide of the green on the 16th, he was left with a difficult chip from out of the left hand rough to save par. To his credit he executed the shot perfectly but on the 17th, a 205-yard par-3, he was immediately faced with yet another tricky chip from the fringe of the green. Once more he held his nerve managing to get up and down to save par. Then, with Van de Velde still failing to take advantage, Björn came to the last needing just par to win. So, with the tournament almost won, the Dane knew that one last solid drive off the 18th tee would make it safe.

> I think my drive on 18 was the key shot to the whole round. Even though I was leading, it is such a difficult hole you could miss the fairway and run up 6, 7 or even 8 quite easily. Standing on the tee, I just tried to convince myself that one good swing would settle everything. I knew that from the middle of the fairway I would make four and that was all I wanted to do. Looking back it was probably the best drive I have ever hit in my life, considering how nervous I felt at the time. It went off brilliantly. After that I knew I was going to win and really started to enjoy the whole atmosphere.

Now left with little more than a short iron to the final green, Thomas almost finished in the most spectacular fashion possible by nearly holing his second. It was not to be, so when he walked smiling onto the final green hard by historic Rossdhu Castle to receive the applause of the large and enthusiastic Scottish gallery he still had a little work to do. He had finished 20 feet away and could afford to take two from there for his maiden Tour victory. Sensibly, he used both his strokes. A model of consistency, his one under par round of 70 was just enough to beat off the challenge of Van de Velde who birdied the last for 71.

> I learned a lot about myself during that round. I learned that all it takes to win any tournament, maybe even a major like the Open, is going out and playing your own game. Forget what anybody else is doing and as long as you can do that under pressure you will be fine. I think maybe I choked in the past because I wasn't ready to win. Or perhaps I was not on top of my game as much as I would have liked to have been.

It was an historic moment, the first ever win by a Danish professional on the European Tour. As the evening closed in, Björn was bagpiped onto the final green to accept his first prize of £125,000. And the story does not end there. Building on his success at Loch Lomond, Björn finished 6th and 8th the following two weeks to secure his top ten place in the Ryder Cup standings. The next year he went one step further and earned enough to qualify automatically for the European side to face the Americans at Valderrama in Spain. Once there his invaluable 1½ point contribution would help secure a hard earned victory against the United States. Björn's rise has been little short of meteoric and he is now considered one of the brightest young stars in world golf.

A real case of bringing home the Danish bacon.

Fred

Couples

70 in the final round of the US Masters at
Augusta National, Georgia, 9–12 April 1992.

Couples came to Augusta in 1992 still looking for his first major championship win. Disconcertingly he was forced to return to Augusta National early on Sunday morning to finish off his third round. A three-hour rain delay on Saturday meant that he still had four holes to play and to his credit he played them in some style, finishing with two birdies and two pars. This meant that for his final round in the afternoon he trailed tournament leader, Craig Parry, by a single shot. Then when he returned with question marks still hanging over his ability to win the 'big one', the hugely talented American came through in a tense final round to take the Masters by two strokes from the veteran Ray Floyd.

From the moment Fred Couples birdied the final hole at Hazeltine in the 1991 United States Open he was a changed man. Among the most naturally gifted golfers of his generation, his tournament record up to that point had been disappointing. He had performed well enough in the majors but appeared to lack the vital spark of confidence which transforms fine golfers into great champions. Accused of being too laid-back for his own good, Couples' relaxed on-course manner gave the impression of not caring whether he won or lost. Of course it was never true, but that failed to stop other players voicing their criticism, including Tom Weiskopf who commented, 'Great talent. No goals in life. Not one.' Even Jack Nicklaus weighed in with, 'Here's a guy with tremendous talent but you never see him do much.'

There were also question marks over his competitive nerve following a disastrous appearance in the 1989 Ryder Cup at The Belfry. With the overall match balanced on a knife edge going into the last day singles, Couples had come to the 18th hole level with Irishman Christy O'Connor Jnr. Left with a simple short-iron approach, compared to his opponent's difficult 2-iron, it was clearly advantage

Couples. Then somehow he contrived to lose the match by missing the green to the right, chipping badly and two putting for bogey. As the Europeans celebrated around him, Couples left the green looking dazed, and could only reflect on losing a match he should have won.

With the score tied 14-14 the trophy stayed in Europe and Couples was berated in the American press for the mistake which cost his team the Ryder Cup. Even team captain Lanny Wadkins was not pulling any punches when he commented, 'Freddie was just not prepared for the enormity of the situation.' In his defence the amiable Couples replied to the growing criticism by saying, 'I didn't know what to expect. Lanny and I are two different people. He's real aggressive, wants to kill 'em right off the bat. I was scared to death and he didn't make me feel any easier.'

Something had to change if Couples was going to compete at the highest level. His golf game was obviously good enough but he lacked the confidence which a top player needs to carry him through to victory. But in the three years between the disaster at The Belfry and winning the US Masters in 1992 he would eventually find that vital spark. Following the 1991 United States Open his competitive outlook was transformed.

Taking confidence from his third place finish behind winner Payne Stewart and runner-up Scott Simpson, having bounced back from a disappointing 75 in the third round to challenge for the title over the closing holes, Couples had at last performed well under pressure. His record over the next ten months was truly remarkable and the change was almost immediate. Two weeks after Hazeltine he strolled to victory in the St Jude Classic before following it up with another third place in the prestigious Western Open.

Fred Couples tapping in on the final green at Augusta National to register his first victory in a major championship.

Maintaining his rich vein of form, he came over to Britain for the Open Championship at Royal Birkdale and, after challenging well, finished third behind the run-away winner, Ian Baker-Finch. Couples was on a roll and it seemed only a matter of time before he would win a major of his own. In September he won the BC Open before rounding off the season with his third tournament victory of the year at the Johnnie Walker World Championship in Jamaica. He finished 1991 with the lowest scoring average on the United States PGA Tour and continued in similar fashion the following season.

In the five tournaments he entered leading up to the 1992 Masters Couples recorded four top-three finishes including two victories. His aggregate for the events played was a record-breaking seventy-one under par and perhaps the most impressive part of this were his totals in the third rounds, when so many tournaments are lost and won. Here he racked up a stunning sequence of 64, 69, 65, 63, 63. The most in-form golfer in the world, it came as no surprise when he was made odds-on favourite to win his first major at Augusta in April. Indeed, Nick Faldo had summed it up best when he said, 'He's so hot, he should be wearing asbestos underpants.'

The tournament itself began to take shape on the Saturday. Along with Couples, the main challengers for the title were Australian Craig Parry and the equally diminutive Welshman Ian Woosnam, joint leaders after the opening two rounds on nine under par. The Popeye-like Parry was looking to make it a Masters double after capturing the Australian version earlier in the year, while the tigerish Woosnam was determined to make it back-to-back victories, having won at Augusta twelve months earlier. Couples started the day in third position, one stroke behind, after rounds of 69 and 67, so the stage was set for some real weekend fireworks.

Then, as the third round began to warm up with the leading protagonists throwing birdies back and forth, the Georgia skies darkened and the heavens opened.

The Masters was thrown into confusion. The rain imposed a three-hour delay in mid-afternoon and the threat of the leaders not completing their round became a distinct possibility. Forced to wait patiently inside the clubhouse until play finally resumed, the effect on both Parry and Woosnam, who were paired together, was devastating. Having begun the third round in blistering fashion both players found it impossible to pick up their previous momentum. They resumed their round at the 4th and each promptly made double bogey. While Parry would eventually recover his composure to record 69, Woosnam slipped out of contention with a heart-breaking 73. (A journalist asked him what he had done during the three-hour break. 'I had ten pints,' joked the former champion.)

Like the others, Fred Couples returned to Augusta at 8.15 on Sunday morning to complete his third round. Unlike Woosnam, who had dismissed his chances of staging a final round comeback, the American seemed totally relaxed about the whole affair and completed his round with the minimum of fuss. In simple terms, he turned up, made birdies at 15 and 16, par at 17 and 18, signed his card for 69, and went back to bed. Now eleven under par for the tournament, he came back a few hours later to find himself playing in the last pair with tournament leader Craig Parry. He trailed Parry by one and, in turn, was one stroke ahead of past Masters champion, Ray Floyd, in third.

Couples knew exactly what was required. Not only would he have to beat Parry, he would also have to control his own attacking instincts on a course which threatened disaster at every turn. The record books show how well he would complete his task but not before some heart-stopping drama at Amen Corner had threatened to turn his dreams into dust. That was why he would select his final round at Augusta as the 'Round of My Life'.

> That round will always be special in so many ways. It was my first win in a major after coming close in the British Open a few times and I guess you could call it the 'Round of My Life'. I remember it wasn't the best round of golf I have ever played – that was probably my 64 at Royal Birkdale in 1991 – but it was certainly the most memorable.

Yet for all the plaudits which followed it was Parry who took the early advantage in that final round at Augusta. After the opening two holes he had more than doubled his lead for the hapless Couples found trouble on the par-5 2nd after driving into a bush. Parry made birdie to the American's bogey and the gap was now three strokes. It seemed the Masters would have its first Australian winner after all. Perhaps weighed down by the expectation of the Augusta crowds, Couples looked unsettled and seemed incapable of making a charge. Then almost without warning came a collapse so spectacular and so inexplicable that Parry would suffer from its consequences for years to come.

It started on the third green. Having putted quite brilliantly throughout the week, Parry missed a straightforward six-footer for par. Nothing too disastrous when you consider his lead, but the effect on his confidence was devastating. Three putting the next two greens, he then hit a tree with his approach to the 7th. Obviously shaken, by the time he reached the turn, his three-stroke lead had turned into a three-stroke deficit, with Couples making birdies at the 8th and 9th. After turning for home, any lingering hopes the Australian may have had of staging a comeback were soon dismissed after more strokes went early in the back nine.

Eventually limping over the finishing line with a six-over-par score of 78,

With his ball balancing precariously on the bank in front of the 12th green during the final round, Couples played a superb chip to within a few feet to save par.

Parry had some harsh words for the partisan American crowds. 'They kept making snarling remarks and coughing on my backswing,' said the frustrated Australian. 'When I had the three putts they started clapping.' Then speaking about Couples' reaction to the whole affair he said, 'Freddie was great, but he was a little embarrassed by the way the crowd were reacting.'

Couples for his part disagreed, 'There'll always be a lot of noise out there in the final round of any major championship. But people were not pulling against him.'

With his playing partner falling back, the stage was now left clear for Couples to complete the most important nine holes of his career. Therefore it was somehow ironic that Ray Floyd, the man acclaimed as Couples' mentor after their glorious winning partnership in the 1991 Ryder Cup, was now his closest challenger. Couples certainly had a lot to thank Floyd for. Having made the United States team for Kiawah Island, it was the 50-year-old veteran who had effectively nurse-maided Couples throughout the entire event, passing on his vast wealth of experience.

The pair had been christened 'Butch Cassidy and the Sundance Kid' by the American media. Performing in the same heroic manner they had contributed two wins out of three in the series of foursomes and fourball matches and were instrumental in Europe's final defeat in the so-called 'War on the Shore'. But in many other ways they were complete opposites, with the laid-back attitude of Couples contrasting with the in-your-face competitive nature of Floyd. Yet Couples had benefited enormously from Floyd's help, not only during the Ryder Cup but in the months which followed. Now as they battled each other down the stretch at Augusta National, Raymond Floyd could be forgiven for wishing he had not been quite so generous with his time.

With barely a breath of wind to disturb the dogwood and azalea, the 1976 Masters champion had made steady progress throughout the final round. Having lost in a play-off to Nick Faldo two years earlier, he seemed determined to win in regulation time with every holed putt, or well struck iron, greeted by a sharp clench of the fist. Only five months from his 50th birthday, his desire to win seemed to burn as bright as ever. At the 14th, he pitched in from off the green for a magnificent birdie then nearly holed his putt for eagle on the par-5 15th. With yet another birdie putt on the par-3 16th, it seemed that Floyd might be doing to Couples what Nicklaus had done to the demoralised Seve Ballesteros half a dozen years before. But this was not 1986, and Raymond Floyd was not Jack Nicklaus.

Indeed, unlike the Spaniard, Fred Couples actually seemed to be enjoying the struggle. 'You'll laugh,' he said, 'but I was kind of relaxed because it was Ray making the charge. I don't know why, just because of everything he's told me.'

No matter how relaxed he appeared, it did not make Freddie Couples immune from the odd crisis which inevitably came his way. For any player who has ever won a major there is always going to be an element of good fortune involved. According to Nick Faldo, luck does not exist, it is only the random bounce of a golf ball hit from A to B. Yet even Faldo might have changed his mind after watching Fred Couples play Augusta's treacherous par-3 12th that fateful day.

With the flag tucked into the right hand side of the impossibly narrow green, Couples made the cardinal error of going for the pin. Hitting nothing more than an 8-iron, his shot came up fractionally short and pitched into the bank only feet away from the hole. Watching from the tee, his heart must have been in his mouth as he watched his ball bounce once then roll slowly back toward the infamous Rae's Creek. Couples was looking at a dropped shot, or even worse. But the bank was steep and tightly mown and the heavy rain of the previous day held the ball up long enough to take its momentum away. Somehow it came to a halt only two feet away from the lapping water, and Couples breathed a huge sigh of relief.

> Standing on the tee at 12 I was more nervous than I have ever been. I said to myself 'just knock it over the bunker' but I couldn't help myself shoving the ball towards the flag. It was a natural thing. It was unbelievable that it stayed up like that. That was the biggest break of my life. I don't know what would have happened if it had rolled in like everyone else's that day.

Moments later the crisis was over. Unable to ground his club because he was in the bounds of the water hazard, Couples still skilfully chipped up to within a few inches and gratefully tapped in his putt for par. 'That's how you win tournaments,' said Ray Floyd afterward. 'Everything you do in 72 holes is not perfect. You need some breaks.'

Compared with the high drama on the 12th, the rest of Freddie Couples' round was relatively uneventful. Typically, he failed to make his birdie on the relatively simple par-5 13th, then proceeded to birdie the tough par-4 14th. Floyd in turn missed his birdie on the 16th and would ultimately fail to improve on his eleven under par total. Other challengers like Corey Pavin (67) and Jeff Sluman (71) played well in the final round, but their efforts had come far too late. Yet, needing only to avoid disaster over the closing four holes to win the 56th United States Masters, Couples did take an unnecessary risk on the par-5 15th.

Hooking his 7-iron second around the trees in an attempt to make the green, Couples' ball managed to clear the lake by only a matter of feet. He escaped with a safe par, but it was yet another case of fortune favouring the brave.

By the time he reached the par-4 17th, Couples was thirteen under par and holding a two stroke advantage over the rest of the field with just two holes left. No one really envisaged him doing an 'Ed Sneed' and blowing up within sight of the winning post. Yet having hit the 17th in regulation his birdie putt from ten yards finished an unhealthy five feet past the hole! It was just the sort of nerve-stretching situation tailor-made for the old Fred Couples, but it was a test he passed with flying colours. Remaining focused on the task in hand, he calmly slotted home a putt he might previously have missed. It was a crucial moment which Ray Floyd expressed best in the post-match interview. 'Believe me,' he said, 'you cannot ever imagine what he was going through with that putt. You have no idea, and he hit it right in the middle.'

The par on 17 meant that bogey would be good enough to win at the last. Yet even the final hole was not without its drama. Couples drove into the same bunker down the left side of the fairway that Sandy Lyle had fallen foul of en route to his dramatic 1986 triumph, but he followed the big Scot by whacking his 7-iron approach onto the green. Another risky shot, but it paid rich dividends. Two putts later and Frederick Steven Couples was the champion.

With delays for rain and having played twenty-two holes on the Sunday, it had certainly been a roller-coaster tournament for the 32-year-old but the rewards of success were not long in coming. Along with his newly presented green jacket, his hard-earned victory also gave him the number one spot in the world rankings. At the end of the year, he also led the United States Money List for the first and so far only time in his career. Looking back, it was something Freddie Couples is happy to have achieved even once in his career.

Fred Couples receiving his green jacket from the previous winner, Ian Woosnam.

> Nowadays the competition for the majors is so strong with maybe 30 or 40 players able to win. Thirty years ago only about ten could win. It's the same with regular Tour events. I think you have to be happy with winning one tournament a year, let alone a major.

Having fulfilled the potential which everyone thought he had, more recent years have seen very little of Couples at his imperious best. Plagued by severe back problems, and some highly publicised personal ones, he has failed to add to his single Masters victory. Yet he remains one of the biggest draws in world golf. Even after recording fourteen PGA Tour victories, and seventeen victories worldwide, he remains remarkably easy going about life in general saying, 'It's the oldest cliché out here, but there are more important things than golf.'

As for winning another major, his attitude is refreshingly simple. 'I win tournaments when I putt well and I lose them when I don't. That is the way my game is. I am a much better ball-striker now than I was at the Masters back in '92. I wish I could putt like I did when I was younger but that is not going to happen. So if another major comes along that's great, if not . . .'

John

D a l y

71 in the final round of the US PGA
Championship at Crooked Stick Country
Club, Indiana, 8–11 August 1991.

In one of the most unexpected major victories of recent years, John Daly arrived at Crooked Stick after driving through the night from distant Memphis. Ninth reserve at the start of the week, he was brought in on the eve of the tournament as a late replacement for Zimbabwean Nick Price. With no time to get to know the course by playing a practice round, the man from Arkansas set about demolishing the tough 7,289-yard layout on his way to leading the tournament after three rounds. Moving into the final day holding a three stroke advantage over the rest of the field, doubts still remained whether he had the game to win under such tremendous pressure. But the big-hitting Daly would prove his critics wrong. Bringing the same devil-may-care attitude into the final round he had throughout the tournament, he fired a solid 71 on his way to winning by three clear strokes. Not only was it his first major victory, bringing him instant superstar status, but his first ever win on the United States Tour.

It was the stuff of fairy tales. The final round of the 1991 United States PGA Championship at Crooked Stick, Indiana, and here was an unknown 26-year-old looking to win himself a major championship.

Hugely popular with Indiana galleries who flocked in their thousands to watch him play, John Daly's motto throughout the week had been simple, 'grip it and rip it'. The advice from his caddie was even simpler. On any hole that required a driver he simply told his boss, 'Kill'. Now as Daly shuffled his feet nervously back and forth on the 1st tee, the golfing pundits all advised caution. 'He could win,' they said, 'but only if he puts away his woods and plays it safe.' But the big-hitting pro from Dardanelle had other ideas. Having come so far playing his own brand of fearless golf, why should he change now? Besides, he said later, 'I'm not sure I could, if I tried.'

Brought in as a last minute replacement for Nick Price, Daly had driven eight hours across the country to take his place among the golfing elite. Starting the week as ninth alternate for the championship, John Daly seemed an unlikely candidate for major glory. More used to socialising with Jack Daniels than Jack Nicklaus, most of his career had been spent playing in professional tournaments which barely rated a mention in the local paper. Mostly self-taught, he had picked up the basics of the game from watching golf videos as a youngster. Yet as he proved at Crooked Stick, here was someone with a very special talent.

Armed with a backswing that would give a chiropractor nightmares for weeks, Daly was hugely long off the tee. With drives averaging around the 300-yard mark, he literally pounded the monster 7,289-yard course into submission in the opening three days. The only player in the field to have recorded three consecutive rounds in the sixties, he had enthralled the PGA crowds with some wonderful shotmaking. And like Beauty and the Beast, his raw aggression off the tee was complemented by a putting stroke about as tasty as the hamburgers which appeared to make up his staple diet.

Moving into the final round of the championship, Daly held a three stroke advantage over second place Kenny Knox. With none of the acknowledged superstars like Norman, Faldo or Couples making a concerted challenge that week, the tournament was there to be won and the 26-year-old was in pole position. But in the interviews which followed his third round 69, he appeared totally unaffected by the enormity of what he was about to achieve. Reporters asked about his strategy; he hadn't got one. They wanted to know how nervous he would be; he smiled and just shrugged his shoulders.

A rare putt slips by for John Daly during the final round at Crooked Stick in 1991.

In fact, the only problem which concerned John Daly after round three was the very real threat of incurring a two shot penalty for a possible rules infringement. Someone had accused his caddie Jeff Medlen of touching the line of Daly's putt on the 11th green with the flagstick in an attempt to show the correct line. But after rules officials consulted with Daly's playing partner Bruce Lietzke, and looked at video evidence, the possibility was finally removed. Daly could now concentrate on the last round and winning his first major. It was certainly the most important round he had played in his short career, and it comes as no surprise when he describes it as the 'Round of My Life'.

I've played some really great rounds in my life. I remember shooting 62 in Las Vegas one year. At the Open at St Andrews in '95 I played pretty good, especially on the first day when I shot 67. But I guess, if I had to pick out the most memorable, it would be the final round at Crooked Stick in the PGA. That was my first big win and really made the difference for me. It wasn't my best round of the week. I had two 69s, and a 67 in the second round, but with everything going on around me it was really special. It was a round I will never forget.

In the light of Daly's brilliance in the opening rounds at Crooked Stick, one obvious question begs to be asked. Why had no one heard about John Daly before this? The truth is they had, but perhaps not for the right reasons.

Hailing from Dardanelle, Arkansas, Daly had always been as unconventional as he is powerful. Nicknamed 'Wild Thing' long before his more recent well-publicised bouts of alcoholism, hotel room redecoration, paternity suits and serial wedlock, the blond-haired golfer always had the reputation of living life to the full. Drinking his first beer at eight, his young life has been one long battle with booze. Balanced against this was his lasting love for the game of golf. But even after picking up his first golf club at the age of five, his early years were spent annoying the neighbours.

> I used to wade into the ponds on a little nine-hole country club that I grew up on. I wasn't old enough to play on it. But I used to take the balls I found onto the baseball field and there was this little guy who I used to fight all the time when I was four or five years old. He lived just across the neighbourhood so I used to take the balls and try and hit his house with them. When I got to about six or seven I started to hit the windows. I was a little bigger than he was, but his dad was a lot bigger, so I quit.

Educated at Arkansas State and a member of their golf team for three years, John Daly turned professional at 21. From there his progress was steady but not spectacular. Playing in a baffling array of satellite tournaments, local events and pro-ams, his first substantial win came in the Missouri Open in 1987. He followed this up with a successful spell on the Hogan Tour in 1990, during which a surprise victory in the Utah Classic went some way to helping him qualify for the main PGA Tour the following season. And it was there he would meet up with some of the golfers he had worshipped as a boy.

> The guy I loved to watch was Fuzzy Zoeller. Watching Fuzzy play was probably the biggest influence on my life but of course there was Nicklaus and Palmer. It was just awesome to watch them win every week. It's something I haven't been always able to do, but pretty much I started golf watching them on TV.

Little known outside of his home state of Arkansas at first, the big-hitting Daly became an instant success with fans on the practice ground. Smashing his driver out of sight to the delight of everyone, he came into the second half of 1991 leading the Tour driving distance statistics. Unfortunately, he also rated 185th in driving accuracy and 174th in putting, certainly not figures which hinted towards a possible major winner at the forthcoming PGA Championship.

It is now part of major championship history that John Daly had begun the week well away from Indiana. Designated ninth alternate, the chances of his getting into the tournament were slim to none. Choosing to spend the week hundreds of miles away in Memphis with girlfriend Bettye, he then received the news that he had moved up to number one. Immediately jumping in the car for the long eight-hour journey, the two of them arrived in the early hours of Wednesday morning. In the end it proved to be the right decision. Nick Price had pulled out on the eve of the tournament with his wife due to give birth and Daly gratefully took his place.

Also taking the opportunity to borrow Price's experienced but unemployed caddie, Jeff 'Squeaky' Medlen, Daly set about learning the course as he went along. With not enough time even to play a practice round, Daly's opening score was a competitive 69 that left him tied in seventh place behind joint leaders Ian Woosnam and Kenny Knox. Following up with a magnificent 67 in the second round, his name now sat proudly at the top of the leader board one stroke ahead of veteran American Bruce Lietzke.

Not surprisingly, his sustained run at the title caused panic in the press centre as journalists scrambled to find something to say about him. As things turned out, they probably need not have bothered. By the end of the week, John Daly would give them enough copy to last a lifetime.

In the third round, Daly took his overall score to twelve under par after shooting 69. Now leading by three strokes over journeyman pro, Kenny Knox, and by four over Lietzke, the title was effectively his for the taking. Yet at times like this, doubts always persist and Daly knew that, come the final round, he would have to shoot par or better. Trying to banish any thoughts of major championships, he took the unusual step of going out on Saturday evening to watch the Indianapolis Colts play a home game in the National Football League.

Yet as he teed off that day, there was still the nagging doubt he might fail. The opening holes at Crooked Stick were notoriously long and difficult and Daly would need to get off to a solid start, said the experts. Never one to take advice, Daly immediately dropped a shot at the 1st after finding deep rough with his driver. Then almost before anyone could sense a collapse in the making, he bounced back with birdies at the 2nd and 5th.

Twelve under par for the championship, Daly's cause was further helped at the next when playing partner Kenny Knox faltered with a double bogey to fall six strokes behind. Making par himself, Daly then took the chance to glance up at the scoreboard for even more good news. His next closest challenger was Bruce Lietzke at eight under but, like the rest of the field, he was showing few signs of making a charge.

Still blasting away with his driver when it suited him, Daly went into the final nine holes knowing that only a disaster would prevent him winning. But it was never going to happen. Birdies at 13 and 15 to go even further ahead effectively closed out the rest of the field with the back nine looking more and more like a victory march. Indeed, as the round drew to a close, Daly began striding down the fairways twirling his metal wood in his fingers like a football cheerleader. Acknowledging the southern-style hog-calls with a gentle wave of his hand, Daly knew he was home in more ways than one.

A consistently long hitter off the tee, Daly winds up for another drive during his spectacular final round.

Now fourteen under par with just three holes remaining, the only thing left was to thumb through the record books as to the lowest winning aggregate. Moments later, though, everyone could have saved themselves the effort. After struggling to make par at the 16th, Daly three putted the short par-3 17th for a double bogey. Thankfully for him it would make no lasting difference to the final result.

> I told myself before the round not to think of it as a major, but just another tournament. I realised I couldn't tell myself that any more when I got to the 16th. I just knew it was a major and instead told myself, 'Hey you can win this.' I felt comfortable until I got to 16, then I felt the pressure. I never got nervous until I got to three holes from the finish.

Standing on the tee of the par-4 finishing hole with a comfortable three-stroke cushion, John Daly dragged his driver out of the bag for the final time. Certainly the most demanding hole on the course, the right side of the fairway was bordered down its entire length by a lake. Having provided a watery grave for many good rounds throughout the week, Daly had shown it scant respect having made birdie two out of the three times he had played the hole. Amazingly, it was almost the same story last time around. Blasting his ball over the hazard into the left-hand rough, Daly played from there into the middle of the green and just missed his putt for birdie.

It had been a remarkably composed performance. Indeed, he could have been playing with his friends back in Arkansas for a few dollars for all the pressure he showed. The enthusiastic cheers which greeted his final putt also showed what a hugely popular winner he was. In a tournament not particularly noted for its high drama his was truly a remarkable story. In less than a week, the unknown John Daly had gone from rank outsider, to underdog, to contender and finally to major champion.

Accepting the famed Wanamaker trophy, he noted some of the legendary names who had won the United States PGA Championship before him: Sarazen, Hagen, Snead, Player and his own personal idol, Jack Nicklaus. It even appeared to humble him for a moment. 'This is a dream come true,' he commented. 'It's just the greatest feeling in the world.'

Presented with his winner's cheque of $230,000 his thoughts must have drifted back to those hard times scratching a living on the Hogan Tour. To his credit, his first move was to donate $50,000 of it to help establish a scholarship fund to pay for the education of two girls whose father had been tragically killed by lightning on the opening day at Crooked Stick. It was straight from the heart stuff and endeared John Daly to the American golfing public even more.

Sadly it would prove only a fleeting moment of glory. The lurid newspaper reports of his activities in more recent years prove that there were hard times ahead for Daly, many of which would have nothing to do with golf. But for now, he could reflect on the multitude of rewards which a major victory brought with it. Apart from the multi-million dollar endorsement deals which inevitably followed, it also included a ten-year exemption on the US Tour plus an automatic invitation to all the other major championships for the following season, including the Open Championship which Daly would win at St Andrews in 1995.

Not long after the PGA Championship, John Daly was invited by the great Jack Nicklaus for a sociable nine holes. It was hoped that some useful advice would be passed from one golfing generation to another on how to handle the pressures winning a major brought with it. Incredibly Daly never asked Jack a thing. Speaking about Daly and their uneventful few holes together Jack said, 'He could have a great career and he could be great for golf, but he has to have focus.'

Only time will tell if Nicklaus is right.

Laura

Davies

66 in the final round of the Du Maurier
Classic at Edmonton Country Club,
29 July–4 August 1996.

Davies began the final round five strokes adrift of leader Meg Mallon. Playing in extremely windy conditions, she was the only player to break 70 en route to winning her second major championship of the year by two clear strokes.

Everything about Laura Jane Davies is larger than life. Without doubt the most recognisable figure in women's golf today, her desire for risk and excitement is also well documented. Despite the potential distractions of her love of fast cars and her high-roller's passion for gambling, she still manages to play golf in a style most people can only dream about. With booming drives around the 300-yard mark she also boasts an enviable playing record. The winner of over 50 tournaments worldwide, including a handful of majors, she has accumulated close to £3 million in official prize money since turning professional in 1985. Today she remains the only golfer, man or woman, to finish top in both the US and European money lists.

Ranked by *Golf Monthly* magazine as the sixth best British golfer of all time, Laura continues to cut an imposing figure on the course. Yet away from the rarified world of professional golf, the Coventry-born player is curiously shy with anyone outside her immediate circle. A fanatical football fan and supporter of Liverpool, golf also often seems to take second place to some of her other leisure interests.

During the European Football Championships in 1996, she was observed watching the England versus Spain match on a portable television stuffed in her golf bag during the final stages of the Evian Masters tournament. It was an incident that might have gone unnoticed except for the fact that she was leading by four strokes at the time. Eventually going on to win, Laura later complained about how annoyed she was having to miss the penalty shoot-out because of the prize giving!

Her love of sport in general is unbounded. The Surrey home she shares with her mother and stepfather is reputed to be a veritable pleasure dome of sporting excess. Apart from the countless television sets, most of which are tuned into the Sky Sports channels, it contains pinball machines, its own tennis court, swimming pool, snooker table, dart board and for good measure, a golf green with nine tees measuring anywhere from 40 yards to 87. But Laura, you feel, would not have it any other way.

> I love it when I'm at home. And then when I'm away, I love it. When I'm at home, I get up and play a bit of tennis, then go shopping with my mum, kick a football about the garden, go for a swim, maybe watch a bit of racing on the TV in the afternoon, play around on my golf course, have another game of tennis.

Apart from sport, her second greatest passion is gambling. Competitive in everything she does, one notorious occasion saw Laura and some friends fly to Las Vegas for a night on the blackjack tables before flying back the next morning – this in between the first and second rounds of an LPGA tournament in San Diego. Despite coming back from Vegas around £10,000 richer, the trip was not a complete success. Her enthusiasm for the odd wager got into the press and provoked some fairly strong criticism, not least by the tournament sponsors. While the whole incident passed by without further comment, worse was to come not long after.

Back in Britain, she found herself on the front pages of the tabloids after admitting gambling away around £500,000 in the past few years. Describing it as a hobby rather than an addiction, the comment which had sparked such controversy was little more than a throw-away quote from her autobiography *Naturally Laura Davies*. Though the actual figure had been plucked out at random, the press and anti-gambling organisations had a field day at her expense. While no doubt adding to her already colourful image it still proved an uncomfortable time for the publicity-shy golfer.

> It really came home to me when one of my best mates [Lisa Hackney] thought I was dead because she saw my picture on the front page of the *Daily Mirror*. She was in the airport and her heart stopped. She thought, 'Laura's killed herself in that bloody car.' [Davies had recently bought a top-of-the-range BMW 850.] Then she read the story and laughed her socks off. What I find annoying is not that I made the front pages for that, it's more to do with how little space you get when you win two major championships as I've done this year. If Monty or Faldo had won two majors in 1996, they'd be royalty by now.

While it was her fame as a golfer which had led the tabloids to seize on the story, the portrait of Davies as reckless and out of control could not have been further from the truth. As charming off the course as she is aggressively powerful on it, her comments about her own record in 1996 were also well made. In August, she had beaten a top-class field to win the prestigious du Maurier Classic at Edmonton Country Club. Her second major triumph of the season, she had come from five strokes behind going into the final round. Faced with windswept conditions more suited to Scotland than Canada, Laura was the only player to shoot in the sixties. Winning the tournament by two clear strokes, her six under par 66 was considered among the best rounds in LPGA history. It would also be her selection for the 'Round of My Life'.

I would say the round of my life was the final round of the 1996 du Maurier Classic. It wasn't the lowest score I've ever had but it was great to shoot a 66 to win a major championship in bad weather. But what made it so special to me was that I was five shots behind [Meg Mallon] starting Sunday morning and not really considering I had any chance of victory. The first three rounds I had struggled badly with my putting but on that last day everything started going right. So to come through under such circumstances really made it something I will always remember.

37

Laura Davies launching into another massive drive, this time during the 1995 Ford Golf Classic at Chart Hills.

Destined to become one of the best women golfers of all time, Laura Davies was introduced to the game by her elder brother Tony at the age of 14. Following him around Merrow Golf Club in Guildford, she first learnt by mimicking the action of her single figure handicap brother and his friends. Then, as her own game took shape, she began paying attention to European stars like Langer and Ballesteros, Langer for the drives and Seve for the short game. In the period that followed, Laura progressed to such a degree that she was playing off scratch less than three years after she started.

One unique aspect of the Davies game is her total reliance on natural ability to see her through any swing problems or dips in form. Her reluctance to take on a full-time coach is still looked on as something odd by her fellow professionals. But Laura has never been one to do things that are expected of her. Even during one particularly bad spell which lasted over a year from February 1991 to May 1992, she resisted the temptation to go and find professional help. Even after losing confidence in her driving, she battled through despite using little else than long irons off the tee.

I've never had a coach. Most of the players can't seem to play without ringing up their coach every day. The way I look at it, if you can't sort out problems for yourself, then what's the point. Most people make everything far too complicated, in life as well as in golf. You can pick up a club and just get on with it.

After a short amateur career Davies turned professional in 1985. Helped along by a £1,000 loan from her mother, Rita, she surprised everyone by finishing runner-up in her first event to American superstar Jan Stephenson. Then, building on her success, she won the Belgian Ladies' Open before taking top spot in the European WPGA Money List. Not surprisingly, she was the most cast-iron certainty for

Rookie of the Year in the award's short history.

> It came as a bit of a shock the first year after not doing much in the amateur game. And then to do it the following year was even more surprising. As an amateur I had played Curtis Cup, so I had obviously been reasonably good, but apart from that, I was nothing special.

Two years later any lingering doubts she may have had about her own ability were swept away for good. In 1987, she followed up a victory in the British Open by winning the most highly prized event on the LPGA calendar, the US Ladies' Open. Confirmed in her new found status as a world-class player, her presence at British events was often enough to ensure good TV and press coverage, something the fledgling European Tour needed desperately to survive in the late eighties and early nineties.

In 1994 she won her second major title, the LPGA Championship and as the first woman to win on all five circuits in one season, her worldwide domination was astounding. With three victories in the United States, two in Europe, and one each in Australia, Japan and Asia she became the first British golfer to top the US Money List. She would also be the first woman in history to win over $1 million in a single season.

By her own high standards, 1995 was a relatively quiet season for Davies with seven tournament wins but no majors. Yet having worked hard on her game it proved a springboard to an exceptional 1996 with nine victories, four on the LPGA Tour, three in Europe and two in Japan for a record-breaking year earnings total of $1,383,003. Not only

Laura relaxing at home with her King Charles spaniels, Benji and Dudley.

that, she doubled her career major wins by picking up her second LPGA Championship and her first du Maurier Classic in Canada. Without doubt, the win in Canada was the highlight, especially considering how well she played in the final round.

Coming into the du Maurier Classic in late July, Laura had received some bad news about the death of a good friend.

> About a week before, I was told that Karen Lunn's father had passed away. [Lunn is one of two Australian sisters who play on the LPGA Tour.] He was a wonderful bloke and it was a sad time for all of us who knew him. When I told them I was coming to Australia for the funeral they told me to do something better and win the du Maurier for their dad. They said the same thing to Karrie Webb and Brandie Burton because we are all pretty close.

In the week that followed, Laura Davies set about doing just that. After three steady rounds of 71, 70, 70 she was in good position but no longer expected to win. Five shots behind leader Meg Mallon starting the final round, there seemed to be many quality players between her and the championship. While her ball striking that week had been excellent, her putting had let her down badly. Yet she still felt confident about her chances.

> On Sunday morning the weather was really nasty, blowing a gale with a little bit of rain. When I woke up and saw how windy it was, I thought, if I could shoot a 69 or better, something good might happen. After all, I had played quite well in Dublin to finish third behind Ally [Nicholas] in the Guardian Irish Open the week before and had managed to keep that form going throughout the week.
>
> I remember starting the day in sixth place, three shots behind Nancy [Lopez], four behind Karrie Webb and Pat Hurst and five behind Meg. I think both Liselotte [Neumann] and Annika [Sorenstam] had one shot on me. But it was one of those days where I just started off solid and it just got better. I think what was so good about my game that day was my control of the golf ball in the wind because it really was howling. I also made some crucial putts on the last few holes which I knew I had to make if I wanted to win the championship.

Having picked up three birdies on the front nine, including holing a bunker shot on the par-4 3rd, Davies turned for home in confident mood.

> Probably the key shot of the day was my high drawing 2-iron over the trees into number 8 using the wind. It was a par-5 and it set up a possible eagle which I missed, but it gave me an easy birdie. It was one of the shots of the week – of the year maybe. It was just a cracking shot which you remember for a long time and it helped set up my whole round.

Now eight under par for the tournament, even dropping her first stroke of the round on the 139-yard par-3 11th failed to unsettle her rhythm. Bouncing straight back with two consecutive birdies on the 12th and 13th, Davies closed on the tournament lead with yet another on the 470-yard par-5 15th. Following this up with two pars, Davies came to the 18th green in good shape after hitting just a 6-iron as her second into the 465-yard par-5 hole. Moments later, she walked off the green with a spectacular closing eagle and an equally spectacular round of 66.

> Maybe what I was most proud of was that I was the only person to shoot in the 60s that day. [Meg Mallon slipped to a 74 to finish third.] Perhaps what made it so memorable was that it was one of those incredibly rare rounds where I had complete control of my game for a day. The windy conditions were tough but having played in Europe most of my life, I guess I was used to it.

Waiting while Nancy Lopez finished off her round was probably the most difficult part of Laura's day. But while the American legend would shoot the lowest score among the leading pack (71) it was only ever good enough for joint second place with Karrie Webb. Eventually taking the title by two clear strokes, Davies described her win as 'fabulous'. She then said how much she looked forward to picking up the only major event she had not won, the Nabisco Dinah Shore.

It had been a superb performance from the 32-year-old English golfer. Now all that was left was the evening flight back to Scotland for her next tournament. 'I told Tony [her brother and caddie] that if I won the bloody thing, then I was going to sit in first class. It was a year to the week since the last time he caddied for me, when we missed the cut in the du Maurier!'

As for the final round itself, how does Laura Davies rate it among the other great ones she has played in her career?

> It was probably the best. People have asked me could it have been lower, but of course any round you play could always be lower. Unless you shoot something like a 55, 56 or 57, you can never actually come off the course and say you have shot your absolute lowest round. You are always going to miss makeable putts and obviously they could always have been lower. And while I'm not a great one for looking back, my uncle taped it for me so it will always be a great memory for me when my career is over.

For many, Laura Davies MBE is the face of women's golf as we approach the new millennium. Travelling, as she does, countless times around the globe each year in pursuit of even more golfing glory, the big-hitting girl from Surrey looks set to be a major force in the game for years to come. And for that reason alone we should all be grateful.

Ernie

E l s

69 in the final round of the US Open
Championship at Congressional Country
Club, Bethesda, Maryland, 12–15 June
1997.

*After the completion of the storm-delayed third round, Ernie Els found
himself in joint second place with American Jeff Maggert. Two strokes
behind leader Tom Lehman, he was partnered in the penultimate match
with a determined Colin Montgomerie who was looking for his first
major title. With all four players on top of their game, it was to prove an
absorbing battle all the way to the final holes. With Els ultimately victorious by a single shot over Montgomerie in second, the championship had
rested on how well the leading golfers negotiated the treacherous 457-
yard par-4 17th. Els later described his 5-iron approach to the green as
'the shot of his life' and it certainly went a long way to securing the
second United States Open title of his short professional career.*

There can be few more naturally gifted golfers in the world than Theodore Ernest
Els. At 6 feet 3 inches he stands head and shoulders above many of his closest
rivals and hits the ball further than most people go on holiday. Winner of 23
international tournaments before his 28th birthday, his heady mixture of power and
skill have made Els one of the biggest draws in world golf. No longer considered
just a rising star, his hard-earned victory at the 1997 US Open at Congressional
Country Club near Washington, DC, confirmed him as a genuine contender for
the game's major honours in the years to come.

Yet, away from the golf course, Ernie Els is as relaxed an individual as you
might find. Known widely in the United States as 'The Big Easy', what you see is
what you get. In keeping with the slow, almost lazy way he swings a golf club, he
prefers nothing more than retreating back to his tranquil home near Fancourt, two
hours from Cape Town. Here, away from the goldfish bowl existence of tourna-

ment golf, this often shy individual is able to open up a few cans of beer, throw some food on the barbecue and spend time with friends and family.

In contrast to the fist-clenching aggression of his fellow South African, Gary Player, Els has often appeared to lack that vital competitive spark. Yet it would be a big mistake to underestimate the seeming lack of ambition behind the image. One of his long-time friends, sports journalist Rudi Lake, once said, 'Yes, he is a pussy-cat. He is very easy-going but he is also intensely ambitious to be as good a golfer as he possibly can.'

Now challenging American Tiger Woods for the crown of best younger golfer in the world, Els has come a long way. After his second US Open victory in less than three years, his first coming in a play-off against Colin Montgomerie and Loren Roberts in the 1994 Championship at Oakmont, he now stands on the threshold of golfing greatness. Having shown himself to be remarkably cool under pressure, there seems little to stop him adding to his growing collection of tournament victories. So what is his choice for the 'Round of My Life'?

Winning a tournament like the United States Open doesn't come easy and winning it twice is very special. I know from my own experience it's among the toughest of the majors to win. While I played some great golf to win at Oakmont in '94 and Congressional in '97, if I had to pick one round it would be my 69 in the last round at Congressional. Apart from having to come back and finish off my third round, that was probably my best ever round under pressure. I think that would be the one I would describe as the round of my life so far.

Arms aloft, Ernie Els acknowledges the cheers of the large US Open crowds after holing his winning putt on the final green at Congressional Country Club.

Ernie Els was born in Johannesburg on 17 November 1969. The youngest of three, after brother Dirk and sister Carina, his upbringing was nothing short of privileged. With his father Neels owning a highly successful truck haulage company, Ernie was given every advantage any young, white South African could possibly want, including ample access to sport.

A talented all-round athlete with an abiding love of all sports especially cricket and rugby, Ernie was Eastern Transvaal tennis champ at 14 – senior not junior! But having played golf since he was eight, he was ultimately forced to choose between Augusta National and Wimbledon Centre Court. Fortunately he chose golf and shortly after, his father set about digging up the family tennis court and replacing it with a practice green complete with bunkers. 'I still wonder sometimes what I might have achieved at tennis,' said a reflective Els, 'but I've no regrets about becoming a golfer.'

Yet considering some of the problems he faced after turning professional in late 1989, Els could have been forgiven for having second thoughts about his final choice of career. With much expected from him after his second place finish in the prestigious South African Open as a 16-year-old amateur, Els struggled badly early on. Originally looking to make his name in the United States, he failed twice at the Tour Qualifying School to get his player's card and was forced to play on the second-string Hogan Tour. Invitations to senior Tour events in America and Europe would occasionally come through but indifferent performances only added to the pressure. It was a bleak time for the talented youngster.

Out of form and out of his home country, rumours began to circulate that perhaps all was not well with the golden boy of South African golf. Stories about all-night drinking sessions, plus two minor car accidents, neither with Els driving, only added fuel to the fire. The pressure began to build. With fellow South Africans David Frost little more than a bit-part player on the United States Tour and Gary Player no longer the superstar he once was, huge expectation had fallen on his shoulders. Instant success was demanded and Els, obviously taking time to adjust to his new environment, sadly failed to deliver.

Perhaps the most widespread accusation coming out of his homeland was that he was simply not hungry for success because of his wealthy background. The criticism obviously hurt and Els sought refuge by playing for a spell on the 1992 South African Sunshine Tour. It proved a major turning point in his young career. In January, his road to glory began with a three-stroke win in the South African Open after leading in the early rounds. Perhaps more importantly, it also won him a gilt-edged pass into the World Series of Golf at Akron, Ohio, later in the year.

Without even taking time to celebrate his first tournament victory as a professional, Els headed off to America and showed his versatility the following week by coming from behind in the final round to win the Lexington PGA. One week later, now batting two for two, Els just missed out on an unprecedented treble by finishing third in the Bell's Cup at Cape Town. But even then Ernie was not finished. In the Tournament of Champions at Kensington Golf Club the next week, he missed a six-foot putt on the 72nd green that would have put him in a play-off with the eventual winner, Bobby Lincoln. Cashing in on his rich vein of form, Els finally achieved his third victory in five weeks after coming from two strokes back to win the prestigious South African Masters. His critics silenced and confidence fully restored, Els had time to reflect on an incredible five tournament run. Perhaps most impressively, he had missed out on registering an amazing five straight tournament wins by only three shots.

Having now equalled Gary Player's long held record as the only golfer to win the South African Open, PGA and Masters titles in the same year, Els was becoming unbeatable on his home continent. Then, looking further afield, he achieved his first success outside South Africa by winning the Dunlop Phoenix event in Japan in 1993. The same year at Royal St George's, Sandwich, he became the first professional to record four sub-70 rounds in the Open Championship. Greg Norman became the second minutes later on his way to winning. Ernie had to settle for joint sixth but it seemed he had arrived in the big time at last.

Making his United States Open debut at Baltusrol that year, Els finished with excellent rounds of 68 and 67 for a highly creditable share of seventh place. Despite finishing seven strokes behind the eventual winner Lee Janzen, the championship offered the young professional some much needed experience in the majors. He would use this to great effect the following year when he turned up to compete at Oakmont.

The 1994 season itself had started in spectacular fashion. Shooting a record twelve-birdie round of 61 (eleven under par) on his way to winning the Dubai Desert Classic at the end of February, Ernie then finished tied eighth in the US Masters in April after rounds of 74, 67, 74 and 71. Further wins later the same year in the World Matchplay at Wentworth, the Johnnie Walker World Championship and the Sarazen World Open confirmed his place among golf's elite. But it was at the US Open at Oakmont where people finally began to take notice of the blond giant from Johannesburg.

After playing some of the finest golf of his career, rounds of 69, 71, 66 and 73 left him in a three-way tie at the top of the leader board with Colin Montgomerie and American Loren Roberts. The US Open is the only major championship to still employ an 18-hole play-off on the Monday. In this Montgomerie played poorly for 78, effectively knocking himself out of the running. Meanwhile Els went on to beat Roberts at the second hole of sudden death after tied scores of 74. Among the youngest champions in US Open history, Els' victory acted like a springboard to further success in the coming months.

Carrying his winning form into 1995, early season success in South Africa was followed by his first regular US Tour win at the Byron Nelson Classic. Back in Europe, the big-hitting Els then retained his World Matchplay title in September, beating Australian Steve Elkington in the final. Progress in Els' own words had been 'solid if not spectacular'.

Although he was now hot property in marketing terms, Els had a surprisingly lean time on the course in the two years following Oakmont. Winning majors was his stated priority and after missing the cut at the 1995 Masters, he was doubly eager to defend his US Open title at Shinnecock Hills, New York. Unfortunately, a spell of poor driving resulted in far too many missed fairways and inevitably another missed cut after opening scores of 74 and 73. Three weeks later in the Open Championship at St Andrews, Ernie's long game was back in shape and so were his scores. Opening scores of 71, 68 and 72 left him high up the leader board, but a disastrous last round 75 pushed him back to joint 11th. (A solid 70 would have won the tournament by one stroke from John Daly.)

Later in the year at the United States PGA Championship at Riviera Country Club in Los Angeles, another loose score of 72 in the final round left him in third place, just two shots behind eventual play-off winner Steve Elkington, and Colin Montgomerie who had to settle for second. It was yet another huge blow for Els especially as he had led the tournament after three wonderful rounds of 66, 65 and 66. Having come so close to picking up another two majors in 1995 was a disappointment which Els would carry with him for some time.

It was a similar story for Ernie Els the following season. Failure in the four majors, including a tied second place behind Tom Lehman in the Open Championship at Royal Lytham, balanced out against further worldwide success. In South Africa, he picked up the national Open and the World Cup team event with Wayne Westner, in the United States it was the Buick Open, and in Europe, his third consecutive World Matchplay Championship (where he beat Vijay Singh in the final).

While the previous two years would be described as highly successful for anyone else, Els felt changes were needed. In February 1997, he signalled his desire for hard work by rejoining the European Tour and became the only golfer to be a Member of the three Tours at one time: European, United States and South Africa. He also hoped a change of clubs from Lynx to Taylor Made would help make the difference – and it seemed to.

Early success at the Johnnie Walker Classic in Singapore gave Ernie just the start to the season he was looking for. Even a level par score in the Masters to finish a lowly seventeen places behind winner Tiger Woods failed to dent his confidence. With his powerful drives and accurate iron play, he knew the United States Open, scheduled for Congressional Country Club, was his best chance of major success. Consequently, he went into the event full of confidence and looking to win.

Playing solidly, Els opened up with rounds of 71 and 67. At the halfway stage he was in second position, one stroke behind leader Tom Lehman, and well placed to make a challenge over the weekend. Along with Els in the chasing pack were Americans Jim Furyk and Jeff Maggert, and his old rival Colin Montgomerie. Monty, who began the championship with a course record 65, had fallen away on day two with a 76. But where Ernie was, Colin would follow, and as the tournament started to shape up on Saturday, the big Scot would pull himself back into contention with a third round 67.

With scores in the mid-seventies littering the leader board in the early rounds it was thought unlikely that anyone would break par over four rounds on the tough 7,213-yard course. With hard luck stories commonplace in the press room, the main topic of conversation centred around one subject, the severity of the par-4 17th hole.

The course layout had been altered somewhat since the last time the US Open had been held at Congressional Country Club. When the heat-exhausted Ken Venturi staggered down that fairway in 1964, it was his last hole. For 1997, the championship committee deemed that the dramatic 480-yard par-4, with water almost surrounding the green, would play as the 17th. Made possible by making the short par-3 1st into the 18th, it offered a suitably dramatic backdrop with the two last greens less than 80 yards apart. It was a gamble which ultimately paid off but the switch would not be without its problems, or critics.

With the scoreboard behind the 18th detailing his second US Open triumph, Els lifts the trophy moments after producing a wonderful closing round of 69 to win by a single stroke from Colin Montgomerie.

Severe local thunderstorms interrupted play towards the end of the third round. Montgomerie, who had been distracted by a rowdy crowd during a similar delay on Friday, burst into the lead after going to the turn in 31 on Saturday afternoon. But like Els and the other leading contenders, he was forced to return to the course early on Sunday morning to complete his final two holes. (Which he did in level par for a 67.)

Lehman in turn kept up his record of leading going into the final round of the past three US Opens by making two birdies in his remaining five holes for 68. But it was Ernie Els who made the most dramatic start on the final day with three consecutive birdies for 69. 'I knew I could be aggressive because it was early in the morning and that gave me a lot of confidence,' he said. 'Then I came out and made some good par-saving putts in the afternoon to keep that momentum.'

Partnered with Montgomerie, Els had taken the lead at the 8th but failed to match the big Scot's birdie at the par-5 9th. A bogey at the 6th and birdie at the 7th meant that Els had gone through the first nine in a level par score of 35. Montgomerie in contrast had played brilliantly to go out in 33, one shot better than Maggert, and three better than the luckless Lehman.

A chip-in birdie from off the green at the par-4 10th would be a turning point for Els. It put him in a four-way tie for the lead at four under par, and then he holed a nine-foot putt at the 12th for yet another birdie. Like Maggert and Lehman in the group behind, he dropped a shot at the 13th but followed this with three solid pars. The predictions that the tournament would be settled on the difficult 17th were about to come true in a most dramatic way.

Els and Montgomerie both hit perfect drives. Els' 260-yard 3-wood was just a few paces further from the hole and so he was first to hit the tricky downhill approach to the tiny water-bordered target. Els had 213 yards to go. During practice from this exact spot on the Wednesday he had hit three shots to the difficult back left pin position that had actually been chosen for the final round. One had gone left into water, one went right and the other was spot on.

Hoping to produce the one good one, Els now struck a majestic 5-iron to within 15 feet of the pin. Describing it as the 'best shot I have ever hit', Els said,

> I just felt the shot was right. My whole mental attitude was right on that occasion and the shot came off. At other times things could have been different. There's a very fine line between victory and defeat, and you've just got to try and be as positive as you can and play the shot you feel comfortable with.

In what now resembled a matchplay situation, the shaken Montgomerie failed to commit to his own second shot. A little quicker than normal on the backswing, he caught the ball thin with his 6-iron approach, leaving it short and right of the green. Then, playing out of the tangly semi-rough which had enveloped his ball, he managed to stab his chip to around seven feet in the hope of saving his par. But, with his mind in a whirl, he was forced to wait while the huge crowds settled around the last two greens. In the end it probably cost him at least the chance of a play-off.

Often proving vulnerable in such pressurised situations, Monty paced about waiting for his chance to putt. Then while Els and his caddie Ricki stood quietly by the side of the green, the red-faced Scot took it upon himself to start marshalling the crowds. 'I didn't quite understand the reason for the commotion,' he complained later. 'I felt I had to wait to hit the putt. I didn't want to rush the most important putt I've ever hit.' Moments later he would miss.

Surprisingly calm under the circumstances, Els' own birdie putt had neither matched the accuracy or quality of his wonderful second. Slipping by on the low side, it would still be enough to take him to the 72nd hole one stroke ahead of Montgomerie.

The change in the layout of the course meant that Els and Montgomerie were able to watch from the final tee as Lehman and Maggert played their approach shots on the 17th. 'I don't think I've ever been in a situation like that,' said Els, 'where so many golf shots meant so much to me. One mistake and you're out of the championship.'

Maggert, en route to a poor round of 74, had dropped out of contention over the closing holes, but Lehman was still in with a good chance of winning. A bogey at 14 had been quickly followed by a birdie at the par-5 15th, where he hit his third to within 12 inches. Having played erratically throughout his final round, Lehman dropped another shot at 16 but it was at the 17th that his challenge finally came to an end. His approach shot splashed into the water and he ran up a disastrous double bogey. Lehman was plainly devastated. 'I would give anything in the world for a mulligan [a replay of a shot under no penalty],' he said afterwards. 'I caught it just a bit heavy. I am bitterly disappointed that I did not pull it off.'

Knowing that a final hole par would probably give him his second United States Open title, Els played safely to the middle of the green. With Monty then failing to threaten the hole with either his tee shot, or approach putt, the South African effectively had two putts for the championship. Dramatic to the last, he stroked his first putt five feet past then, with the pressure at its most intense, he calmly rolled the return in. 'Maybe on the exterior I am very calm,' he said, 'but inside I was very tense. But I had the confidence in my game that comes with experience.'

Ernie Els had achieved his dream of winning a second major title. His round of 69, matched by a hugely disappointed Colin Montgomerie in second place, had been enough to win by one stroke. 'The US Open is not easy to win,' he said. 'I really worked hard on this one. I tried to believe in myself and my game. I was just trying to stay positive, be myself. Three years ago when I won, it was like a war and I knew it would be again.'

Having played the greatest round of his life, Els reflected on what was the most important win of his professional career.

> Obviously the US Open was the highlight for me, and my career, especially in the style I won that tournament. All those good players on the last nine on Sunday afternoon, and to come through in that kind of way was really pleasing to me. It's probably the best I've played in a two-week stretch ever.

(The following week, Els made it two-in-a-row by winning his second Buick Open.)

As a bonus to the week, Ernie Els was declared the number one ranked golfer in the world. Asked if he felt like the best in the world he said, 'Winning the US Open down the stretch like I did was very satisfying. Then winning the week after, I really felt like I was the best player in the world.'

And who would argue with him?

Nick

Faldo

67 in the final round of the US Masters at Augusta National, Georgia, 11–14 April 1996.

Without a major win since the 1992 Open Championship at Muirfield, Nick Faldo went into the final round of the 1996 Masters six strokes behind overnight leader Greg Norman. Before the final round, victory for Faldo had seemed out of reach, with the Australian playing some of the finest golf of his career. Yet, after being paired together in the final group on Sunday, Faldo gradually overpowered, then overtook the hapless Norman in one of the most dramatic final rounds in Masters history, eventually winning by two clear shots. It meant that a European had won at Augusta ten times in the previous seventeen years.

Of all the great players in golf history, few can be as intimidating to play against as Nick Faldo. Widely known as a cold-blooded competitor, he is fashioned in the same mould as the legendary Ben Hogan. Tough and uncompromising, he has dedicated himself over the past two decades to the science of tournament play. Meticulous in both practice and planning, he has also exhibited throughout his career an awesome will to win. Holder of six major titles, three Masters and three Open Championships, he is not the player you want breathing down your neck in the later stages of a golf tournament.

One of the few players to translate strokeplay success into matchplay domination, Faldo's head-to-head record in both the Ryder Cup and World Matchplay events shows just how hard he is to beat. The world's number one player in the early nineties, Faldo often dominated his opponents through sheer force of will. And unlike the great Jack Nicklaus, whose matchplay record was little short of abysmal, Faldo relishes the individual challenges and the problems they often present during a round.

Perhaps the best example prior to the US Masters of 1996 was his singles win over Curtis Strange in the 1995 Ryder Cup at Oak Hill. Matched against the experienced two-times US Open winner, Faldo literally grabbed victory from the jaws of defeat. Coming back from one down with two holes remaining, he was forced to hole a vital putt from five feet on the last to win. European captain Bernard Gallacher later described this putt as the 'turning point of the entire match'. Like all his major triumphs, this was an emotional victory for the tall Englishman. Even though he was mobbed by his relieved team-mates, including a tearful Seve Ballesteros, it was to Faldo's credit that few people watching that day ever felt he was going to miss. After all, he had spent most of his professional career coming through under such enormous pressure.

During the presentation of the trophy to the victorious European side Curtis Strange looked understandably subdued. Perhaps wondering how he let slip such a golden opportunity, he was then only the latest in a long line of golfers who had lost out to Nick Faldo. Following hard on the heels of Scott Hoch in the 1989 Masters, and John Cook in the 1992 Open Championship, Strange was not the first to fold under pressure exerted by the Englishman. As the two-times Open champion Greg Norman found out less than six months later in the 1996 Masters, when Faldo is chasing, nothing can be taken for granted.

Of course, like the others, Norman would contribute to his own downfall at Augusta. Having compiled three wonderful rounds of 63, 69 and 71, he had led the tournament going into the final day. Faldo, in contrast, had struggled with his putting on day three but managed to rally at the end of the round to finish in second spot. Yet, despite being a massive six strokes behind, it would be Faldo who would come out the winner that fateful Sunday.

On his way to a magnificent final round of 67, Faldo stalked the hapless Australian from the very first hole. It would be a golf lesson Norman will probably never forget. Losing out by two strokes at the end of the day, he could only look on in anguish as his closest rival collected his third US Masters title in eight years. For Faldo, it was an equally important victory. His first major since the Open Championship at Muirfield in 1992 came at a time when people were just beginning to write him off as a force in world golf. Among the lowest last round winning scores ever seen at Augusta, his 67 would also be Nick Faldo's choice for the 'Round of My Life'.

Nick Faldo holing his winning putt on the final green to take the 1996 Masters title at Augusta.

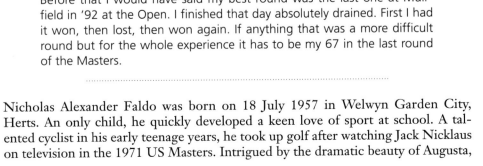

The round of my life was the obvious one at Augusta in '96. My final round was special for a number of reasons. Being so far behind; the pressure; then playing so well; I think it was the whole package really. Before that I would have said my best round was the last one at Muirfield in '92 at the Open. I finished that day absolutely drained. First I had it won, then lost, then won again. If anything that was a more difficult round but for the whole experience it has to be my 67 in the last round of the Masters.

Nicholas Alexander Faldo was born on 18 July 1957 in Welwyn Garden City, Herts. An only child, he quickly developed a keen love of sport at school. A talented cyclist in his early teenage years, he took up golf after watching Jack Nicklaus on television in the 1971 US Masters. Intrigued by the dramatic beauty of Augusta,

Faldo soon enrolled for lessons at a nearby club and within two years had reduced his handicap to low single figures.

Intensely competitive by nature, golf no doubt appealed to the young Nick Faldo because it was a sport where success was rarely compromised by the fallibility of others; a game where long hours of solitary practice actually pay off and the term 'loner' is not necessarily considered a derogatory one. Maintaining his initial rapid progress, Faldo made an immediate impact on the amateur game by winning both the British Youths' Championship at Pannal, and the English Amateur Championship at Royal Lytham in 1975.

Coming to the fore just too late that season to make the 1975 Walker Cup side to face the Americans at St Andrews, Faldo turned professional the following year and would go on to become the most successful British golfer of his, or possibly any other generation. His career can be split into two periods, before 1984 and after, or, as some golfing pundits have described it, before and after David Leadbetter.

Long before he met up with the renowned golf coach, Faldo had already carved out a highly successful career in the paid ranks. He represented Great Britain and Ireland as the youngest professional in Ryder Cup history at Royal Lytham in 1977, where he beat reigning Open champion Tom Watson in the singles, and had risen to the top of the European game only six years later. An established professional with a string of wins to his name, Faldo was crowned Order of Merit winner for 1984 with earnings of £140,761. Then, despite being widely tipped as the first home-grown Open champion since Tony Jacklin in 1969, Faldo turned his back on everything he had achieved.

Having long since dedicated himself to winning the Open, Faldo instinctively felt his willowy swing with its slight looping motion would not stand up to the intense pressure of being in contention for a major championship. He was probably right. Later that year he turned to the little-known Zimbabwe-born coach, David Leadbetter, for help. It was to prove an incredibly brave decision.

He spent the next couple of seasons in a frustrating attempt to remodel his entire game and his Money List position plummeted to a woeful 42nd with earnings of £30,140. In what must have been a difficult time, Faldo found himself giving up almost every privilege he had earned as a top professional. Morale boosting invitations to events like the Masters dried up, and various lucrative sponsorship deals were not renewed, but he vowed to carry on in typically single-minded style.

With the light at the end of the tunnel often proving nothing more than an oncoming train, Faldo finally got rewarded for his efforts in 1987. He had been without a victory on the European PGA Tour since the Car Care Plan International in 1984, but played well to win the Peugeot Spanish Open. His first post-Leadbetter victory, it would prove a major turning point in his career.

Looking back, it is hard to imagine events like the Open Championship, the Masters or even the Ryder Cup without Nick Faldo. Leadbetter had been given orders by Faldo to take his game apart, and rebuild it in championship-winning style. Nothing like this had ever been attempted before and both men had effectively put their reputations on the line.

At the time the decision was announced, and for months after, Nick Faldo had been almost vilified in the golfing press for attempting such a foolhardy idea. But, in the Open Championship at Muirfield in July 1987, all the mind-numbing hours of practice finally bore rich fruit. Holding off Paul Azinger in the final round with eighteen straight pars, Nick Faldo was crowned British Open champion.

This opened the floodgates to even more success and the past decade has seen Nick Faldo add two more Opens to his name, St Andrews 1990 and Muirfield 1992, as well as a host of other professional titles. After finishing runner-up to

Severiano Ballesteros in the European Order of Merit in 1988, he finally regained his old number one position in 1992 with record earnings of £1,220,540.

Faldo also became only the second British-born golfer, after Sandy Lyle the previous year, to win the Masters at Augusta in 1989. Tied with Scott Hoch on a score of 283 (five under) he survived a scare on the first extra hole of the play-off when the American had a two-foot putt to win. Crisis over, Faldo bounced back at

the next with a birdie to capture his first green jacket. Then, in typical style, Faldo made it two the following year by beating American veteran Ray Floyd, in exactly the same circumstances, winning with a birdie on the 11th in the second hole of a play-off.

Wins like these gained Faldo the number one position in the world rankings. Having thus achieved his early ambition to be 'the best golfer in the world', Faldo's desire for a third Masters green jacket nonetheless remained undiminished. Coming into 1996, however, Faldo's confidence was not at its best. In fact, since his decision to play more golf on the United States PGA Tour in 1994, his game had gone through a particularly barren patch in terms of tournament wins. However, by the start of the 1996 season, there were some encouraging signs.

Faldo launched that season by finishing joint second in the Mercedes Cham-

Watched by Greg Norman, Nick Faldo driving off the 10th during the final round. Recovering from six shots behind the Australian going into the final day, his spectacular closing 67 secured his third Masters victory in eight years.

pionships behind Mark O'Meara and the old confidence started to come back at last. By the time the Masters came round, his bank balance had been further boosted by a number of other good finishes in the United States. Swinging well and, perhaps more importantly, putting well, Faldo's new-found confidence was reflected in his opening scores at Augusta.

Like the rest of the field, Faldo had been forced from round one to chase an in-form Greg Norman. Having scored a course-record equalling 63 on the opening day, Norman had followed it up with rounds of 69 and 71 for a 13-under-par total. Faldo, in reply, had performed well for his three rounds of 69, 67 and 73 (seven-under). This left Faldo one stroke clear of American left-hander, Phil Mickelson, in third, but Faldo still found himself six shots adrift of the world number one. Most people considered this a winning lead at any tournament, and thought that Norman would win his first Masters at a stroll. Having already won two Open Championships, in 1996 at Turnberry and 1993 at Royal St George's, the 'Great White Shark' had looked confident and relaxed throughout the week. Yet going into the final round, Greg Norman must have had his doubts.

As the tournament leaders Norman and Faldo were paired together and were already long-term adversaries. They had crossed swords as long before as the 1990 Open, with the Englishman coming out on top in their tense third round encounter then. Not only that, Norman had also previously been in a winning position at Augusta and blown it, perhaps most notably in 1986 when he came to the last needing a birdie to beat Jack Nicklaus only to take bogey. Now with a six-stroke lead to defend, the last round took on a matchplay feel with Faldo doing the chasing. It was destined to be an uncomfortable few hours for the Australian. For Nick Faldo, it would be the 'Round of My Life'.

For Norman, trouble started as early as the opening hole. After a nervous drive into rough, he failed to make the green with his second and dropped his first shot. Faldo, in contrast, made his regulation par 4 and the lead was immediately cut to five; first blood to Faldo. At the par-5 2nd, Norman looked to have recovered his composure and matched his partner's birdie to go back to thirteen under.

Pars at the 3rd were followed by poor tee shots by both men at the par-3 4th. Faldo found himself through the green, while Norman was in a bunker short and right. Chipping up to around four feet, Faldo immediately put the pressure on Norman whose splash shot from sand had finished at least double that distance from the hole. Not surprisingly Norman missed and Faldo holed to reduce the deficit to just four.

With Norman remaining at twelve under par for the next four holes, Faldo had chipped away yet another stroke by the 8th. Despite dropping a shot himself on the 5th after failing to get down in two from a greenside bunker, he birdied both the 6th and 8th to pull himself up to nine under. By now, Norman was looking increasingly at odds with himself. He was obviously struggling with his game, but worse was yet to come.

Hitting what looked to be a good short-iron approach into the 9th green, Norman could only look in anguish as the ball spun back off the front edge. Faldo was on the green in two and completed a regulation par while Norman once more failed to get up and down from the front. As both players headed off to the 10th tee, it was impossible to see from their attitude who had the two-stroke lead. Head down, Norman seemed about to explode, while Faldo marched forward without any hint of emotion. Yet even he was feeling the strain of the occasion. 'From 10, 11 and 12,' he said, 'it was just so nerve wracking it was unbelievable.'

At most major championships commentators almost inevitably trot out the hackneyed old phrase about the 'tournament really starting on the back nine on Sunday'. This time, they may even have been right. Norman and Faldo both hit the fairway on the long, downhill par-4 10th. However, Norman pulled his second shot left and was lucky not to run down a steep bank. Meanwhile, Faldo had played his approach perfectly and was only 20 feet below the hole, with a good chance for birdie.

With his short game having deserted him, Norman's chip ran around ten feet past the whole. Watching Faldo two-putt for par, Norman obviously recognised what a crucial putt this was and took extra time looking at the line. Sadly it made little difference. Showing the signs of pressure, his putting stroke let him down and he missed his chance for par: Faldo nine under, Norman ten under.

At the par-4 11th, the scene of past Faldo play-off triumphs, both men hit the green in regulation. Norman was slightly closer at around 20 feet but was positioned above the hole leaving a treacherously fast downhill putt. Faldo played first and safely two-putted for par, still giving Norman the outside chance to move two clear. It could have been a real turning point in the match. Instead Norman hit an aggressive first putt a yard past, then missed the return. The six-stroke lead which he had enjoyed at the start of the final round was now gone.

Moving on to the difficult par-3 12th, Faldo had the honour. With Rae's Creek lapping the bank at the front of the green, he knew how vital it was to hit a good tee shot. Ignoring the flag positioned front right, he gladly settled for the heart of the green. Norman decided to gamble and paid the price. Just fractionally short of perfect, his 7-iron tee shot pitched on the bank and fell back into the water. Dropping under penalty, he chipped on the green, two-putted and walked off with a double bogey 5. Moments later, Faldo calmly two-putted for par and Norman's disaster was complete. In a complete reversal of fortune, it was now the Englishman who found himself two shots in the lead.

Having suffered throughout the final round, a gracious Greg Norman congratulates Nick Faldo on the 18th green. An emotional moment for both men, Faldo has always refused to elaborate on what was said that day.

Repairing at least some of the damage, Norman matched Faldo's birdie on the 465-yard par-5 13th to go back to eight under. In an odd change of attitude, Norman seemed far more comfortable chasing a lead than defending it. He had cut a forlorn, almost embarrassing figure over the past few holes and now he was fighting back.

At the 14th, both players made regulation pars after missing long range efforts for birdie. Pushing hard for the first time, Norman found himself just short of the green in two at the 500-yard par-5 15th. With Faldo over the back of the green in two and facing an impossible downhill chip towards water, Norman saw the glimmer of a chance. After carefully reviewing his shot, the Australian hit a low, skidding chip which brushed just past the hole narrowly missing his eagle. Thinking it had gone in, Norman fell dramatically to the ground. Moments later, Faldo played a brilliant chip to match Norman's tap-in birdie and the tournament was effectively over. It had been Norman's last throw of the dice and now he was finished, drained of emotion.

Faldo also knew how important the last few holes had been.

> I think the key shots for me were hitting a great shot on 12. On 13 I wanted to go for the green but I was on such a steep slope [with his second]. I thought the shot was to hit my 5-wood but then I thought I didn't like the look of it. But I felt the lie was so good I've got to go for it. And then I made my great up and down on 15. But he was still there and the rest you really know about.

Faldo found the middle of the green on the 170-yard par-3 16th. Norman then pulled his 6-iron shot miles left into the water. It was a desperately tired stroke and any lingering hope he had of coming back into the tournament was sunk without trace at that precise moment. Taking three shots more to get down, his double bogey took him even further behind. For Faldo it was now a matter of making no mistakes. But mistakes were never really on the cards. After making par at 16, he added another at 17. With nobody else in the field even remotely close, the final few holes had become a victory march.

Faldo's obvious pleasure in winning his third green jacket was also tinged with sadness for his long-time rival. After making a wonderful birdie three at the last after being bunkered off the tee, he turned towards his ashen-faced opponent and offered some words of sympathy. It was a side of Faldo which few thought had existed. Never the greatest of friends, it was a special moment as both these great players hugged each other on the 18th green.

Norman finished with three pars for 78, compared with Faldo's brilliant round of 67. Almost impossible to contemplate before the round began, there had been an incredible eleven-shot swing. With Phil Mickelson falling back to a level par round of 72 for third, Faldo's five-shot margin of victory was among the largest in Masters history, beaten only by Cary Middlecoff in 1955, Arnold Palmer in 1964, Jack Nicklaus in 1965 and Ray Floyd in 1976.

With his sixth major championship since his comeback year of 1987, Nick Faldo had put himself back where he is happiest, competing for and winning golf's greatest prizes, and while the 1997 Masters will long be remembered for Norman's collapse, it is also certain that Faldo's six-birdie round will long be considered among the very best ever played in championship golf.

> It's obvious that people will tend to look at Greg's downfall, but I've had a very positive reaction to my own round. Those I've spoken to seem to recognise that 67 as one of the best rounds ever played in a major. I have got an awful lot of pride and satisfaction from that. I regard it as a very great round. I did it, I competed and I won.

Max

Faulkner

74 in the final round of the Open
Championship at Royal Portrush,
2–6 July 1951.

In the days when the final two rounds were played on the Friday, Max Faulkner went into lunch leading the Open by six strokes from Argentinian Antonio Cerda. Despite having two-times Open champion Bobby Locke in the chasing pack, the extrovert Faulkner felt confident enough before the final round to sign one autograph 'Max Faulkner, 1951 Open Champion'. Looking back, it was a flamboyant gesture which he almost came to regret as he stumbled to a 74, his worst score of the week. Yet it carried him over the winning line and made him, until Tony Jacklin in 1969, the last home-grown winner of the Open for almost eighteen years.

Max Faulkner was one of Britain's greatest golfers and, almost certainly, British golf's most colourful personality. Bringing a dash of colour to drab post-war Britain, he was an engaging mixture of Hollywood good looks and outgoing personality. In raising the profile of professional golf in the late forties and early fifties, he was even considered outrageous at times. As well as entertaining the crowds by walking down the fairway on his hands, he would appear in major tournaments dressed in a blaze of bright colours when sombre browns were the accepted norm. A true golfing maverick, he remains the only player to have won the Open dressed in canary yellow plus-twos with matching shoes and socks!

Physically powerful, as befitting an ex-RAF gym instructor, he was a solid ball striker and frequently brilliant putter. Despite being a keen student of the golf swing, Max was not a classic champion in the Bobby Jones mould. A shade under six feet, he revelled in giving the ball a hearty swipe and often played to the large crowds who always followed him around on competition days. The winner of several long-driving competitions, he was also skilled enough that his desire for distance rarely compromised his accuracy – an important element in any future Open champion.

Max Faulkner early in his career receiving the winners' trophy for the Addington Open Foursomes in 1937.

Winner of many professional titles throughout his long career, including the 1957 Spanish Open at the age of 53, Max had the reputation of being an inspirational player with a big heart. Probably the most naturally gifted golfer of his generation, he often lacked the consistency to put four great rounds together. Even today, Faulkner himself admits there should have been more than one Open Championship medal in his trophy cabinet.

'Looking back, the amazing thing was my [four-round] scores, and Bobby Locke's scores, were identical for the '49, '50 and '51 Open Championships, yet he won two titles to my one. I often think it could so easily have been the other way round.'

Yet, in looking back, Max knows the value of winning just one Open Championship. Now in his eighties he enjoys reminiscing on his past glories from the comfort of his picturesque Sussex farmhouse. 'When I think of all the great golfers who didn't win the Open like Dai Rees, Charlie Ward, Ken Bousfield and even Peter Alliss, I just shudder and thank God for Portrush. I think that is why I would pick my final eighteen holes in the '51 Open as the "Round of My Life".'

Certainly, the defining moment of Faulkner's career did come at Royal Portrush in Northern Ireland in 1951. Played close by the famous landmark of the Giant's Causeway in County Antrim, it was an historic and unique occasion, the first and only time the Open Championship has been taken outside mainland Britain.

Actually, I nearly won the Open at Sandwich in '49. I rattled off three consecutive 71s and with the last round left to play, I shared the lead with [Bobby] Locke and [Harry] Bradshaw. Unfortunately, they both finished with 70 to go into a play-off against my 74. I was just as consistent the following year at Troon, but this time my rounds of 72, 70, 70 and 71 left me four behind Locke. So by now I could taste victory and when 1951 came around I had a gut feeling I was going to win it. Even as a youngster, I knew I would win the Open one day and I sensed Royal Portrush would be the one.

Even before the tournament had started, Max had put himself under considerable financial pressure to win, perhaps even deliberately. Never one to let money burn a hole in his pocket, he had recently bought an expensive sports car with a gas-guzzling V8 engine.

I paid £1000 for this car. That was a lot of money back in the fifties and it was equally expensive to run. So my last words to my wife at London airport were, 'If I don't win the Open, I'll have to sell this damn car!' Well I wasn't going to let that happen was I?

Fortunately, as the history books record, Faulkner won the Open and kept the car. Coming into the final round with a massive six-stroke lead over Antonio Cerda, and eight ahead of Bobby Locke, he would struggle to a 74. Even so, it was this round which carried him to victory and holds his fondest memories. Nominating it as the round of his life he briefly outlines the reason why. 'For me it was the only choice. Obviously I've bettered the score countless times in my career but, after all, how many times in your life do you get to play a winning round in the Open?'

Born in Bexhill in Sussex on 29 July 1916, Max Gustavus Faulkner was the son of the respected professional at Bramley Golf Club in Surrey. Having spent his early years learning to play golf with hickory shafts, he was actually encouraged by father, Gus, to skip school lessons in favour of golf practice.

> I was only 14 when my dad went to see the headmaster at my school in Guildford. I don't know how he did it, but he arranged for me to play in the afternoon when everyone else was in class. So I was very lucky in two respects. Golf always came absolutely naturally to me and I had a father who had great faith in my ability to succeed in golf.

After some local success in the Surrey and Sussex area, Faulkner had his first taste of big-time competition just weeks short of his 17th birthday. Technically too young to play in the Open, his father somehow wangled a place for him in the 1932 Championship at Royal St George's. 'Lord knows how he fixed it,' said Max. 'You could not enter the Open at 16 in those days, but my old dad was a popular chap and he must have talked somebody into letting me in.'

As apprentice golf professional, he was schooled in the art of club-making and repairs but, having played at Sandwich, he never lost sight of his main ambition. 'I remember following Gene Sarazen who won that year. I never forgot the way he hit the ball and from that moment on I set my heart on winning the championship.'

Like many aspiring young professionals, losing valuable years out of his career because of World War II was obviously a major blow. 'Not only did it take six years out of our lives,' he said, 'it took several years to get going again.' But, like his future Ryder Cup team-mates, Dai Rees and Charlie Ward, Faulkner quickly set about re-establishing himself on the tournament scene.

Having survived many narrow escapes during the conflict, including an air raid while on guard duty at Wentworth Golf Club (then being used as a military base), Max began his post-war golf career 'a bit shaky but fit as a fiddle'. Leaving the Royal Air Force in 1945, an acrimonious few months working with Henry Cotton at Royal Mid Surrey ended after a disagreement concerning the type of ball he was allowed to use. Prepared to forgo the security of a paid club pro's job, Faulkner's decision to play full-time tournament golf was soon vindicated after he won the first professional event held after the war, the 1946 Dunlop Tournament at Southport.

Using his first place prize money of £450 to fund his chosen career, the next few years were spent playing all over the world. As well as in the United States, he also gained invaluable experience by playing in far-off locations like Egypt. Having already achieved some success by the start of the fifties, Faulkner was now ready to challenge for the biggest prizes. By 1951, he knew he had the game to compete with the best.

Always the joker, Faulkner entertains Ben Hogan and the rest of the 1951 American Ryder Cup team with some impersonations of their swings.

I had a premonition I was going to win the 1951 Open. In 1949, at Royal St George's, I'd been tying with one round to go. A year later at Troon, I was one behind going into the last eighteen holes. I might have been playing rubbish for the rest of the year, but the Open brought out the best in me. Royal Portrush, on the Northern Ireland coast, was ideal for my power fade. It was also a favourite of mine since I'd come third there in the Irish Open on my 21st birthday.

In 1951 the greens at Royal Portrush were faster than many players had ever experienced in an Open Championship. Fortunately for Faulkner, he had come across a light blade putter only weeks before which played a great part in his eventual triumph. 'Putting, to my mind, is all about feel and I gripped this putter so lightly anyone could have knocked it out of my hands. Anyway, I simply loved this one, and my putting at Royal Portrush was absolutely incredible.'

It certainly was; just 27 putts in the first round, 24 in the second and 29 in the third had helped put Faulkner into an almost impregnable lead. With the last two rounds played on Friday, to allow the majority of the players time to get back to their weekend duties as club professionals, he scored 70 in the morning. Partnered for the day by top American amateur Frank Stranahan, Max was now six strokes ahead of second place Argentinian Antonio Cerda.

His greatest threat, the great South African Bobby Locke, was eight shots behind and as Faulkner prepared to tee-off in the afternoon round, all seemed well. Playing some wonderfully controlled golf, Faulkner looked certain to pick up his first major title and his confidence was high. So high, he almost made the worst mistake of his career.

Putting on the style: Faulkner driving during practice at the 1951 Open in Portrush.

A large crowd was milling outside the clubhouse as I made my way across to the first tee. I was lost in my own thoughts until a young boy and his father approached me about an autograph. 'Will you sign my ball, Sir?' he asked, 'and could you sign it "Max Faulkner, 1951 Open Champion"?' I said, 'Blimey, steady on,' but he said, 'Well you are six ahead, Mr Faulkner.' I considered this for a moment and thought, 'He's right.' So I asked for a pen, signed it, then stared at it for a second or two before handing it back. As I walked to the first tee, the words kept appearing in front of me. As I prepared to drive, I suddenly felt terrible and I nearly parted the hair of a spectator as my drive flew low and left, finishing near the out of bounds fence.

Long iron shots were the worst part of my game and I needed to hit a good one now. Fortunately the lie was good, so I took a deep breath and hit a great 4-iron to the green. I then two-putted for par which helped settle me down a bit. My putter saved me time after time on the front nine that round. I was eventually out in 37 and knew that par figures coming in would keep the chasing pack at bay. In fact, Stranahan looked over and asked me, 'Have you got the book written yet Max?' I laughed but I knew the strain was beginning to get to me.

The rest of the round was a real struggle. I made five at the 10th, then dropped a shot at the short 11th, which was bad. I thought, 'Blimey, this won't do.' I managed to get a four at the 12th from out of a cavernous bunker short of the green. I could only see the very top of the flag and I played it out to five feet and made my par. I was pleased with that. I then got four at the 13th where I rimmed the hole for a three. I was happy to get my par at the next, a really nasty hole that one, right across a valley with a 50-foot drop. I remember Stranahan missed it down there and took two to get out! But having got my three, things were a bit up and down after that.

I made bogey five at the 16th having knocked it into a bunker. But then I got a birdie four at 17 after hitting a brassie up close to the green then chipping it up within a few inches. I thought, 'That's not bad.' Then I teed up my ball on the last hole, knowing I had to make four or five to win the Open. I know I felt nervous. My knees were shaking and I had difficulty getting the ball to stay on the tee peg. I kept telling myself, 'Trust your swing. Just swing it naturally like your dad taught you.'

Under all that pressure I hit my best drive of the championship, perhaps my entire life. With deep bunkers on the left and heavy rough on the right I hit this thing like a bullet down the middle. Then I took out a baffie (3-wood) for my second. That's when the trouble started.

I was setting up for my shot when I heard this hissing sound coming from behind me. I stopped, set up again and blow me if it didn't happen again, 'Pssssss!' I looked around and spotted my old Ryder Cup partner, Jimmy Adams, in the crowd – he was trying to tell me I had too much club. First I tried to ignore him but he hissed again. I was so damn nervous that I told him to shut up and let me play the shot my way. Bloody near put me off completely it did. Almost lost me the Open!

I know he wanted me to hit a 5-iron or so, but I thought I had the right club. Of course I hit this thing too faint-hearted and it cut out to the right thick rough well short of the green. When I got to my ball I had a real shock. The ball was on a down-slope, teed up on a tuft of grass, almost defying gravity. I then had to hit it precisely with my bunker iron with a full swing. Of course there was a very real danger of blasting out of bounds or just leaving it there. When I finally hit it, the ball just made it to the edge of the green. But from the muted applause, I don't think the crowd appreciated how good a shot it was in the circumstances.

From there I managed to putt it up to around a couple of feet. Looking at the crowds, I thought, 'If I miss this I am going to look a right bloody fool.' But I was feeling more and more nervous. Suddenly the hole looked like it had filled up with cement and my ball swelled up twice the size! So I gave it a quick tap and it went straight into the hole. After I signed my card for 74 my friend Dai Rees escorted me through the crowd to the press room, where I asked for a cigarette. I'd deliberately left mine in the hotel to give myself the best possible chance on the final day. But after all that tension I nearly passed out on the first drag. Bloody fool!

But the Open wasn't over yet. This was in the days where players were drawn and the tournament leaders didn't go out last like today. I still had to wait to see how the others were doing and I had learnt a long time ago not to count my chickens. So it was over an hour before I was finally confirmed the winner. [Max eventually finished two strokes ahead of Antonio Cerda in second place.]

It still remains the most exciting week of my golfing career even with all the pressure that went with it. As for that final eighteen holes, it was not the best golf I have played in my life but it was certainly the most memorable. That is why it has to be the 'Round of My Life'.

Tony

Jacklin

70 in the final round of the US Open
Championship at Hazeltine National Golf
Club, Chaska, Minnesota, 18–21 June 1970.

In the weeks leading up to the 1970 United States Open Tony Jacklin's form had been patchy at best. His ball striking was top class but his putting had been erratic and, after a series of indifferent finishes, his confidence had plummeted. Lacking the vital spark which had brought him British Open glory less than a year earlier at Royal Lytham, he arrived at Hazeltine National with very little thought of winning. Then on the eve of the tournament, he received a putting lesson which transformed his game. Shooting three sub-par scores on his way to leading the tournament, he took a four stroke advantage going into the final day over American Dave Hill. Looking to become the first man to hold both Open titles simultaneously since Ben Hogan, the outcome depended on whether the young Englishman could hold his nerve or not. Thankfully, for him, he could. In what was the first American tournament ever televised in Britain, Jacklin put together a controlled final round of 70. It was enough to make him the first British golfer to win the United States Open since 1920.

When a fresh-faced Tony Jacklin won the Coombe Hill Assistants' tournament back in 1964, few people could have predicted what a remarkable impact he would have on British and European golf over the next thirty years.

Winner of the Open Championship at Royal Lytham & St Annes in 1969, Jacklin made it a glorious double by capturing the United States Open 49 weeks later at Hazeltine National in Minnesota. He returned to a celebratory banquet in his home town of Scunthorpe, but his boyish good looks had already established him as a household name throughout Britain. Taking his place alongside other sporting superstars like George Best, this working-class son of a lorry driver could have been forgiven for thinking he had finally arrived in the big time. Indeed like

Best, he was popular enough to cut his own album of cover versions. Entitled *Tony Jacklin Sings* it was destined never to reach number one in the music charts. Which, sadly for the talented Jacklin, would apply to his own career over the next few years. After scaling the pinnacle of golfing success, his decline was equally swift and dramatic. Rated among the world's best golfers in the period from 1969 to 1972, the incredible desire which had driven Jacklin to such heights of brilliance had all but disappeared by the late seventies.

He would still challenge for the occasional European title – even winning the Sun Alliance PGA Championship as late as 1982 – but the brash arrogance which singled him out as someone special was no longer there. Golf, in his own words, had become hard work and while he was still in demand, winning major championships was now a thing of the past. Curiously his long game remained as good as ever, but the lack of a consistent putting method became so mentally draining that Jacklin would consider giving up the game on more than one occasion.

Yet the memory of his former glories would always drag him back – and what triumphant times they were.

Having picked up his first golf club at nine, his passion for the game was all consuming for many years. Later he would spend every lunch hour cycling the three miles from his job as an apprentice fitter in the local Scunthorpe steelworks to the practice ground at Holme Hall Golf Club. There he would have just enough time to hit a bag of balls before making the return journey. Indeed, such was his dedication, that one of the members later gave him a part-time job paying a princely £6 per week. Jacklin was delighted – at least he would have the afternoons off to play golf!

After winning almost everything in sight in his native Lincolnshire, the confident youngster turned his sights on a career in the professional game. He wrote away to Bill Shankland at Potters Bar Golf Club, a former Australian Rugby League international turned club pro, who offered him his first assistant's post. Theirs would be a stormy relationship, but the time spent at the Hertfordshire club yielded one main benefit for the ambitious Jacklin, a sponsor to help launch his tournament career.

Having shown such determination to succeed it perhaps came as no surprise when he informed *Golf Illustrated* shortly after turning pro that his main ambition was to become 'the best golfer in the world'. That was in 1963 and in the next eight years Tony Jacklin would all but achieve his target. Starting with Rookie of the Year his next few years were spent travelling the globe in search of golfing success. After victories in South Africa, New Zealand and Australia, his first notable victory in Britain came in the Pringle Tournament in 1967. In what had been a remarkable rise he returned two years later to the scene of that triumph, Royal Lytham & St Annes, to capture the Open Golf Championship.

The first British professional since Max Faulkner in 1951 to capture the most prestigious title in golf, his victory was not totally unexpected. Already the top golfer in Europe, he had won the Greater Jacksonville Open on the US Tour in 1968 and looked set to challenge the very best America had to offer in the coming years. Yet it was his victory in the 1970 US Open at Hazeltine National, or rather the manner of it, that launched him to superstar status.

Before the tournament he had been rated a lowly 20th among the leading contenders by American magazine *Golf Digest*. No doubt looking to make them eat their words, Jacklin put together three sub-par rounds to take a four-stroke advantage into the final day when his round of 70 was enough to secure victory. In what was a seemingly nerveless performance, he thrilled all those back home who stayed up to watch the action on their grainy black and white television sets right up to the moment when he holed a monstrous putt for birdie across the final green to secure victory. That final round will live long in the memory of those who watched it, as it does for Jacklin himself. Almost three decades later, it would be his choice for the 'Round of My Life'.

Picking out one round is very hard. They are all meaningful for different reasons. Obviously my Open win at Royal Lytham was very special but my last round against Bob Charles wasn't exactly spectacular in scoring terms – 72. It was just a round which got the job done and essentially that is what being a professional is all about, getting the job done. It was fantastic coming to the last hole knowing I had it won, but I have certainly played far better rounds than that in my career.

What most people forget is that 1969 was my worst ever year in terms of tournament wins. I won the Open and nothing else! In fact, I actually played better over four rounds at Muirfield in 1972 and didn't win. I remember returning to America after the Open at Royal Lytham and missed four cuts in a row. Perhaps that's why I don't really rate any of the four rounds among my best ever.

I think in pure ball-striking terms my best round was probably my third round 65 in the Wills Tournament at Dalmahoy in 1973. I played wonderfully well that day. I also remember shooting 62 around the West Course at Wentworth against Lee Trevino in the World Matchplay one year and losing! That is something you don't forget in a hurry. There was also the round at St Andrews that got washed out in the 1970 Open. I had got to the turn in 29 and was playing some of the best golf of my career when the heavens opened. That could have been a spectacular round in scoring terms.

Yet if I had to pick one it would be my closing round of 70 in the US Open at Hazeltine in 1970. It was just one of those fantastic weeks when your game comes together and you can do little wrong. I putted really well and I established a lead on the first day and increased it every round after that. I remember leading by two strokes after the first round, three after the second, four after the third and finally by seven at the end. It is that part of my victory of which I am most proud.

Even before the 1970 United States Open had got underway there were rumblings about the newly created course at Hazeltine National. Many of the top players criticised the number of dog-leg holes, with the controversial Dave Hill commenting how the whole course should be ploughed up. 'All it needs,' he said during one of the practice rounds, 'is eighty acres of corn and some cows.' Perhaps understandably, some of the locals took exception to this and Hill would be haunted throughout the week by derisory shouts of 'Moo!'

In contrast, Tony Jacklin had little time to worry about the course. He had more fundamental problems to deal with. In the weeks leading up to the tournament, his short-range putting had been erratic and his scores and confidence had both suffered badly. His rating at a lowly 20th behind favourite Billy Casper among the contenders for the championship was probably a fair assessment of his chances that week.

After finishing second earlier in the season behind run-away winner Frank Beard in the Tournament of Champions at Rancho la Costa (Jacklin's entry being courtesy of his victory in the Jacksonville Open the season before) his overall form had plummeted. With his putting becoming gradually worse, Jacklin had had a poor finish in the Atlanta Classic, followed by a missed cut in Memphis and equally

frustrating performances in the Kemper and Western Opens. It was obvious that something drastic had to happen if he was going to add the American Open to the British one he had won less than a year before. Then came a chance meeting which was to transform not only his US Open chances, but possibly his entire career.

> On the second practice day, I had really got the feel of the course with its seemingly endless run of dog-leg holes and blind shots but I was still not holing those putts. Then came a meeting on the practice putting green with Jim Yancey, the brother of Bert, who had been one of my closest friends since I went to play regularly in the United States at the beginning of 1968.
>
> Jim watched me putt and suggested that having lined up the shot and set the blade behind the ball, I should hit the ball with my eyes still on the hole. The putts began to drop from all over the place and I could feel the confidence rushing into me. If any one thing helped me win it, it was that chance meeting with Jim Yancey.

The transformation in his play was immediate. The only golfer in the field to break par on each of the first three days, Jacklin carded rounds of 71, 70 and 70 for a five under par aggregate. Seemingly playing a different course than the rest, the quality of his golf was best illustrated on the blustery opening day when his one under par score contrasted with the 79 taken by Arnold Palmer, the 80 by Gary Player and the 81 for the Golden Bear himself, Jack Nicklaus. (Indeed, Jack was quoted as saying that he fully expected the winning total to include at least one score in the 80 region!)

With the players' locker room at Hazeltine National echoing to tales of disaster throughout the entire week, Jacklin had gone about his business calmly and with the minimum of fuss. Having stretched out the field, he led by four strokes over the controversial Dave Hill in second, six from Gay Brewer in third and seven from Julius Boros in fourth. The result looked a foregone conclusion but, with such a high level of expectation, doubts inevitably began to creep in before the final round.

I slept fairly well after taking a few calls. It is amazing the number of people who want to reassure you that 'everything is going to be fine, Tony'.

Britain's first Open champion for 18 years, Jacklin went on to add the US Open title less than one year later.

Yet the evening was not without its moments. Having suffered from severe leg cramp the night before, no doubt brought on by the mounting tension, Jacklin also had to contend with his son, Bradley, cutting his first tooth. Dinner at their rented home in nearby Thunderbird was cordial but neither he nor wife Viv broached the subject which had consumed them both all week. 'Both of us knew,' said Jacklin, 'just what victory would mean in terms of cash and our future but tried to steer clear of the subject.'

Arriving at Hazeltine the following day, Jacklin found a note pinned to his locker with the word 'Tempo' printed on it. From his good friend, Tom Weiskopf, it contrasted with some of the animosity he had faced as a 'foreigner' playing on the American Tour. In golfing terms it was also a timely reminder not to fall into his old habit of swinging a little quicker under pressure. A few hours later, Tony Jacklin stepped onto the first tee and began what he would later describe as the 'Round of My Life'.

With Dave Hill playing in the group ahead, Jacklin was partnered with the less demonstrative American pro, Gay Brewer. After spending the morning being grilled by the golfing press about his strategy for the final round, the opening holes must have offered some respite from all the attention. It certainly seemed that way as he got off to a steady start making five pars and a birdie in the first six holes.

At the 7th, however, things started to go wrong. After hitting a tree down the right with his tee shot, his second to the long par-5 hole came to rest on a patchy piece of ground. He needed a fairway wood to get him somewhere near the green, but it proved too ambitious a shot from such a bare lie. Inevitably in these situations, one bad shot followed another and the result was a disastrous bogey.

> I had hit my first bad shot of the afternoon and was paying for it. Certainly I had a six to drop back to level par [for the round] but even now what happened is wrapped up in some sort of memory fog. I wanted to win so much, and to win by as many shots as I could. And with eleven holes to play, I felt that I might be going into some sort of skid which would wreck everything.

Standing on the tee of the short par-3 8th, with water protecting the front part of the green, the nerves started to show. And even worse, a solid 5-iron into the heart of the green was quickly followed by three putts for yet another bogey!

> Having three putted for only the third time in the tournament, I could not have chosen a worse time. With Hill out in a level par 36 my lead had been cut to three. The next few minutes were perhaps the most critical I had ever known.

The 9th hole was a lengthy par-4 requiring a drive and long iron to a well bunkered green. Jacklin set his drive off on what looked a good line but the ball ended up in the rough on the right. Fortunately the lie was good enough to hit a 4-iron safely onto the green, finishing about 30 feet away. Then having survived what looked a potential disaster off the tee, the hole suddenly became a major turning point when Jacklin rattled his putt in for an unlikely birdie three.

> This was without doubt the most vital putt of the week. I hit it a little strong and, as it raced for the hole, I had the horrible mental picture of the ball missing and finishing four or five feet past. But it hit the back of the hole, bounced fully a foot in the air and then bolted down out of sight again like a rabbit going underground in the face of danger.

Having weathered the storm, Jacklin was now back in control. Another birdie at the par-4 10th stretched his lead even further and, while the final nine holes of any major championship could hardly be described as smooth sailing, the tournament was effectively won.

> I often find myself thinking back to those three holes when it seemed so likely I would blow my lead, or much of it. And of that putt charging across the green, slamming against the back of the hole, up and down again, and in. From that moment life seemed good again. From thinking it was going to be a bit of a slog after the 8th, I actually enjoyed playing the last nine holes and the nearer I got to the end of this marvellous four-day battle the more I enjoyed it.

Par figures over the next seven holes meant Jacklin came to the final hole needing only to avoid disaster to become the first British winner of the United States Open since Ted Ray in 1920.

> I have been asked hundreds of times since that afternoon how it felt to stand on the 18th tee with such a huge lead. I knew that the BBC were transmitting the American ABC pictures by satellite and all I could think about was my family and friends who would be watching. And of the celebrations in the bars of Potters Bar and Scunthorpe Golf Clubs.

Like his spectacular closing tee shot in the Open at Royal Lytham less than a year before, when his drive had threaded its way through a necklace of bunkers to finish dead centre of the fairway, Jacklin again resolved to finish in style. He launched his drive over a bunker on the left leaving himself little more than a 4-iron approach to the green. Moments later, his second shot landed safely on the putting surface about 30 feet away to a huge cheer and he was almost home. But the work was not quite over yet.

> The reception was fantastic, and as I walked into that huge horseshoe of people I knew I could now take six putts and still win. But winning was no longer enough. I wanted to win by as many as possible, stay under par in each of the four rounds and make this final moment as memorable as I could. At Royal Lytham I had left my first putt half an inch short of the hole. Now I was determined to be strong enough and from the moment I hit it I knew the putt was in.

His third consecutive round of 70 had been enough to win and, with an English-run restaurant in nearby Minneapolis providing a crate of beer, the post-tournament celebrations went with a swing. In typically petulant style, Dave Hill, who finished runner-up, had refused to attend the presentation ceremony, but it was only a minor distraction in what had been a glorious triumph for the young Englishman.

The next morning the British newspapers proclaimed his incredible victory in banner headlines. Golf was now front page news. The country had a new sporting hero and what a champion he was. Talented, youthful and highly charismatic, he had caught the imagination of everyone who witnessed his triumph.

Looking back, we can now see that that glorious day at Hazeltine was the pinnacle of his career, though nobody imagined it at the time. In 1972 the wise-cracking Lee Trevino would rob Jacklin of perhaps his best chance of winning another Open after chipping in outrageously time after time in both the third and final rounds at Muirfield. It would be a blow which Jacklin would always struggle to recover from.

Of course more recently he has recaptured some of his former glory by captaining the Europeans to Ryder Cup victory over the United States. And while the years in between held their share of triumphant highs and tragic lows for the amiable Jacklin, no home-grown golfer has yet followed him into the history books as joint United States and British Open champion.

Barry

Lane

Beating David Frost 2-up in the final of the
Five Tours Andersen Consulting World
Championship of Golf at Grayhawk Golf
Club, Arizona, 29–31 December 1995.

Barry Lane qualified for the matchplay final of the inaugural Andersen Consulting event in some style. Having already beaten Sam Torrance, Bernhard Langer and Seve Ballesteros in the European qualifying section earlier in the year, he travelled to the United States where he defeated Japan's Massy Kuramoto in the semi-final. With the final stages held at Grayhawk Golf Club in the Arizona desert he then faced the experienced South African, David Frost, in the final. With an astounding $1 million on offer to the winner, Lane played some of his best ever golf under pressure going round in an approximate 67. Beating Frost on the 18th green, he walked away with the largest prize ever offered in the professional game.

In the rarefied world of top professional sport, the value put on winning is often measured in millions of dollars. Indeed, the very word million gets bandied about quite casually when discussing the earnings of top-class footballers or boxers. But in cold, hard terms, how many sportsmen actually get to play for $1 million over the course of a day? Certainly not many, but among those who did was golfer Barry Lane.

The tournament which offered such a huge inducement was the grandly titled Five Tours Andersen Consulting World Championship of Golf in 1995. This was the first playing of what has since become a highly prestigious event, a worldwide matchplay competition with qualifying rounds taking place in Europe, Asia, Africa and America. With one winner emerging from each event, the four finalists would then battle it out in the Arizona desert in a semi-final and final to find the eventual champion. The prize for the winner – a cool US $1 million!

When the event was first announced in the press, the huge winner's cheque obviously attracted a great deal of publicity, and not all of it good. Debate about the large amounts of money on offer at the top end of the professional game raged on but the event itself had other problems to contend with. Scheduled for the last two days of December the sponsors had hoped to attract top-name players like Greg Norman and Nick Faldo. Yet, despite the obvious attractions of playing for such a valuable prize, both turned down invitations to play so late in the year. Each had a young family and the thought of finishing off the Christmas turkey and then hurrying to Arizona to play in a golf tournament plainly did not appeal.

It was the same story in the qualifying rounds. Having made it through the European section by beating Sam Torrance, Bernhard Langer and Seve Ballesteros,

Englishman Barry Lane was perhaps not the big-name draw the sponsors were looking for. Despite this, he was among the most naturally gifted golfers on the European PGA Tour. A proven tournament winner, the highlight of his career had come in 1993 when he represented Europe in the Ryder Cup match at The Belfry. And while he failed to pick up a point against the Americans, his match-play skills had been put to good use in recent World Cup and Dunhill Cup matches.

Blessed with a long rhythmic swing and good putting touch, Lane had broken through in 1983 by winning the World Assistant Professionals' Championship. Then, having made seven return trips to the Qualifying School, he recorded his first professional win in the 1987 Equity and Law Challenge at Royal Mid Surrey. This opened the doors to further success. A year later, he won his first 72-hole European Tour event, the Bell's Scottish Open at Gleneagles. Since then, he has rarely finished out of the top fifteen in the Order of Merit. Golfing success has been hard won for the Berkshire-born professional, so having got to the final stages of the Andersen Consulting tournament, Lane was determined to make the most of his opportunity.

Having come through the European qualifying round at The Oxfordshire, I felt I had already achieved something. After all, it's not often you get to beat Seve and Bernhard Langer in one day! It was a good performance over the two days, and so the finals in Arizona held no real fear for me. Besides I've often thought, if I can play at my best I can probably beat most players on the day. It is just a matter of self belief.

After seven visits to the European Tour Qualifying School early in his career, Barry Lane went on to become one of the Tour's highest money earners with nine victories worldwide including the 1995 Andersen Consulting World Championship of Golf.

Obviously aware of what $1 million would do for his bank balance, Lane already had some idea of how he would use the money. In the long term, it would smooth the path of an extensive swing rebuilding programme which he was planning to undergo, one which would help him become a better player, perhaps even one capable of challenging for the majors. In the short term, he had a more pressing ambition. Having won the Mercedes German Masters in 1992, the Canon European Masters in 1993, and the Turespaña Open in 1994, his record of picking up at least one title a year was important to him. But as Lane arrived at Grayhawk Golf Club, he was still without a win for 1995. And with the final of the Andersen Consulting scheduled for New Year's Eve, it would be his last opportunity to keep his run going. But as for most players, the festive period had offered little opportunity for serious practice.

> When I arrived in Arizona, I hadn't played for five weeks and it was important to get in a couple of practice rounds. The draw was already set so I knew I would be playing the Japanese player, Massy Kuramoto, in the semi-final. I think in some ways that helped me focus my mind on what I had to do. That was important because the match was over the sprint distance of eighteen holes and over just one round anything can happen. In the match itself I wasn't exactly flushing it but I did just enough to get through. In fact out of my two matches at Grayhawk that was probably the most nerve-wracking. After all, you cannot start thinking about the million dollars until you are in the position to win it.

Beating Kuramoto by two holes set up a final with David Frost who eventually got the best of American Mark McCumber by 2 & 1 in the other semi. Despite the lack of any of golf's superstars, the final itself proved a high quality affair. With the runner-up's prize $½ million less than the winner's, there was obviously an unusual edge to the match. But neither player let it affect the quality of his golf and, with Lane driving and putting well, the final looked to be over long before the closing stretch.

> I got three up early on but David Frost battled back around the turn. I was leading one-up playing the 11th but a bad approach had left me in a greenside bunker. That was the time I really started to feel the pressure.

Needing to get down in two to retain his lead, Lane left himself a twisting 12-foot putt for par. Then he and his long-time British caddie, Gary Tilston, disagreed about the line for the putt, but the last words he heard before lining up were, 'Go with what you see.' It proved good advice. Lane holed the putt and retained his slender advantage going to the next tee. Tilston later described the incident as 'a key moment' in the match. From the 14th hole onward, Lane pushed hard for victory.

> We were all square at 13, then I birdied 14 and 15 to put some daylight between me and him. But still it wasn't enough. I was three under for the last five holes but only won two of them. I somehow knew it would go down to the wire.

Coming to the final par-4 hole one-up, Lane pushed home his advantage by playing a match-winning approach to around 12 feet for a birdie chance. With Frost almost double the distance away for two, the match was almost won but like most good dramas, this one had an unusual twist in the end.

> The situation on the final green passed off without anybody really noticing. But at the time I was fairly concerned about what would have happened if my first putt had slipped by down the slope and left me with a tough one back. You see, Frost had already putted up and missed. Obviously thinking that it was all over he then whacked his ball off the green and into the water. I hadn't conceded it, so technically it was still in play.

But it got me wondering what would have happened if I had putted down then just picked up my ball! I was still going to win but it might have led to all sorts of hassle with the rules officials. In the end it didn't matter after I holed my putt for birdie. But looking back, if it had missed, it would have gone at least four feet past.

For his caddie and friend the situation was equally tense. Perhaps looking forward to picking up his 10 per cent caddie's fee for a win, Gary Tilston later commented, 'When we were on that final green, I couldn't stop thinking that if Barry was to three-putt we might never get over the shock.' Thankfully for his bagman's nerves, Lane's final putt gave him an approximate round of 67 and his second winning margin of 2-up.

Known for his short game skills, Lane executes a pitch to the green during the 1993 Dubai Desert Classic.

The tournament over and the cheque presented, it was not long before everyone wanted to know the answer to the question: 'What is it like to win a million dollars in a day?' 'That's a difficult one to answer,' Lane said afterwards. 'A million is a lot, but professional racing drivers earn that every race. It's hard to believe how much American basketball players pick up and in comparison, I don't think golfers are all that highly paid. Besides the actual money didn't really enter my head when I was on the course. Anyway once the tax man, my agent and my caddie have all had their share, then we are down to about $400,000.'

Returning to the European Tour, the publicity his victory generated surprised even Barry Lane. In the months that followed, invitations for tournaments all over the world started appearing through his letter box including four early season tournaments on the US Tour which opened up the possibility of a career in America. Rumours began to circulate about the Englishman leaving his home Tour, rumours which were quickly quashed by Lane himself, 'I enjoy everything about playing in Europe: the courses, the other guys on Tour. There's a lot of camaraderie and it would always be difficult for me to play over there although it was nice to be invited.'

For the likeable Barry Lane, the period since his million dollar victory has not proved quite the stepping stone to success he obviously hoped it would be. The promised swing changes, which saw him attempt to replace his natural draw with a more reliable fade, have proved unsuccessful so far. Despite working with some of the top golf coaches in the world, he plummeted down the Order of Merit from 8th in 1995 (with £936,845) to 76th (with £139,198) a year later.

Continuing through 1997, his loss of form has proved a painful lesson in fortune for Lane. There are always the occasional shafts of light for this talented professional, like his three wins out of three in the preliminary rounds of the 1996 Alfred Dunhill Cup at St Andrews, but he now lacks the consistency he once had. Always the player for the big occasion, winning tournaments, not just prize money, has always been the driving force behind a career which has taken him to a creditable 9th in the all-time European Money List. Yet despite the Andersen event looking increasingly unlikely to continue in its present form (due to the emergence of a series of 'World Tour' events over the next few years) Barry Lane looks back with obvious pride at his million dollar win in just this way.

I think the title itself was the most important thing at the time and nobody can ever take that away from me. While the prize money was great, it was a real honour to be the first ever winner of what looks like being a prestigious event. I think that reason, probably more than anything else, is why I would choose it as the 'Round of My Life'.

Bernhard

Langer

62 in the final round of the Benson & Hedges Spanish Open at Campo de Golf, El Saler, Valencia, 11–14 October 1984.

Having already survived a career-threatening bout of the putting 'yips', in 1984 Bernhard Langer was bidding to become Europe's leading money winner for the second time in four years. Trailing Howard Clark by seven strokes going into the final round of the Spanish Open, he suffered the misfortune of having £3000 stolen from his hotel room the night before. Perhaps taking his annoyance out on the course, Langer's course record score of 62 brushed aside all opposition to win by two shots. At ten under par, it remains one of the lowest ever individual rounds in European PGA Tour history.

For many Bernhard Langer is the grey man of European golf. A seemingly cold individual, he goes about his business quietly, efficiently, and, more often than not, very very slowly. For him there is none of the air-punching drama of American Tiger Woods or the in-your-face aggression of Welshman Ian Woosnam. When the ice-cool German holes a tournament-winning putt, which he has done over fifty times worldwide, little more than a tight-lipped smile will break across his face. And the only thing he will do with his right hand is wave it gently in the air.

One of the best ball strikers in the modern game, Langer has also built a formidable reputation as a rock-hard competitor. Certainly a record that includes two US Masters wins and nine Ryder Cup appearances has made him one of European golf's most enduring figures. Yet behind the cool and calm exterior, you are left with the impression there is so much more to Herr Langer. Therefore it comes as no surprise to discover that, when interviewed, he puts the game of golf a distant third behind God and his family.

I have been very fortunate in my life. I've got wonderful parents, a wonderful wife and have been blessed by God with three wonderful kids. I used to be pretty selfish in the past and my priorities were all wrong. Golf was the most important thing in my life and, if it wasn't good, my entire world was miserable. But now I have things in balance. I'm certainly not a saint out there on the golf course. In fact far from it. Like when you make a three putt and become upset. I take one step back and try and remember there are more important things going on in the world than golf.

Of course, there was one uniquely famous occasion when golf did take most of his attention. Playing in the final singles of the Ryder Cup at Kiawah Island in 1991, Langer was battling it out with the equally tough American, Hale Irwin. In a match that has been labelled forever as the 'War on the Shore', Langer had pulled himself back from the brink of defeat by winning three of the last four holes. Now with the entire match result resting on his shoulders, he faced the ultimate golfing nightmare, a six-foot putt on the last green to achieve game, set and match for the Europeans.

Normally reliable under such circumstances, Langer later described how the putt had caught the edge of an old pitchmark and swerved away from the hole at the last possible moment. But as the putt slipped by on the low side, the German reeled back and let out a shout of anguish. Langer, it seemed, was human after all. Like missing a penalty in the football World Cup final, his failure had been at the same time both highly public and deeply personal. According to some golfing pundits, the miss would probably haunt him for the rest of his career – and possibly even destroy it.

But in the chaotic scenes which followed, amid all the whoopin' and hollerin' and flag waving, Bernhard Langer stood out as possibly the most composed person there. Seemingly oblivious to the excitement around him, he actually took a few moments on the final green to speak to the badly shaken Irwin before heading off to the European team room. Only hours later, he came out with a statement which was somehow typical of the man.

Drawing on his deep religious faith, he said how pleased he was that it was he, and not any of his fellow team-mates, who had missed the putt. After all, he would be the best person to handle such a setback. Anyone who had followed the German's long career knew this was no casual boast. A two-times major winner and twice European number one, he had survived the dreaded putting 'yips' not once, but three times when they threatened to ruin his career.

The involuntary jabbing action had haunted Langer almost since he first turned professional back in 1972, and had become the bane of his life, often appearing under the pressure of competition. For Langer it became so bad at times that he was hardly able to draw the putter back. Even worse, the problem often appeared quite unexpectedly, with perhaps the most notorious occasion coming in the Open Championship at Royal Lytham in 1988. There Langer would take five putts on the par-4 17th, four of them from inside a few feet.

It was an impossible position for any professional golfer to be put in. Before leaving for America a few weeks later, Langer had informed his long-time caddie Pete Coleman not to bother making the trip, 'because I won't be making any money.' Once there, he quietly set about rebuilding both his confidence and putting action from scratch. Looking to take all wrist movement out of the putt, he

Twice US Masters champion, Bernhard Langer.

developed an unusual technique that attracted a certain amount of ridicule. It involved holding the bottom of the grip with his left hand, with the right hand clamped to the inside of his left forearm. With the right arm acting like a lever, Langer was eventually able, with much practice, to give the ball a stiff-arm push towards the hole.

It would be a frustrating struggle at times, but once more he exhibited the amazing strength of will which had taken him to the top of the European game. 'I have always known that I have too much ability to let the yips beat me,' he once said. 'If I can play the touch shots as delicately as I do, then I must be able to putt.' He was right and when the post-Kiawah test did come, Langer was at least ready for it. Incredibly the test of nerve came much sooner than anyone expected, exactly

Drama at Kiawah Island during the 1991 Ryder Cup. Langer, faced with a shortish putt to beat American veteran Hale Irwin and retain the trophy for the Europeans, reels back as the ball slips agonisingly past the hole.

one week later in fact. Standing over a similar length putt on the final green to win the German Masters, Langer once again took it in his stride. With the question marks hanging over his competitive nerve, he calmly stepped up and rolled it in dead centre. It was yet another victory against the odds.

A few years later he would perform the same feat again but under far happier circumstances. This time, another win in Germany followed hard on the heels of his winning performance in the Ryder Cup at Valderrama in 1997. There his two putts on the 17th green had been enough to defeat Brad Faxon in the singles and ensure the trophy stayed on the European side of the ocean.

An unusual putting style along with hard, unrelenting practice had been the answer to Langer's putting woes in the late eighties. In the mid-nineties it would be a broom-handle putter. In between he would capture his second US Masters title in 1993, to go with his first in 1985, and accumulate over £3 million in official prize money in Europe alone.

Today Langer remains one of only four Europeans to have recorded four rounds of 62 or better in an official 72-hole event. (The others are Nick Faldo, Ian Woosnam and Darren Clarke.) So what is the one round which he would select as the 'Round of My Life'?

> Selecting just one round out of my career and calling it the 'best' is very difficult. What is an important round under one set of circumstances, a major like the Masters for example, may not be the same for another competition. In my career I have played really well under difficult conditions for a 71 and not played half as well for a 66. That is the problem. If you ask me what is my most memorable round I would probably refer back to one of the victories at Augusta. But if you ask me to define what is the best golfing round in terms of overall ball-striking then the choice is between three. My 60 in the Linde German Masters in 1997 was obviously special, as were my 62 at Valderrama in the 1994 Volvo Masters and my 62 in the last round of the Spanish Open at El Saler in 1984. But on reflection I would choose the earlier round in Valencia as the 'Round of My Life'. That was a great round in many ways and one which still brings me some pleasure when I think about it.

Born on 27 August 1957 in Anhausen, Bavaria, Bernhard Langer originally turned to golf as a way of making some much needed pocket money. Coming from a relatively poor background, his father Erwin had settled in the area north-west of Munich after escaping from a Russian prison train shortly before the end of the war. A bricklayer by trade, he had little money for the luxuries of life and so gave permission for Bernhard to join his elder brother and sister caddying at the local Augsburg Golf Club.

With golf in sixties Germany the domain of the rich and privileged, it proved the right decision. At nine years old, Langer would cycle five miles each way to the village of Burgwalden where the club was situated. Learning much about social etiquette from the doctors and professors who made up a good part of the membership, he also learnt how to play the game, with the help of a few old clubs left by the caddie shed.

With no expectation other than making a living as a good golf teacher, Langer turned professional at the tender age of 15. Two years later, he won the German National Championship and seemed set for a more tournament-based life. Early in January 1977, a spell in the German Luftwaffe on National Service saw golf take a back-seat probably for the first and only time in his life. Returning to his career fifteen months later, he fell victim to his first attack of the yips and a remarkable cycle of boom and bust was born.

After conquering his inability to hole even the shortest of putts, Langer achieved his first significant victory by winning the 1979 Cacherel European Under-25s' Championship in southern France. Taking first place by a remarkable 17 strokes, his winning margin remains a record almost two decades later. Building on this success, his first victory on the European Tour came less than a year later at the Dunlop Masters tournament at St Pierre, Chepstow. Since then his playing record is almost unsurpassed. Winning at least one tournament almost every year since 1980, he has been a Ryder Cup regular since Walton Heath in 1981. Yet it was in 1984 that he signalled he was ready to move up a league in tournament-winning terms.

Having won the European Order of Merit in 1981 with earnings of £95,991, Langer appeared set to repeat his feat three years later in 1984. Having already captured the French, Dutch and Irish Opens earlier in the season, he arrived at El Saler in October looking to confirm his top position by winning the Spanish title. The Order of Merit had been a tense battle for most of the year. Locked in a struggle with Sam Torrance for the number one spot Langer only had to remember back to the previous year to know how bitter failure was. Then he had finished third behind winner Nick Faldo and runner-up Seve Ballesteros. At El Saler, Langer had no intention of letting it happen again, but after some fairly indifferent golf in the opening three rounds, he looked to have missed out once more. Going into the final day, rounds of 73, 68 and 72 had left him well down the field, seven shots behind tournament leader Howard Clark.

Langer playing out of a tree on the 17th during the 1981 Benson and Hedges International Open at Fulford.

The course at El Saler had proved a reasonably stiff test throughout the week. Situated on the coast just outside Valencia, it had long been acknowledged as one of the finest golf courses in Europe. Often prone to high winds, it has some wonderful holes which wind their way along the shores of the Mediterranean before turning inland among the dwarf pines. Perhaps not quite the tough test it would become in later years, it was certainly not the easy golf course that Langer made it look in the final round in 1984.

In what was probably one of the finest rounds of golf ever seen on the European Tour, Langer launched himself at the course on the final day. No doubt upset by having the money stolen from his hotel room the night before, he made a record breaking nine birdies in the space of eleven holes starting at the 5th. With his earlier birdie at the par-4 2nd this took him to ten under par standing on the 16th tee. And with the tournament all but won, the possibility of breaking the magical 60 barrier was definitely on with three holes to play. It did not happen, but Langer's remarkable 62 was enough to brush aside the opposition and win by two.

I played very well that day. I am not sure how much losing that money affected me but I was certainly upset the following morning. Of course it always helps to get off to a good start. Making my second birdie at the par-5 5th hole was good. Then to follow it up with eight more over the next ten holes was very satisfying. I'm not sure how close I came, if at all, to breaking 60 that day. If I remember, the closing three holes at El Saler were very long and quite difficult and I was pleased to make par in the end. But I think it is crazy to be upset at shooting 62 any day of the week.

Tom

Lehman

64 in the third round of the Open
Championship at Royal Lytham & St Annes,
Lancashire, 18–21 July 1996.

Having come so close to winning the 1996 United States Open at Oakland Hills only weeks earlier, Lehman came to the Open at Royal Lytham still searching for his first major. Now 37 years old, he shared the halfway lead with Irishman, Paul McGinley, after two consecutive rounds of 67. Then with golfers like Ernie Els and Nick Faldo snapping at his heels, he blasted the quality field apart with a remarkable third round score of 64, seven under par. Going into the final day with a six-stroke cushion, Lehman's faltering two over par score of 73 was just enough to give him the title and the £200,000 winner's cheque.

Like in the old movie saying, it took Tom Lehman fourteen years to become an overnight success. Named United States PGA player of the year for 1996 with earnings of $1,780,159, he could reflect on how far he had come since turning professional back in 1982. From struggling journeyman to number one ranked golfer in the world, the transformation had been little short of miraculous.

Undoubtedly, the highlight of his most successful year to date was his Open Championship triumph at Royal Lytham & St Annes. Having set his sights on challenging at the highest level of the game, the amiable Lehman had cruised home to a two-shot victory over the Lancashire links, leaving quality players like Ernie Els and Nick Faldo in his wake. This had catapulted the Minnesota-born professional to immediate superstar status. Having finished runner-up in the United States Open at Oakland Hills weeks earlier, he went on to confirm his place among the golfing elite by winning the prestigious US Tour Championship and the PGA Grand Slam of Golf later the same season.

Though not exactly a rags to riches story, Tom Lehman had certainly experienced the many ups and downs of a golf professional's life. Six years earlier, he had been struggling just to make ends meet. Repeated failure in the early eighties to retain

Tom Lehman celebrating his 1996 Open triumph after his closing round of 73.

his US player's card had sent him in a ten-year tail-spin of satellite tours and second-rate foreign events. 'Honest, I've played everywhere,' he said. 'In Asia, the Dakotas Tour, the South Florida Tour, the Golden State Tour, the Carolina Tour, the list is endless.'

Standing on the 18th green at Royal Lytham that July evening with a winner's cheque for £200,000 in his pocket, he must surely have thought back to those early days; days spent taking showers in the rain just to save on motel bills, and days spent travelling around America in a battered Volvo and playing golf in backwater tournaments where first prize would often fail to cover his expenses.

Making the best out of what a journalist once described as an 'agricultural' golf swing, Lehman then came within a whisker of giving up. Ranked 425th in the world, short of money and having hit the big 'three-zero', he was offered the position of golf coach at the University of Minnesota in 1990. Now with a wife to support and new baby on the way, the temptation of secure employment was obvious. Then came the moment which changed his whole life.

Reading through his contract, he discovered that his duties would include renting out skis in the winter months! That was it for Lehman. The thought of being nailed to a pro shop in a bleak Mid-Western winter was the final straw. No matter what the cost, he would give tournament golf one more try.

The decision was backed by his wife Melissa, and proved to be the right one. Still without his player's card for the main PGA Tour in the United States, Tom travelled the world looking for golfing success. A few months later he finally found it by winning $25,000 in the South African Open, the biggest payday of his career so far. It proved just the start he was looking for.

Continuing to play his golf on a shoestring budget, Lehman returned to the Hogan Tour in 1992. With the pressure on him to succeed greater than ever, he finally got the breaks he deserved, winning three times that season. Topping the Money List with $141,936 the rejuvenated golfer regained his exempt status for the main Tour the following season. The rest, as they say, is golfing history. His first year on Tour since 1985, he helped himself to nine top-ten finishes, earning over $½ million in the process, and finished a creditable 24th on the Money List. He has hardly looked back since.

Capturing his first major championship at the relatively advanced age of 37 also had its advantages for the quietly spoken Lehman. After years scratching out a living away from the golfing spotlight, his win came at a time when he could appreciate it the most. For him, the journey to golfing glory had been both long and hard. And as he bear-hugged the most famous trophy in golf that warm July evening, he could perhaps reflect on just how far he had come. 'We were never quite completely broke,' he said later, 'but at one point we got down to our last $1,000 which is fairly close.'

Winning the Open Championship had been a dream come true for Tom Lehman. His victory had come courtesy of a final two-over-par round of 73, enough to give him a two-stroke margin over Ernie Els and Mark McCumber in joint second place. It was not, however, that round in his opinion which enabled him to win the tournament – that had come on day three with a magnificent score of 64. His lowest ever round in a major, it had put daylight between him and the chasing pack and given him an almost impregnable six-shot advantage going into the last day. It was a lead he was never going to lose. For Lehman it was the key round of his Open triumph and the one which he nominates as the 'Round of My Life'.

> I have no doubt which was the most memorable round of my career. It was my 64 in the third round of the British Open at Royal Lytham in 1996. I guess some people, if they won a major, would choose the last round as that's the one with most pressure. But for me, all the work was done on the Saturday. I played so well that day it gave me a lot of confidence. Driving, iron play, putting, everything worked well. And even with Nick Faldo in second place, I pretty much knew that unless I had a real disaster somewhere, I was going to win. That's why it was the 'Round of My Life'.

Tom Lehman began his lasting love affair with the majors by finishing runner-up to José-María Olazábal in the 1994 Masters at Augusta. Despite having led going into the final round, only to finish with a level par score of 72, it would be a stepping stone to future major success. 'It was my first time in a situation like that, going into Sunday in the lead,' he said. 'If I could do it again I'd sure do things differently, but all in all, it was a positive experience. At that point, I knew I was capable of winning a major.'

Gaining confidence from his performance, Lehman made his PGA Tour breakthrough by winning the Memorial Tournament at Muirfield Village later the same year, with four record-breaking rounds of 67. His cheque for $270,000 went a long way to securing fourth place in the Tour Money List.

The 1995 season was also a solid one for Lehman with a third place finish in the US Open at Shinnecock Hills. However, there was a small problem. He ended up just three strokes behind eventual winner Corey Pavin, but his habit of posting superb third round scores (67) only to follow them up with poor finishing rounds (74) was finally starting to get to him.

Having now achieved a certain financial security, Lehman was forced to turn his attention to more important matters. A regular health check late in 1995 showed he was in the first stages of cancer of the colon. Surgery followed and after a short time away from competitive golf, he made a triumphant return the following May by winning the 1996 Colonial National Invitation. It was the start of what would prove a remarkable year.

His old last-round problem reappeared in the US Open at Oakland Hills in June 1996. Leading the field by a single shot after his third round 65, Lehman had reached the 72nd tee joint leader at two under with his close friend and fellow Bible class student, Steve Jones. With news filtering back about Davis Love III having three-putted the final green to take him out of a three-way share of the lead, the championship would be decided between the last two players out on the course.

In a decision which effectively cost him the championship, Lehman overruled his caddie, Andy Martinez, on what club to hit off the last. While the experienced Martinez advised a 3-wood, he had chosen his driver. Inevitably, the tee shot came out hot with the ball running through the dog-leg fairway and coming to rest in a deep fairway bunker. Forced to lay up pitching-wedge distance away from the green, Lehman made bogey to Jones' par and lost by a shot. With his poor final round of 71 bettered by the top ten finishers that week, question marks over his competitive nerve were beginning to emerge. (Lehman was also criticised for quoting Bible passages to an increasingly tense Jones to help calm him down.)

Despite the obvious disappointment of leading three majors going into the final round and finishing second, Tom's confidence remained high going into the Open Championship at Royal Lytham three weeks later. The Lytham course has fewer blind shots than other Open venues like Troon and St Andrews. Ignoring the fact he had only played two other links courses in his life because he thought it would suit his long, accurate iron play, Royal St George's and Turnberry, Lehman felt at home instantly. Perhaps more importantly, it was a golf course he knew he could win on.

> Even after the US Open I felt my chances were really good at Lytham. I am never one to say I am going to win a tournament but if you asked me on the Monday of the Open, or even a couple of weeks before, I would have said I had a really good chance. I was mentally ready to play and to win.

Amazingly, he was not the only one who thought he was going to win. In the week before the Open, Lehman had been approached on the practice ground at Sunningdale by Peter Lopez, manager of the world famous band The Eagles, who invited him along to their Wembley concert the next evening. At the concert Tom spotted Nick Faldo sitting only a few seats away. A big fan of the band, the Englishman visibly winced halfway through the show when lead singer Glen Frey announced they had a celebrity in the audience. 'One of our favourite guys, professional golfer Tom Lehman! He finished second in the US Open and we know he's going to win at Lytham.' One week later, Tom Lehman set about proving him right.

With the weather at Lytham more typical of his Scottsdale home in Arizona than the Lancashire coast, Lehman opened up with two consecutive rounds of 67. In the lead after 36 holes, he was tied with Dublin-born Irishman Paul McGinley at eight under par. One stroke ahead of a small group including Ernie Els and Jack Nicklaus, Lehman knew if he was going to make a move it would have to be in the third round.

Like in any other tournament, Saturday at the Open is known as 'moving day', the day when players who have missed the cut move out, and players looking to mount a challenge try to move up. But as Lehman came out for the third round on Saturday, no one could have predicted the fireworks which followed.

With quality players like Nick Faldo, Fred Couples and Greg Norman all hovering within a few shots of the lead, no one had given the quiet American much of a chance, especially after his recent performances in the majors. Yet one look at his third round scores should have given them some idea of the brilliant round which followed. Paired with the inexperienced Paul McGinley, Lehman literally blasted the field apart with some of the most spectacular golf seen on a British links. A seven-under-par round of 64, it would be the round of Tom Lehman's life.

> I think anytime you are in the hunt for a major championship you learn something about yourself. Even though I hadn't won yet, I felt I was getting closer all the time. At Lytham, I was less nervous and more comfortable than I had ever been up to that point. I had also formulated a small game plan throughout the week. I had talked to the head pro [Eddie

Birchenough] and he told me the secret of Lytham was not hitting it far, just to keep it in play. That is what I tried to do all week. I also knew before the third round began, that I was playing really well and if I could just get off to a solid start, I might be able to do something. At the time, I was hoping to score well enough to keep myself in good position going into the final day. I had no idea things would turn out as well as they ultimately did.

Lehman playing out of a fairway bunker on the 18th on his way to a remarkable third round score of 64.

In one of the greatest outward halves in Open history, Lehman made four birdies in the first six holes, to race into a clear lead. With another following at the 9th, he went to the turn in a remarkable 29 strokes, a new record for Royal Lytham. With Nick Faldo leading the chasing pack at nine under par, Lehman now enjoyed a four-stroke lead with the back nine still to play.

At this stage Tom was unstoppable. He went five strokes clear at the 11th after holing a birdie putt from 15 feet. Then, after a solid par at the next, he drew even further ahead after reducing the difficult par-4 14th to a mere drive and pitching-wedge for yet another birdie. As if to confirm his massive superiority, he bolted in a twisting 30-foot putt on the short par-4 16th to record his eighth birdie of the day. With a new course record in the making, he came to the final hole knowing that a par 4 would give him a 63, comfortably beating the 65 by Seve Ballesteros recorded en route to his 1988 win.

Bunkered off the tee, Lehman looked understandably disappointed to find his ball had rolled up against the steep face. Left with no other option than splashing out a few yards down the fairway, his second shot was unlucky to find a small patch of semi-rough off to the right. To his credit, Lehman then managed to scramble his short-iron third to within 15 feet of the hole, giving himself an outside chance of making par. But, faced with a slightly uphill putt for his four, he failed to strike it hard enough and came up two feet short. Moments later he strolled up and tapped in his putt for bogey and a remarkable seven-under-par round of 64. Yet there was still a discernible touch of annoyance at it not being at least one stroke less.

> When you hit it into one of those bunkers, you have a potential double-bogey every time. You can only move it a few yards forward even out of a perfect lie. You are always left with a longish third if it's a par-4 hole for example, and that's when the problems start. When I was in the bunker on the 18th in the third round, I was happy to get it out, happy to get it on the green, but slightly disappointed about missing out on my par. Still it's not often you shoot a seven-under round in a major.

By the close of the third round, Lehman had taken a commanding lead. His 64 had taken him to fifteen under par for the tournament with Nick Faldo second on nine under, Mark Brooks and Vijay Singh joint third on eight under, and Ernie Els and Fred Couples back in fifth position on seven under. While the final round would be a fairly uncomfortable ride at times, especially with his fellow American Mark McCumber shooting a 66 for second place, Lehman would hold on to win. Despite compiling a nervous two over par 73 on Sunday, it was always going to be good enough to give him his first major championship.

> I just felt so proud to win the Open Championship. This is the Olympics of golf, the oldest and the biggest of the majors. In fact the further I got away from the actual Open itself, the more it meant to me. But even then it took a while to sink in. The weeks after Lytham were so busy, my schedule was so hectic, that I didn't have much time to think about it. The Old Claret Jug was sitting on my mantelpiece back home in Arizona but it was so revered by all the family that I hardly touched it, not even to polish it. I think it really came home to me a short time later when some teenage kids came up to my door 'Trick or Treating' during Hal-loween. They knew who I was and asked could they see the trophy. They just huddled around it, reading off the famous names that were on it – Nicklaus, Palmer . . . They were really excited and that made me feel good about winning it. It was then I really felt like an Open champion.

Justin

Leonard

65 in the final round of the Open

Championship at Royal Troon,

17–20 July 1997.

Coming into the Open at Royal Troon many of the top names in golf were set to challenge for the title. With quality players like Ernie Els, Tiger Woods, Greg Norman and home favourite, Colin Montgomerie, all in top form it was thought to be the most open event in years. Instead the final round became a battle between three lesser known players, Jesper Parnevik of Sweden, Darren Clarke of Northern Ireland and Justin Leonard of the United States. With Parnevik leading the tournament at eleven under par and Clarke two shots further back, Leonard stood in fourth place at six under with eighteen holes to play. Then, putting together one of the lowest final round scores in the tournament's history, Leonard battled his way to the top of the leader board to become champion at the young age of 25.

By winning the Open Championship at Royal Troon in 1997, Justin Leonard emerged as one of the brightest young players in world golf. The Dallas-born pro is now rated alongside his fellow 'twentysomethings', Tiger Woods and Ernie Els, as potentially the most dominant golfer of the next decade. Yet for the thousands gathered around the final green for the presentation of the Open trophy, the question many could have been forgiven for asking was, Justin who?

A relative unknown in Europe, Leonard arrived in Scotland with none of the fanfare reserved for some of his better known rivals. Tiger Woods had won the Masters in spectacular style earlier in the season, while Ernie Els was looking to make it an Open double after winning his second US Open title at Congressional only weeks earlier. Yet it would be the fresh-faced Texan who would be grabbing all the headlines come Sunday evening. Not only that but the manner of his victory, with birdies at the 16th and 17th on his way to a wonderful closing round of 65, showed just how much he deserved to be champion.

Extending the run of American winners at Royal Troon to five after Arnold Palmer, Tom Weiskopf, Tom Watson and Mark Calcavecchia, Leonard's twelve-under-par total also set a new Open record for the famous Ayrshire links. His skill and determination were unrivalled that week. Showing a steely maturity well beyond his 25 years, Leonard came from five shots behind on the final day to overhaul third round tournament leader Jesper Parnevik. Leonard's brilliance, combined with mistakes from his closest rivals down the closing stretch, meant he would eventually run out the winner by a margin of three strokes. Taking his place in Open history as one of the youngest ever champions, is it any wonder that Justin Leonard selects that round at Troon as the 'Round of My Life'?

Certainly my final round of 65 at Royal Troon in '97 was among the most memorable rounds of golf I have ever played in my life, if not the most memorable. It contributed to my first major victory and for that reason alone it will always be special to me.

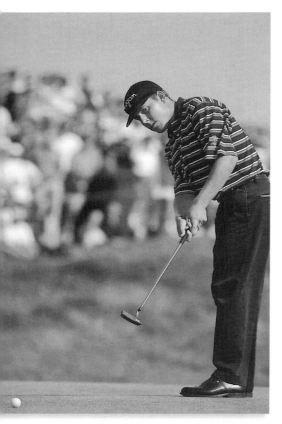

Justin Leonard produced one of the great final rounds in Open Championship history with his 65 at Royal Troon to win by two clear shots over Europeans, Darren Clarke and Jesper Parnevik.

Justin Charles Garrett Leonard was born in Dallas on 15 June 1967. Nicknamed 'Jasper' by his family and friends, he played golf alongside soccer and baseball as a youngster. Later voted among the top 25 most eligible bachelors in the United States by *Cosmopolitan* magazine, his golfing achievements have been equally impressive.

Crowned United States Amateur champion in 1992, he was nominated by *Golf Digest* magazine as the world's number one amateur a year later. Leaving the path clear for another amateur prodigy called Tiger Woods to shine, Leonard turned professional in June 1994 and made his pro debut at the Canon Greater Hartford Open. He quickly earned enough prize money in the thirteen tournaments he played that year to become exempt for the following season. From that point on his career in the paid ranks has been little short of meteoric.

His first professional victory came in the 1996 Buick Open. His three-quarter, round-the-houses swing means that he will never be considered the longest of hitters, but Leonard still managed to pocket over $748,000 for the 1996 season on the way to finishing a creditable 22nd in the official Money List. Having now established himself, his target for the 1997 season was simple: to make enough prize money to get himself into the US Ryder Cup side to face the Europeans at Valderrama in Spain that September. It was an ambition he would fulfil in the most dramatic way possible.

In the weeks leading up to the Open Championship at Royal Troon, Leonard had a series of high finishes in the United States, including a win in the Kemper Open, which had put him on the very fringes of making the team. Knowing that a good finish in the third major of the season would be just enough to take him into the ten automatic places, his spirits were given an extra boost by team captain, Tom Kite, during the tournament.

Tom had said to me in the week that I was tenth on the [Ryder Cup] list and why don't I take care of it this weekend. I thought, 'Why not?' It's been a big goal of mine to make the team for two years, ever since Tom was made captain.

It would be no easy task. Prior to the Open great emphasis had been placed on how many of the world's top golfers were performing at their best coming into the championship. Defending champion Tom Lehman had just strolled to victory in the Loch Lomond Invitational with a 19-under-par total – a score which Colin Montgomerie had said was impossible – while Montgomerie himself had recorded a remarkable 62 on the way to winning the Irish Open at Druids Glen two weeks earlier. Others like Greg Norman, Nick Price and Ernie Els were all in top form and among the favourites to win the championship. Golf, though, can prove a fickle beast and rarely delivers on such predictions.

Playing in only his fourth Open, his first without having to pre-qualify, long odds of 60–1 were given against Justin Leonard lifting the silver claret jug aloft on Sunday. Perhaps it was not surprising, considering that his past record in the event had been fairly dismal. He had missed the halfway cut both at Turnberry in 1994 and Royal Lytham in 1996. The only previous time he contested the weekend was in 1995 at St Andrews, and even then he finished tied for 58th!

In stark contrast to Tiger Woods, who spent the entire week surrounded by a posse of security guards, journalists, photographers and marketing men, Leonard went about his business quietly and with little fuss. His hotel accommodation was private and unassuming and, with no family or friends travelling to Scotland to watch him play, there were few distractions. 'That was probably a good thing,' he said later, 'because it enabled me to really focus on what I was doing.' Which that particular week meant winning the Open Championship.

Having maintained his composure in the strong winds which ripped across the Troon links on the first two days, Leonard came through to complete his opening three rounds in six under par. Like his fellow Texans Tom Kite and Ben Crenshaw, he had the reputation of being a good 'wind' player and so it proved with magnificent scores of 69, 66 and 72. With players like Sandy Lyle having already fallen victim to the conditions with opening rounds of 87 and 75, Leonard now had a simple game plan for the final day.

> The guys with the strongest mental outlook were going to do well. You have to stay patient and realise you are going to make some bogeys. At the same time you have to recognise a good bounce when you see one. I've never had control of the weather so you just wake up, see what it is like and go from there.

Despite finding himself five strokes behind leader Jesper Parnevik of Sweden, and three behind second place Darren Clarke of Northern Ireland, Leonard felt he was in good position to make a challenge. Having recently switched to metal woods he had also found an extra twenty yards off the tee and felt positive about his chances. 'The confidence keeps building,' he said later. 'I had come from five strokes back before and felt there was no reason why I couldn't do it again.'

After starting with 156 competitors, the top-class field had been spread-eagled after the opening three days. With none of the pre-tournament favourites still in the hunt, the Open was effectively reduced to a three man race. (Fred Couples was in joint third with Leonard starting the last day but an ailing back would take him out of the running with 74 in the final round.) Speaking about his attitude prior to the final round at the time, Leonard commented,

> I slept well, in fact my alarm woke me. I think being five shots back meant I had more of a relaxed attitude. I was also thinking about the Ryder Cup knowing I could lock up my team place. But then I would say,

'Hey wait a second. You're in a golf tournament here and you're in good shape.' I knew I had to focus on one thing at a time and that's what I did.

....

With mistakes coming from the leading pack, Leonard got himself into contention by sprinting to the turn in 31 strokes. With some excellent putting the key to his five-under-par total on the front nine, his round had started with a regulation two-putt par at the first from 15 feet. Then having single putted the next three holes from 12, ten and four feet respectively, he contrived to three putt the 210-yard par-3 5th for his first bogey of the day. It was a disappointing end to such a dynamic start, especially as Jesper Parnevik improved his own score, though not quite as dramatically, by playing his opening five holes in one under par.

Thankfully for the young American, the damage did not take too long to repair. A pair of stunning wedge shots at the 6th and 7th holes helped set up two more one-putt birdies and Justin Leonard was back in the chase once more. Quickly followed by another birdie at the 9th, his sixth in nine holes, there was now only one player between Justin Leonard and the tournament lead – Jesper Parnevik.

The final nine holes at Royal Troon proved to be not only a contest of skill but a fascinating battle of wills for the two young professionals. In the final run-in, the big hitting Darren Clarke would eventually recover to finish as joint runner-up. But after shanking his tee-shot out-of-bounds en route to a double bogey at the 2nd and an outward nine of 37, he was never in serious contention for the title. Nor for that matter was any one else.

The most important stretch of golf in Leonard's young career, the back nine, began poorly with a dropped shot at the 10th. Then, with Troon's most difficult holes coming up, a sequence of remarkable putts helped keep him in contention. At the hardest rated hole on the course, the 463-yard par-4 11th, he rescued par from ten feet after missing the green with a 4-iron. Under increasing pressure, it was the same pitch-and-putt story at the next, with the American salvaging par after hitting a wonderful lob wedge to within two feet.

With Parnevik maintaining his lead with some solid iron play, Leonard could only continue making pars and be patient. Managing to keep in touch with Parnevik, he made a vital putt on the par-4 15th from 18 feet to save yet another par. Fortunately it gave him the platform he needed to mount a final assault on the championship. With three holes left and the pressure now at boiling point, Leonard trailed the Swede by just a single stroke. 'I enjoy pressure,' he commented. 'Getting into the middle of a tournament at the weekend is what it's all about. That's when you learn most about yourself and your game.'

Standing on the tee of the 542-yard par-5 16th Justin Leonard knew he needed a great finish and duly delivered. Two solid 3-woods, a full wedge and another wonderful putt from 15 feet gave him the birdie he desperately needed. Walking off the green he glanced up at one of the scoreboards to find he was now tied for the lead. But this was no time for celebration. With Parnevik yet to play the hole, and likely to make birdie, he now needed to play Troon's tough 17th and 18th in no more than par. But as the week-long stroke average for both holes was well above their 3, 4 par, it was going to be no easy task.

A 3-iron to the heart of the tough par-3 17th looked to have set up the par he needed. With the green dried out by the wind earlier in the week, Leonard could probably consider himself unlucky that his ball had taken a hard bounce before coming to rest close to the back edge. Lining up from around 30 feet, he faced a lengthy putt with a ridge halfway along the line. In what proved a major turning point in the championship, he calmly drew the putter head back and knocked the ball straight into the middle of the hole.

> I was expecting to birdie the 16th but I was praying over the one at 17 just to two-putt. I saw the line and it went in. About three feet from the hole it was dead centre. As soon as it went in everyone went nuts! The hair on the back of my neck stood up. I didn't allow Jesper any breathing room.

He was right. Moments later, Parnevik stood over a short putt for birdie on the hole behind and inexplicably pushed it wide. Ultimately it would bring the Swede his second near miss in the Open Championship in four years, the first being when he gave away a final round lead to Nick Price at Turnberry in 1994. 'I felt if I had made that one, I'd win,' he said afterwards. 'I saw Justin had birdied the 17th and the wind went out my sails for good.'

In typically efficient style Leonard played the finishing hole at Royal Troon in a regulation par. Believing that four at 18 would put him in a play-off, he played a safe 3-wood off the tee, followed by an equally safe 6-iron into the heart of the green. 'I don't like crises,' said the young American afterwards.

Acknowledging the applause of the huge grandstands near the green, Leonard calmly two-putted from 40 feet for a wonderful closing round of 65, including a remarkable total of 25 putts. Moments later, he watched from the scorer's hut to the right of the final green as Parnevik (73) and Clarke (71) finished off their rounds knowing by then that the title was already his. Winner by three clear shots, his six-under-par score was the second lowest winning round in Open Championship history.

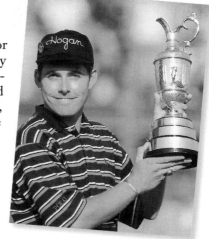

Justin Leonard with the Open trophy, the first major victory of his career.

> Most of the day I was two or three behind but I made a lot of putts. I was surprised how calm I stayed until the 18th. Being able to come through with a tournament on the line like this one is something great to be able to reflect on.

After maintaining a cool exterior throughout the week, Justin Leonard was unable to contain his emotions during the presentation ceremony which followed minutes later. 'This is such a thrill,' he said. 'I hope it takes a long time to sink in.' Then reflecting on what had been the greatest week of his life, he shed a discreet tear for his absent family and friends. 'I was thinking about my family, coach Randy Smith and the people at Royal Oaks, my home course in Dallas, and how crazy the men's locker room would be.'

However there was one friend at hand to share his triumph. Tom Kite had already left Troon on his way home, but dashed back from nearby Prestwick Airport on hearing the news, and was there as his fellow Texan raised the Open trophy aloft. Congratulating him, Kite's next words were, 'Welcome to the team.'

Ultimately, Valderrama would not prove as successful as Troon with the United States losing out for the second consecutive time in the Ryder Cup. But even in defeat Justin Leonard proved what a skilled competitor he had become since his Open victory in July.

Nancy

Lopez

64 in the final round of the Colgate Dinah Shore Invitational at Mission Hills Country Club, Palm Springs, California, 2–5 April 1981.

The Colgate Dinah Shore Invitational was an elite tournament open to women professionals who had achieved a third place or higher on the LPGA circuit during the previous season. Nancy Lopez went into the final round trailing the relatively unknown Carolyn Hill by three shots. Having exploded onto the women's golf scene back in 1978 with a remarkable nine victories in her first season alone, question marks had arisen over Lopez's ability to sustain her remarkable winning streak. Now with only one victory so far in 1981, the Arizona Copper Classic, pressure had been mounting on her to perform, especially after she had lost a strong lead going into the last round of the Kemper Open only a week earlier. Flying in the face of her critics, her eight-birdie round of 64 not only won Lopez the event, but set a new tournament record in the process.

The report about Nancy Lopez in the local *Desert Sun* newspaper could hardly have been more damning. 'After three days of recuperation from her lacklustre finish at the Women's Open at Kemper last week in Hawaii,' read the article dated 2 April 1981, 'the 25-year-old golfer was anxious to begin her defence today of the Dinah Shore Invitational. But there are a few kinks in her game that Lopez-Melton admits she must get rid of to be successful this week at Mission Hills.'

Published on the opening day of the prestigious $310,000 tournament, it was not the only press item which had questioned her ability in the months before the event. Described as 'a one-off superstar who would rather come in fifth than win by playing safe' Nancy Lopez certainly had her problems going into the Dinah Shore. Her putting was out of sorts and her normally reliable long game had been battered by the strong winds at Royal Kaanapali in the Kemper Open. Yet above all, she was the victim of her own incredible success.

The most prolific tournament winner of her generation, Lopez was the hottest thing women's golf had seen since the days of Babe Zaharias. Not only had she won a record-breaking nine events in her debut season of 1978, she had followed it up with another eight in 1979. Blowing through the LPGA tournament circuit like a whirlwind, she was practically unbeatable in her first two years as a professional. But for many the 'problem' had started in 1980 when she won just three tournaments. This was never going to be good enough for the golden girl of American golf and despite her having won twenty titles in just three years the downward slide of 9 to 8 to 3 had some journalists reaching for their typewriters.

Like Arnold Palmer in the sixties, many blamed the arduous nature of her playing schedule for her lack of tournament victories, while others pointed out the many commercial (and often highly lucrative) interests she had taken on since turning professional. Whatever the truth, having completely dominated the women's game in those seasons, by 1981 she was losing tournaments when once she would have won. Yet by the end of that April week, Nancy Lopez would have answered her critics in the most emphatic way possible.

Coming from three strokes behind going into the final day, she blitzed through the top-class field with a record-breaking score of 64, one of the greatest single rounds of golf ever seen in a United States LPGA tournament. She made eight birdies and no bogeys around the tough Mission Hills course in Palm Springs, eventually winning by two clear shots. That was why Nancy Lopez selected this round as the 'Round of My Life'.

> Picking out just one round from my career is tough. I think every round is special if it leads to winning a big tournament like the LPGA Championship or Dinah Shore. Maybe if I had a winning round in the US Open that might stand out above the others but, as it hasn't happened yet, I don't really know. So I guess the round I would probably choose is my 64 in the final round of the Dinah Shore in 1981. That was special for lots of reasons. Not only for the golf I played that day but the whole build-up to the tournament. Like any big event it was played under lots of pressure and I think it's the one single round I am most proud of. But above all it was just a great round of golf.

Nancy Lopez was born on 6 January 1957 in Torrance, California. Long since ranked among the greats of women's golf, she remains one of the most popular and enduring figures in the world game, not only for her remarkable tournament record but for the sparkling way she often goes about her business. Charming and down-to-earth, she was among the first American women professionals to exhibit her skills in Europe. As big a favourite today as she was back in the early eighties, her personality has drawn as many people to the game as the quality of her golf. And when she is not knocking in birdies and eagles she can usually be found offering an autograph and a warm smile to those thousands of loyal fans who still follow her every round.

Still competing at the highest level as we approach the new millennium, Lopez is credited with doing as much for the popularity and growth of the United States LPGA Tour as Seve Ballesteros did in Europe during the same period. Encouraged to take up golf by her Mexican-born father, Domingo, at just eight years of age, Nancy had won her first tournament within a year. Quite what the quality of the competition was is unsure, but she is known to have run out winner by a remarkable 110 strokes!

Confirming the rich promise she had shown at a tender age, she embarked on a brilliant amateur career which saw her capture the United States Girls'

Championship in 1972 and 1974. Not forgetting her ethnic roots, she won the Mexico Ladies' title in 1975 before going on to represent America in the biennial Curtis Cup match against Britain a year later. But despite her wonderful record, the girl from California seemed an unlikely world beater in those days. Mostly self-taught, her painfully slow swing with its strange loop at the top looked unlikely to produce effective results but how wrong we were.

'I have used a slow deliberate swing all my career,' said Lopez, 'mainly because I have seen many golfers with small swing errors that become catastrophic because they swing at breakneck speed.'

A leading figure in the women's game since the late 1970s, Nancy Lopez continues to be among the most stylish golfers playing today.

After turning professional her rise was nothing less than mete-oric. Seven US Tour victories in her first year, including a remark-able five in a row, gave her number one spot on the LPGA Money List for 1978. It also made her the most cast-iron certainty for Rookie of the Year in the history of women's golf!

Lopez's success was not just limited to the lucrative United States Tour. She showed her versatility by capturing both the Far East Open and the fledgling Euro-pean Open at Sunningdale later the same season. Then, before anybody started talking about her being 'a flash in the pan' she came out the following year and did it all again. Winning eight times in total, her scoring average for the season of 71.20 set a new Tour record which would stand for many years to come. Then to cap it all off, she also got married to a well-known sports presenter, Tim Melton.

To the outside world, the newly titled Nancy Lopez-Melton could do little wrong. Big-name sponsors fell over themselves trying to get the golden girl of women's golf to endorse their products. No tournament was complete without her presence and as 1980 dawned she looked set to dominate the women's game well into the next decade. Showing some of the form which had catapulted her to fame and fortune, the year itself was successful enough with three wins in the Kemper Open, Sarah Coventry Tournament and Rail Charity Classic. But the simple arithmetic revealed the large drop from eight down to three, so in the eyes of the golfing media something must have gone wrong. In typically modest style, Nancy offered no excuses but hoped that her game would be a little sharper for the next season.

At the start of 1981 she seemed back to her best with victory in the Arizona Copper Classic, but then came an inexplicable lull. The slow rhythmic swing which had served Lopez so well suddenly developed a hook which threatened to ruin her career before it had really even started. Then the season turned into a real struggle. Her putting went off the boil and started letting her down all too often in the weeks leading up to the Dinah Shore. She finished third behind Amy Alcott in the Kemper Open in Hawaii after faltering in the final round. Losing out on a great chance for victory was certainly not the best preparation for one of the biggest events on the United States LPGA calendar.

Sponsored by Colgate, the Dinah Shore Invitational was the richest event on the Ladies' Professional Golf Association Tour. Still not rated as a 'major' back in the early eighties, it was open to a select group of 86 golfers all of whom qualified for the event by having finished the previous season with a top-three placing. Even in this top-class field, Lopez-Melton had been installed as pre-tournament favourite despite her failures of the past few weeks. But Nancy herself was not quite so confident.

> I'd played in three tournaments in a row and I was probably a little more tired than I would have liked to have been. The course at Royal Kaanapali was pretty hard to walk on. I got worn out by it. Then, flying back, we left Sunday night and got back to Los Angeles at 6 o'clock Monday morning. So you get goofed up. I didn't know whether to go to sleep or stay up or whatever. All I know is that by the time I teed it up in Palm Springs, I felt like I was still flying on that plane back from Hawaii.

Another problem she faced at Mission Hills was the speed of the greens. Incredibly quick with lots of break, they contrasted starkly with the sluggish surfaces of Royal Kaanapali the week before. Competing in the Desert Inn pro-am which took place in the two days preceding the Dinah Shore tournament Nancy's game had looked increasingly ragged. Having been forced to change her putting style in Hawaii after a large downpour soaked the course before the event, Lopez found herself struggling to re-adjust.

> Playing on those slow greens I was jabbing everything. I mean you would take a whole divot on every hole. If you were uphill, 30 feet away, you had to hit like a 60 footer. You had to hit it real hard! My swing also got tired and when my timing changes a little bit, I swing quicker than when I'm not tired. As for the pro-am, you're never really concentrating as hard as you might and that has a lot to do with how well you hit the ball. But I think you start concentrating more when the tournament really starts. Then it all changes.

For Nancy Lopez the change was immediate. Recording rounds of 71, 73 and 69 over the 6,242-yard course, she went into the final round three behind tournament leader Carolyn Hill. Looking to pass through the $700,000 mark in prize money, she was determined to make her presence felt. For once the pressure was not on her shoulders alone and she would take full advantage during the final round.

My swing was smooth and I had a lot of confidence before the final round. Not leading meant I could play aggressively most of the day and coming from behind, as I did, perhaps gave me the edge, especially on the front nine.

A smiling Nancy Lopez at the 1981 US LPGA Championship.

Birdies at the first two holes were quickly followed by two more at 7 and 9, giving her a nine hole total of 32. This took her to seven under par for the tournament. Still trailing the highly inexperienced, but determined Hill, Lopez continued her assault on the back nine with another birdie at the 12th. Holing a testing downhill putt from 15 feet, she walked off the back of the green smiling to the enthusiastic Palm Springs crowd. She felt good and it was to prove the start of a famous charge.

With her putting stroke working like a dream, Lopez quickly followed her effort at the 12th with birdies at the next three holes. Having holed out from 7, 20 and 18 feet respectively on 13, 14 and 15, she was now an incredible eight under par for the fifteen holes played! It had been a remarkable performance and gave her a stranglehold on the tournament which she never looked like releasing. To her credit Carolyn Hill finished strongly for a 279 total, but par figures at the remaining three holes were enough to give Lopez victory by two clear shots. Eleven under par for the tournament, her final round score of 64 was soon declared a new course record.

Playing so well is what made this round special. I've played just as well at times but never under such circumstances. Of course, it was wonderful to win the Dinah Shore but what gave me most pleasure was how I played. My whole game was great that day: putting, drives, iron play, everything. I just wish I could play that well all the time.

Her closest rivals agreed with her. Beth Daniel, whose own round of 65 had been enough for third place behind Jane Blalock, described the score as 'just incredible!'

It also gave Nancy the opportunity to fulfil a light-hearted promise she made just before the tournament had started.

> The caddies wanted to raise some cash to buy softball equipment to help pass the long hours on tour. I told them, 'Well guys, if I win the Dinah Shore, I'll buy your softball equipment.' So I said, 'Now you know what to do with your players. Let me win the tournament!' In the end, I guess I didn't need their help.

The result took Nancy Lopez to the top of the Money List for 1981 but only temporarily. By the end of the season, Beth Daniel had usurped her position as number one and it was not until four years later that she resumed her throne. Now married to her second husband, baseball star Ray Knight, she rolled back the years to become the first golfer in LPGA history to earn over $400,000 in a single season. Winning five times in 1985, she also collected her third Player of the Year award along with her third Vare trophy, given to the golfer with the lowest stroke average.

Nancy was back, and the golfing world rejoiced at the news. Then with just one more victory needed to give her a coveted place in the LPGA Hall of Fame, she took most of 1986 off to have her second child. But it was impossible to keep her out of the limelight for long. In February 1987, less than a month after her 30th birthday, she captured the Sarasota Classic to register her 35th win on Tour and became only the eleventh member of this elite group of women golfers.

Even joining legendary figures like Babe Zaharias, Joyce Wethered and Glenna Collett-Vare, the name of Nancy Lopez is destined to be among the most revered. Today, she is now into her third decade on Tour and seems to show little sign of easing up. Indeed, as recently as 1997, she was runner-up to British golfer Alison Nicholas in the United States Open, an event which she still holds onto her dream of winning one day. But whether she wins another major to go along with the handful she already has is unimportant. Her contribution to women's golf is immeasurable and she will long remain the most celebrated woman golfer of her generation.

Davis

Love III

66 in the final round of the US PGA
Championship at Winged Foot Country
Club, New York, 14–17 August 1997.

Davis Love III went into the final day at Winged Foot level on seven under par, joint leader with the newly crowned British Open champion, Justin Leonard. Having already blown a golden chance to win the 1996 US Open after three-putting the final green, the pressure was now on Love to come through and win his first major. The two were four strokes ahead of their nearest challengers, and so the round took on a match-play feel with the lead swapping back and forth. In what proved an emotional victory, Love finished the better over the closing holes, going on to establish a new championship record for Winged Foot of 269.

D avis Love III must have viewed the final stages of the 1997 Open Championship at Royal Troon with mixed feelings. While delighted for his friend and fellow countryman, Justin Leonard, he must also have felt the odd pang of envy as he watched him come through to win. Everything about his victory was to be admired: the seemingly unhurried way he controlled himself under such enormous pressure to record a final round of 65, the pictures of him with the Open trophy, his acceptance speech, the plaudits, the praise.

It must have been a bitter pill to swallow for the long hitting, 33-year-old from Charlotte, North Carolina. Blessed with a smooth, measured swing, good putting touch and even temper, he had been tipped as a surefire major winner shortly after turning pro back in 1985. Even as an amateur he seemed set for future glory, having been three-times All-American champion, American University champion and 1985 Walker Cup player. But after a decade on Tour and over $6 million in prize money, the road to major success had started to look a little rocky. He knew there was no escaping the truth. It had taken Leonard just under three years to win his first major. Davis Love was still waiting for his.

Never considered a prolific winner, Love had at least begun to play himself into contention in recent major championships. He had led eventual winner, Corey Pavin, by a shot after two rounds of the 1995 US Open at Shinnecock Hills before falling back to joint fifth. Weeks earlier, a sparkling final round of 65 had almost paid off at Augusta before an inspired Ben Crenshaw finally came through to win his second US Masters. But, in some ways, coming close without winning had only added to his frustration.

Perhaps worse still, he had started to get a reputation as a choker in recent months, a reputation which had begun after Love had blown his best ever chance of winning a major at the 1996 US Open at Oakland Hills. After playing some of the finest golf of his career, he had nervously three-putted the 72nd green to miss out on a play-off with the relatively unknown Steve Jones. Curiously, it was Steve Jones who had dropped two shots on the final hole at the 1987 Heritage Classic to hand Love his first ever Tour victory.

It would be a painful, but ultimately valuable, lesson for the 6 feet 3 inches professional, who later admitted shedding more than a few tears over the result. Major championships, he had come to realise, were rarely given away. They had to be won and perhaps it was this aspect which set winners aside from the rest.

I sometimes look at guys who have won majors and they seem different somehow. Justin has gotten to be a good friend of mine, but I look at him and I don't see Justin Leonard anymore. I see Justin Leonard, Open champion, and that's a big difference.

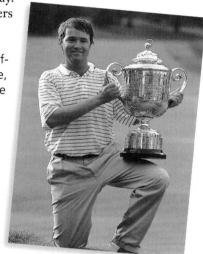

Despite having failed to capture any of the four majors in his previous 35 attempts Love still came into the 1997 United States PGA Championship at Winged Foot with high expectations. At Royal Troon, a closing round of 67 had launched him up the leader board for a share of tenth place overall. Confident and swinging well, he felt he might have a chance in the PGA. But even this most optimistic of players could not possibly have dreamt what would follow.

Within weeks he was battling down the stretch with Justin Leonard in the final major of the season. After his previous disappointments it was perhaps his final chance to write himself into the history books. Question marks still hung over his ability to go that extra mile and win. Yet it was an opportunity he would grasp with both hands. It was also a victory that required him to play the round of his life.

Davis Love III with the famous Wanamaker trophy presented to the winner of the US PGA Championship.

Before the last round at Winged Foot, it would have been tough to know what the greatest round of my life was. After Winged Foot there was no contest. I think probably my lowest ever Tour round was 61 at the Kapalua International in Hawaii in 1989. But I think maybe the best I'd played up to this point was my 65 at Augusta in the last round of the Masters in 1995. But, truthfully, nothing compares to my 66 in the final round to win the PGA. It was a special round for many reasons: the quality of my golf that day, the circumstances, the atmosphere, having my brother as caddie, everything really.

For Davis Love III, the long journey to Winged Foot began almost as soon as he could walk. Playing with cut-down clubs made by his father, Davis Love Jnr, he had decided on a full-time career in golf by the time he was nine. He was brought up in a golfing environment where his mother was an accomplished golfer and his father was a respected golf coach and occasional tournament pro. Growing up beside the 2nd hole at Atlanta Country Club, where his father was based, Davis and younger brother Mark were taught the fundamentals of the game at a young age.

> As kids, my brother and I were taught how to grip the club correctly and how to rip the ball. The only proviso he made was we had to finish the swing on our feet. When I eventually decided to play the game seriously, he told me if I was going to do it, then I should do it right, otherwise just play for fun. He never wanted me to be anywhere in between.

While his single-figure-handicap mother, Penta, stayed at home young Davis Milton Love III would often travel to tournaments in which his father competed. Good enough to claim a top-ten finish in the 1969 Open Championship at Royal Lytham behind winner Tony Jacklin, dad was no stranger to top-flight golf. In 1974 they went to the United States PGA Championship at Tanglewood. While Love Jnr missed the cut with disappointing rounds of 82 and 74, his son had seen just enough to whet his appetite. It was his first taste of a big major championship and one he would not forget.

In between his club duties, Davis Love Jnr continued to coach his son through the early part of his tournament career. A popular figure on the practice grounds, he was a huge influence on not only his son's golf but on his life in general. Therefore it came as a shattering blow to almost everyone he knew when he met his untimely death in a plane crash in 1988. 'After my father passed away,' Love said, 'it was not a lot of fun for a couple of years. He had a lot of friends on Tour and the conversations always led to my dad.'

After a fairly average start, the career which Davis Love Jnr had shaped for his son really took off in 1992. Victory at the prestigious Players' Championship at Sawgrass was accompanied by three other wins, in the MCI Heritage Classic, the Greater Greensboro Open and the Kapalua International in Hawaii. Having already gained the reputation as a long driver of the ball – he recorded the US Tour's longest ever measured drive of 383 yards in his rookie year – he was quickly rated as one of American golf's rising stars.

Moving up to second in the Order of Merit, from eighth in 1991, there was still a sense of frustration that came from having performed poorly in the majors. 'I was [exempt from qualification in 1992] in all four majors, after having made the cut in all four in 1991,' Love explained some years ago. 'I had the experience and I was playing well. I felt like 1992 was going to be my year in the majors.' It was not to be. Instead, it would be another five years before Davis Love would fulfil his greatest ambition.

Three years prior to his great PGA win, Love gave an interview listing the majors in terms of how difficult they would be for him to win. Selecting the Masters as 'the easiest one for me to win,' he continued by saying, 'I like Augusta so I feel the Masters is the one for me. The more comfortable you get with the greens, and with the course, the easier it gets. I've played there enough now to know I can win it, although it might take another couple of years, or it might take the rest of my life.'

Love went on to describe how he might 'have to play perfectly to win the US Open or PGA, but I feel in the Masters or the Open, I can play a good, solid tournament and have a chance to win.' As naive as these sentiments obviously were, at least he was right about having to play a perfect tournament to win a United States PGA.

Despite missing the cut at the Buick Open which preceded the 1997 PGA, Love felt confident that a rain-soaked Winged Foot would suit his game – and hopefully win him enough to ensure his place in the United States team for the forthcoming Ryder Cup at Valderrama in Spain. Going into the week, he was precariously placed in tenth position.

At 6,987 yards long and a tough par-70, pundits believed that Winged Foot

would obviously suit the longer hitters. Setting out to prove them right, Love used his extra length to full effect on the first day. Firing a course-record-equalling round of 66, it left him two strokes clear of Greg Norman, and four ahead of pre-tournament favourite, Tiger Woods. Indeed, the only player to match Love's opening day score was the big-hitting wild boy of golf and past PGA champion, John Daly. But while Daly fell back down the field with subsequent rounds of 73 and 77, Love maintained his rich vein of form with scores of 71 and 66.

Davis Love III acknowledging the gallery gathered around the 18th green during the final round at Winged Foot Country Club.

Moving into the final day, his three-round total of 203 (seven under par) left him a massive seven strokes clear of Lee Janzen and Tom Kite in third place. Indeed, the tournament would have been declared over had it not been for Justin Leonard. Pursuing Tiger Woods for top position on the United States PGA Money List, rounds of 68, 70 and 65 had left him tied for the lead with Love. Having already tasted victory in a major, Leonard was declared the odds-on favourite to match Nick Price's 1994 feat of winning both the Open and PGA in one year. Davis Love, however, had other ideas.

> You might win the first time you are in contention [like Leonard] but you still have to be there a few times to understand it. You have to control your emotions and live through bad breaks and the good breaks. I kept telling myself that Justin had been there a few times just like me. He had won but he has only been there a few times so we were fighting the same battle.

With Love and Leonard the only two players under par and so far ahead of the chasing pack, the final round at Winged Foot took on a matchplay feel. Love struck first with birdies at the 3rd, where he rolled in a huge putt from off the green, and another at the par-5 5th. Poor approach shots by Leonard at the 2nd and 4th led to two dropped shots and, suddenly, Love had gained four strokes on his closest rival in the opening five holes.

When accumulating his course record 65 on the third day, Leonard had not missed a fairway or dropped a shot. Now in the early stages of the final round, he was hardly out of the long grass and began to look tense and a little agitated and was swinging quicker than before. A short-range miss for birdie on the 6th would do little to help his mood. With Love playing solidly, Leonard recovered well on the next to pull a stroke back courtesy of a long putt for birdie. Love came back on the 8th with a birdie of his own and again led by five strokes but with just ten holes left to play.

Into the final stretch it looked like Love had the event all sewn up, but an unexpected two-stroke swing at the par-5 12th would alter all that. After a poor drive into deep rough, a hacked-out second, underhit third and a poor chip, he made bogey. Leonard took advantage with a birdie and brought on a mini-crisis which Love did well to recover from.

The crisis appeared to have worsened at the difficult par-3 13th. Pulling his mid-iron tee shot, Love missed the green pin-high to the left leaving himself with an impossible chip. 'I never let myself hit the easy shot, like I did at Oakland Hills [in the 1996 US Open] and never let my emotions get to my game. I was nervous, but I always thought I could hang on.' In a scruffy patch of deep greenside rough, with only a few paces between his ball and the flag, Love played the shot which would ultimately lead to his first major victory. Laying the club-face wide open as for a bunker shot, his chip actually hit the pin before coming to rest just inches away. 'That gave me confidence,' said Love afterwards, 'that I could get up and down from anywhere.'

After hitting the green, Leonard had seen the possibility of another two-shot swing in his favour disappear in a moment of Davis Love brilliance. And while he cut the gap to just three strokes by the 15th, his chance had come and gone like the brief shower which greeted both players over the closing holes. On the last, a superb mid-iron to 15 feet from the hole by Love all but sealed the victory.

Accompanied by a rainbow as backdrop, his successful putt was greeted by a triumphant shout from the crowd and a hug from his brother and caddie, Mark. 'I couldn't have won without him,' he said later fighting back the tears which had threatened to engulf them both over the closing three holes. 'He did a great job of reminding me of all the things I have worked on over the years, as well as keeping me focused about where I was aiming on every shot.'

Love's birdie on the last gave him a magnificent closing round of 66, while Justin Leonard was left with a disappointing score of 71. Generous in his praise of the new PGA champion, Leonard later said how he had literally to push Davis Love onto the final green to take the applause. 'He is a classy guy and always has been,' said the Open champion.

With Davis Love now assured of his Ryder Cup place to face the Europeans a few weeks later at Valderrama, Jeff Maggert also booked his own ticket with a superb final round 65 for third place overall. But Winged Foot and the PGA Championship belonged to Davis Love.

> I always thought with my distance, majors would be the easiest tournaments for me to win. I never realised how important putting was, and how mentally hard it was. I have lost tournaments by trying too hard. But I knew, if I could play my game and enjoy it, I could win. People have said to me that I am too nice to win, that I don't have the killer instinct or enough meanness to win. But I don't think you need that. I wanted to beat Justin so badly, but I couldn't bring myself to stare him out or anything like that.

Perhaps a measure of how well Davis Love played that week was his 269 four-round aggregate. A new tournament record for Winged Foot, it was seven shots better than the course record established jointly by Greg Norman and Fuzzy Zoeller in the 1984 US Open and fifteen shots lower than Hale Irwin's total in the same championship a decade before. It was something not lost on the amiable golfer when talking about his long awaited victory,

> I'm proud of what I have done. It means a great deal to win a major and it's all the more magical to have done it at Winged Foot. This is a special place, it's a place you want to win a golf tournament. You just have to walk through the front door to feel the history of the place and that makes it all that little special.

Davis Love wasted little time in mentioning the pivotal role his father had played in his victory.

> It's been a rough trip, I've been close a few times, but what a thrill to win. Who would have thought the son of a PGA member would win the PGA Championship. Every day I play golf, I think about my dad. I know he would be extremely proud that I not only won a major, but the PGA.

Having conquered any inner doubts he may have had about winning a major, Davis Love's victory at Winged Foot proved a universally popular one with his fellow players. They knew what a long and often frustrating journey it had been for the highly amiable professional from North Carolina. But in golf, experience is a valuable and hard-earned commodity.

> If it wasn't for the times that I have won, or the mistakes I have made and learned from, I don't think I could have made it. I could have double-bogeyed those [final] three holes the way I was feeling. But I played them good because I had been there before and lost it before and knew what the feeling felt like.

Sandy

Lyle

69 in the final round of the US Masters at
Augusta National, Georgia, 7–10 April 1988.

Going into the last round at Augusta, Lyle led by two strokes from Amer-
icans Ben Crenshaw and Mark Calcavecchia. Attempting to become the
first British player ever to win the US Masters, he struggled throughout
most of the final round yet still continued to maintain his challenge.
Then, with the pressure at its most severe, he came to the 72nd hole
needing a birdie to win. But having driven into a fairway bunker, he
played one of the greatest recovery shots ever seen in championship golf
to set up one of the most dramatic finishes in Masters history. Lyle then
holed his ten-foot downhill putt to beat Calcavecchia by a single stroke.

Sandy Lyle is a golfing enigma. Possibly the most naturally gifted golfer of his
generation, the past few years have seen his career plummet from the dizzy
heights of two major victories in the eighties to frustration and failure in the
nineties.

For many, it must seem like ancient history to recall those glory days at Sandwich and Augusta National. In 1985, following a meteoric rise through the paid
ranks, Lyle became the first home-grown golfer since Tony Jacklin to win the Open
Championship. Then, almost three years after beating Payne Stewart into second
at Royal St George's, he exceeded even his own expectations by winning the prestigious US Masters. A truly world-class golfer, Sandy became a huge draw wherever
he played. Hugely long off the tee, talented and seemingly nerveless under pressure, it seemed only a matter of time before even more major silverware would
grace the Lyle trophy cabinet.

Yet amid the growing collection of professional titles the alarm bells were
already beginning to ring. Casual often to the point of carelessness, his tendency to
miss short putts had even his most ardent fans pulling their hair out in frustration.
Add to this a powerful three-quarter swing which would suddenly become wildly
erratic for no apparent reason, and you had a recipe for disaster. But for many
British golf fans, this was the charm of Sandy Lyle. Unpredictable yet often

brilliant, stories about his early extremes are now part of golfing folklore.

In 1985, he needed par up the last to break 90 in the opening round of the Carrolls Irish Open at Royal Dublin. Moments later he dumped his second shot out-of-bounds and promptly walked off. Having struggled to break the century, he returned four weeks later and won the Open. Perhaps Seve Ballesteros summed him up best when he said, 'When Sandy's at his best he is the best, but when he plays bad, he can be almost the worst.'

Sadly, the last few years have seen only brief glimpses of Lyle at his imperious peak. This slump has seen the likeable Scot slip from three-time European number one to his present position among the 'also-rans' and 'never-have-beens'. His fall has sent shudders through the comfortable world of modern professional golf. Before Sandy's example, most players could afford a few months playing off-form golf confident it was only a matter of time before their game returned. But now . . .

In truth, few top players ever make it into their mid-thirties without some problems. Even the great Ballesteros, the most prolific tournament winner in the late eighties, has threatened to pack away his clubs on more than one occasion if things did not improve. What made Lyle's demise so dramatic was the speed with which it happened. In his Masters-winning year of 1988 alone, Lyle picked up victories on both sides of the Atlantic winning almost £1 million in official prize money and culminating in the 2 & 1 defeat of Nick Faldo in the final of the World Matchplay event at Wentworth. The decade which followed has been a barren desert by comparison with three wins in total, the BMW International Open in 1991, and the Italian Open and the Volvo Masters in 1992.

It can happen pretty quickly and is very frightening for a golfer who has won a major title. All of a sudden it's not there in the morning. You just reach the first tee and get butterflies just wondering whether you are going to get through without having a disaster. Then you knock it out-of-bounds or something and the tournament is over for you after just a few holes. You go to the next tournament and there it is again. You reach the stage when you finally do shoot a good round that you start to question whether it was good golf or pure luck. It takes a very strong mind to shut out such thoughts.

Of course, it has not all been doom and gloom for Alexander Walter Barr Lyle. Up until the late eighties, his professional career had read more like a Hollywood film script than a horror story. Son of the Hawkstone Park club professional, Alex, his interest in the game had grown enormously after watching Tony Jacklin win the Open Championship at Royal Lytham in 1969. Enjoying the action from the grandstand next to the 18th, he had almost caught the winning ball when Jacklin had thrown it after holing his last putt. From that day on Sandy knew what he wanted to be – a tournament winner like his heroes.

Playing off scratch at 15, he made the same rapid progress through the amateur ranks as he would later do in the professional game. In 1977 he defeated Nick Faldo and Ian Woosnam among others on the way to winning both the English Amateur Strokeplay and British Youths' Championships. Then, after representing Britain in the Walker Cup, he finally achieved his long-held dream to turn professional later the same year. In 1978, he won Rookie of the Year after finishing a highly creditable 49th in the Order of Merit. The following season he would go forty-eight places better by virtue of winning three events including the prestigious European Open. Still only 21, the big-hitting Lyle was European number one for the first time. It was a title he would retain the following year with record earnings of £66,060.

Having continued to dominate the European scene in the early eighties, Sandy turned his attention to the United States. In 1984 he beat a world-class field to win the Kapalua International in Hawaii. This was the climax to a glorious eight-week spell in which he also won both the Trophée Lancôme in France and Casio Open in Japan. It seemed Sandy Lyle had finally arrived in the big time. But before any player can lay claim to golfing greatness he also has to win a major, and for the Shropshire-born professional that would come the following year at Royal St George's at Sandwich.

Going into the final round of the Open, Lyle was not considered among the hot favourites. Despite sitting only three strokes behind joint leaders Bernhard Langer and David Graham, his looping swing was thought susceptible to failure in the windy conditions. But after three solid rounds of 68, 71 and 73, he finished stronger than any of his nearest rivals to win the £65,000 first prize. Despite dropping a shot at the last, where he dramatically fell to his knees after underhitting a chip from the left edge of the green, his 70 was good enough to make him the first British golfer to win the Open in sixteen years. And from the cheers which greeted his victory, there could never be a more popular winner.

The next three years saw Sandy Lyle at his magnificent best. After his win at Sandwich, he concentrated his efforts on winning more tournaments on the United States PGA Tour. Success came quickly with a win in the Greater Greensboro Open in 1986. A year later he went one better by capturing the highly regarded Tournament Players' Championship at Ponte Vedra. The talented young Scot then set his sights on winning another major – next stop Augusta National.

Looking back, we can now see that Sandy Lyle reached his playing peak in 1988. Even before the Masters it was looking like his most successful season to date. The build up to Augusta was perfect. An early season victory at the Phoenix Open was quickly followed by his second win in the Greater Greensboro only just before the big one. So, coming into the first major of the season, his game was good and his confidence high.

At Augusta, rounds of 71, 67 and 72 took him into a two-stroke lead over Mark Calcavecchia and former champion Ben Crenshaw. With the hopes of millions of British golf fans riding on his broad shoulders, the final round would be played under the most intense pressure he had ever faced. It would turn out to be the most memorable round in Sandy Lyle's career.

> It was certainly a proud moment for myself and my family to win the Masters in 1988, as it was three years before in the Open at Sandwich. Both were really special in their different ways. As for Augusta, I probably played much better on the Friday for my 67 than I ever did for my 69 on the Sunday. That was a great round, perhaps my best. But it's not often you get to play a winning final round in a major and that's the one most people remember. So I guess it would be my choice for the most memorable round of my life.

With the opening two holes playing downwind on the final day at Augusta, Lyle opened up with a superb drive on the 1st. Splitting the fairway, he left himself with a simple 9-iron into the green. Two putts later and showing none of the nerves most had expected, the amiable Scot got the solid start he wanted. Another huge drive down the par-5 2nd left him a 7-iron approach which he duly played to within 20 feet of the hole. Two putts later and he had his first birdie of the day.

Walking up the 3rd, Lyle glanced over at the scoreboard to the left of the fairway. It showed that Greg Norman had reached the turn and now was five under for the day and level par for the tournament. With Lyle at seven under with sixteen holes remaining, the Australian should not be in the running. But Lyle knew how quickly someone could catch him should he slip.

Indeed, the mere thought almost brought a mistake on the par-4 3rd, even though it was playing far shorter than its 360 yards. Lyle went for safety by using his 1-iron off the tee and duly found the fairway, but his sand-wedge approach hardly glanced at the green before bouncing over the back. With Crenshaw putting for birdie the pressure was on the big Scot to get down in two. Moments later, a good chip to within a few feet left him with a simple putt for par which he tapped in with ease. With his American playing partner holing out for a three the first mini-crisis of the day had been averted. Unfortunately, the second was not long in coming.

At 210 yards, the par-3 4th hole was playing no more than a solid 5-iron for the powerful Lyle. But after watching Crenshaw come up short with a 4-iron, he gave his tee shot a little bit extra in the hitting area. It proved to be a mistake. When Sandy and his caddie, Dave Musgrove, arrived at the ball, not only had it cleared the green but it had found a poor lie in a tiny furrow. Still 20 yards from the hole and looking at certain bogey, Lyle then holed his chip for a two.

Sandy Lyle dancing around the 18th green at Augusta moments after holing his winning putt.

After his remarkable shot, a rules official from the Royal and Ancient, who was following the match, congratulated Sandy as he left the green. 'You deserved to hole that because that's the only ball the crowd have allowed to go through this afternoon.'

Continuing to ride his luck, Lyle did well to two-putt from the very front edge of the next green for par. As with the previous tee shot, he had attempted to force an 8-iron approach and it had worked against him. Despite being two under for his round, he was struggling to find any sort of rhythm. His driving seemed good enough but the quality of his iron play was beginning to give him trouble.

On the par-4 6th, the flag was in its traditional final day position of back right. Left with another 8-iron second, Lyle hit it well enough but failed to make the same level as the hole. It was a crucial mistake. With a steep incline halfway up the green, his ball inevitably rolled all the way down to the bottom finishing over 40 feet away. It came as no surprise when Sandy three-putted for his first bogey since the 16th the previous day.

Still a little shaken, Lyle approached his tee shot on the 7th with obvious trepidation. Facing undoubtedly the narrowest of all the fairways at Augusta, he decided to stick with his 1-iron. It was a good decision under the circumstances, but the shot itself was poorly executed. He did well to reach a greenside bunker with his second after finding the trees down the left off the tee. From there, Sandy splashed out to around ten feet before holing the putt for par.

The importance of the putt was evident moments later when Craig Stadler eagled the 9th to go five under. Walking off the green Lyle's experienced caddie Dave Musgrove noticed the increasingly anxious look on his boss's face. 'They're going to be making charges all day,' he said looking to calm him down. 'You just have to live with it. There are six former champions behind you and they all know they can win.'

On the next, the pep-talk looked to have worked wonders. A booming drive by Lyle comfortably cleared a fairway bunker at 260 yards out leaving him with a long-iron second on the par-5 hole. Downwind and with only 230 yards left to the hole, it was an obvious chance for birdie or better. Then, like before, he got a little quick in the downswing and pulled his shot well left of the green. From there, despite finding himself behind a large mound, he played a good pitch but sadly not good enough to make his birdie.

For Sandy Lyle, a golden chance to extend his lead had gone begging. At seven under par he still led the tournament, but with Americans Craig Stadler and Mark Calcavecchia playing well in the chasing pack, he could afford no more mistakes. Fortunately, a birdie on the tough par-4 9th gave him some breathing space. It was also the hole which effectively ended the challenge of his playing partner, Ben Crenshaw.

On a hole where a good drive is a must, Lyle hit perhaps his worst of the day. Completely out of the heel, it had the saving grace of being down the right hand side of the fairway on this right to left dog-leg. With Crenshaw coming up short and right with his second, the young Scot selected his trusty 7-iron for a shot of exactly 173 yards. It proved to be the right choice.

Landing on the back level of the green, with the flag on the very front, his ball spun back to within two feet of the hole. Having risked leaving himself an impossible downhill putt from around 30 feet, Lyle was now left with little more than a tap-in birdie.

Having now moved to eight under par, his unlikely birdie also put him out of range of his partner Crenshaw. With the American looking to keep some pressure on Lyle going into the back nine, his excellent chip at the 9th had brushed the edge of the hole before finishing inches away. Frustrated at not making birdie, he tapped in for par and remained at three under. He would no longer be a threat.

For Sandy Lyle, the par-4 10th proved simple enough. A good drive followed by a solid 7-iron gave him a regulation par and he was now in sight of the finishing post. Another fine drive at the next also looked to have put him in good position but having finished close to its own pitch mark, the second was longer than he might have expected.

With 180 yards to the flag, the same yardage as he had for his approach shot to the previous hole, Lyle went with his 7-iron once again. Perhaps mindful of the lake guarding the front left quarter of the green, he let his second drift off onto the right fringe. The shot looked simple enough but, arriving at his ball, Lyle found it had picked up some soil. Unable to clean it under the rules, the long putt presented Sandy with a unique problem – how would it react once it got rolling? There was also another difficulty.

'Sandy was interested in watching what Langer and Calcavecchia were doing on the 12th,' said Musgrove. 'It was the key hole on the back nine, he hadn't got his mind one hundred per cent on the 11th.' His caddie was right. After leaving his approach putt short, Sandy missed the next one to make bogey.

Standing on the 12th tee moments later, Lyle and Musgrove discussed the all-important club selection. A shot over water to a horizontal, hour-glass shaped green, it was a difficult stroke at the best of times but after dropping a shot at the last . . . Musgrove urged him to concentrate. With no wind it was the perfect distance for his 8-iron, 160 yards. But once again, the Scot let the result of Crenshaw's tee shot affect his own judgement. After watching Ben find the back bunker on this treacherous par-3 hole, he eased back on his own shot. It almost proved a fatal mistake. Despite his caddie urging the ball to, 'Go on, get over the water,' it landed on the steep bank in front of the green before rolling agonisingly back into Rae's Creek.

Walking towards the green, Lyle cursed himself for the error which looked to have cost him the Masters. 'That was a shit shot,' he kept muttering while Musgrove calmly went about his job – which at this moment meant getting the exact yardage to the hole from any potential dropping point. 'This is when I earn my money,' said the caddie later. 'Sandy's got to plan again and I've got to keep a cool

THRU 17

LYLE
CRENSHAW   4

4 CALCAVECCHIA
2 LANGER
2 COUPLES
0 WATSON, T.
POOLEY
1 STADLER
5 NORMAN
2 FROST

head, otherwise we'll make another mistake. I told him, "Don't worry about what's happened. That's done, ancient history. Just make sure you make a five." '

But even making double bogey was never going to be easy from where they were. Even pitching on with a wedge, the same set of problems existed. Too short and it was in the water. Too long and the golfer was forced to play a difficult chip down a green described as hard as 'baked clay'. Musgrove later called it 'the hardest shot in the world' and as Lyle prepared to play from 55 yards out, the possibility of running up a cricket score was definitely on.

To his credit, Lyle landed his ball between the front edge of the green and the hole. It was a wonderful shot but even then it rolled just off the back edge. Two putts later and it was good enough to give him the five his caddie had asked for. Despite this, his mood on the next tee was black. 'What have I done?' he kept saying. 'I've chucked it all away.'

Once again Dave Musgrove came to the rescue, reminding Lyle there were still six holes left. Lyle took a few moments to regroup his thoughts, no doubt helped by the time taken by Mark Calcavecchia to play his shot from the trees down the right hand side of the fairway. Risking his driver on the par-5 hole, Lyle hit a huge shot across the corner of the dog-leg leaving himself in perfect position. Then, no doubt conscious of the creek which cut into the right edge of the putting surface, he pulled his 7-iron second into a greenside bunker.

Playing back downhill towards the water, Lyle looked at his shot with obvious

After playing a remarkable bunker shot from the side of the 18th fairway, Lyle acknowledges the applause of the Augusta gallery around the final green. Minutes later he holed his putt to become the first British winner of the US Masters title.

disappointment. 'I've got a lot to do to stop this on the green,' he said to his caddie looking at the lump of sand behind his ball. Knowing another trip to the creek would definitely put him out of the running for the Masters, he did well to get his ball somewhere near the hole. However it was never close enough to make birdie and moments later, Lyle tapped in his short putt for five.

Under any other circumstances, it was like a shot dropped. Most of his closest rivals had made four there but for Lyle, par at the 13th had the effect of steadying his nerve for the final few holes. No longer in the lead, as he had been since the 9th hole on the second day, his entire attitude suddenly became more positive. To win the Masters he now had to attack the lead instead of defending it. For Sandy Lyle it was a crucial difference.

A solid par at the 14th would keep up the momentum despite him missing a ten-foot putt for birdie. But now, as they approached the last four holes, par figures were no longer going to be good enough and Lyle knew it. The next hole, the eminently reachable par-5 15th, was now crucial. A long drive down the middle of the fairway left Lyle with just under 200 yards to the flag. Having played from almost the same spot during the practice round on Wednesday, he knew a strong 5-iron would be the right club. This time, however, the shot was hit with draw and the extra run was enough to take his ball a few yards over the back of the green.

Once again, Sandy Lyle was forced to chip the ball down a steep slope towards a water hazard. To his credit he played the shot well but, coming out of rough, the ball failed to grip and despite actually hitting the hole, it came to rest over five feet way. The chip was then followed by a totally under-read and seemingly casually hit putt. A great birdie chance suddenly became an unsatisfactory par and Lyle's Masters challenge was beginning to flounder under the pressure.

If there was a turning point for Sandy Lyle it came on the par-3 16th. With the flag positioned back left, and close to the lake which ran down the entire length of the green, his tee-shot finished 15 feet beyond the hole. A brave shot under the conditions, it was followed by an equally audacious putt for birdie. Choosing to hit it firmly to lessen the effect of the severe right-to-left slope, the ball literally rammed into the back of the cup. Watching it accelerate as it neared the hole, the undemonstrative Lyle punched the air in delight as it disappeared from view.

Standing on the tee of the par-4 17th, Lyle was buzzing with excitement. Looking for another big drive, he opened up his shoulders and hooked it left. Fortunately it struck a spectator, and finished just off the fairway, leaving him with a fairly straightforward wedge shot to the green from just under 130 yards. Sandy suspected he might need at least one birdie in the last two holes to win, but his underhit approach came up well short of the flag. Playing from just off the front of the green, two good putts were enough to save his par. The birdie, if it were to come, would have to be made on the tough final hole.

Standing on the 18th tee the options were plentiful. A long drive over the two fairway bunkers situated at the elbow of this left to right dog-leg would offer a shorter second but the angle to the pin was more difficult. Equally, a safe 3-iron would avoid the bunkers but leave an impossibly long second to the green. Lyle decided to take the middle route, a 1-iron aimed at the bunkers with a little fade to take it away from them and nearer the green. Sadly for Lyle, the intended fade became a faint draw and, as he hopped from leg to leg in frustration, the ball drifted into the sand.

Walking up the fairway, it was obvious that Lyle felt any chance for birdie had gone. Turning to his caddie he muttered, 'If it's in that first bunker I've had it. I can't get on the green. I should have hit a driver.' Fortunately for him it was in the other trap and as he arrived at his ball a new possibility emerged.

I thought it was all over when my 1-iron shot finished in the bunker. It was the last place I wanted to be and I didn't think I had a chance of reaching the green from there. Luckily the ball was up the slope of the trap and I had a good lie. I had 140 yards to go and with the pin on the bottom level I knew, if I could get it past the pin, it would roll back towards the hole. That would give me at least a par and a play-off with Mark Calcavecchia.

He selected his 7-iron for the task, and the ball came out well. Almost immediately, Lyle charged out of the bunker and began jumping in the air to get a better view of the ball landing on the green. Coming down 30 feet beyond the hole, it began rolling back down the slope, slowly at first then gathering pace. Then, accompanied by huge roars of encouragement from the crowd around the green, it finally came to a halt around ten feet away.

Having chipped up closer, Lyle's playing partner, Ben Crenshaw, asked for permission to finish off his own putt for par. That done, the stage was now clear for the drama which followed. Looking at the scoreboard, Lyle knew what he had to do. Calcavecchia had finished the day on eight under par. He had this putt to win the Masters.

While no putt at Augusta National is ever easy, this one was fairly straightforward. Downhill with little break, Lyle knew all he had to do was get the ball rolling on line. Pace was vital and as it made its journey down the green, caddie Dave Musgrove admitted thinking it was going to miss on the right. Thankfully for Lyle and the millions of British golf fans following the action late at night on television it didn't. As it fell into the side of the hole, Sandy jigged his way around the green in delight and Britain had its first ever United States Masters champion.

I managed to keep my nerve on the putt. I had a perfect line-up. All that was needed now was a clean strike and to get the pace right. Happily it disappeared into the hole for a three.

Moments later, Dave Musgrove passed by the clubhouse balcony where the BBC had set up their interview area. Among the excited on-lookers that day were Sandy's mother and father, Nick Faldo and Tony Jacklin. It was a proud moment for all concerned and in typical style, the Lancashire caddie called up, 'Did you get all that? Did you have enough film in your camera?' They did and no matter what happened in the future, Lyle's greatest moment had been recorded for posterity.

Today no one really knows if Sandy Lyle will win another major to add to his spectacular Open and Masters triumphs. The chances are stacked against him in most pundits' opinions. But, like his large band of loyal admirers, we can only hope. As for the future, Sandy himself remains philosophical.

At times the past few years have just flown by. Other times, they have dragged. Now I look back and think, well if someone had said when I was 16 that you can have the Masters and the Open, I would have snapped their hand off.

Colin

Montgomerie

61 in the third round of the Canon

European Masters at Crans-sur-Sierre,

5–8 September 1996.

Chasing his fourth consecutive number one spot in Europe, Colin Montgomerie was eight strokes behind tournament leader Sam Torrance at the halfway stage. Needing something special, he shot a career-best 61 in the third round to bring himself within just one stroke of the lead. Following it up with a last day 63, his 124 total was a new European Tour record for 36 holes. This gave Monty his third tournament win of the season, and took him to the top of the Order of Merit where he remained until the end of the year.

Self doubt is not something you would normally associate with Colin Montgomerie. In fact the opposite is probably true. European number one for the past five years, he carries himself on the golf course to the manner born. A perfectionist at heart, even to the point of petulant frustration, he exhibits an indomitable confidence in his own abilities. Yet just over a decade ago during his first trip to Crans-sur-Sierre as a rookie professional, he actually considered packing the game in and playing just for fun.

In contrast to the first-class travel arrangements he now enjoys, Colin attempted to make his own way to the 1987 Swiss Open, later renamed the Canon European Masters. Flying to Geneva, via Glasgow and London, he found no sign of either his golf clubs or suitcase on arrival. Living in hope of being reunited with his goods, he hired a Peugeot 205 and decided to drive the three-hour journey to Crans Montana in the Swiss Alps. Then, after losing his way several times, he failed to locate the hotel he was booked into. In desperation he picked out the first reasonable looking establishment, only to find the next morning that its nightly rate was akin to the national debt of a third world country. Recalling the journey in a magazine interview he gave some years ago, he said,

The next morning I drove back to Geneva, collected my luggage and arrived back Wednesday night with no time to play a practice round. I shot 79 in the first round playing with Andrew Murray and a Swiss amateur, and 68 the next day to miss the cut by eight. I thought, 'What is all this about?' I drove back to Geneva for the second time, got on a plane and came home having spent nearly £2,000 in the process. I decided this was not for me. I was going to ask for my amateur status back again but my dad talked me out of it.

Time has since shown what wise counsel it was from Montgomerie Snr. Competing at Crans-sur-Sierre almost a decade later, his talented son would be on the way to his fourth consecutive European number one spot. A Ryder Cup regular, he had emerged from the relative obscurity of his earlier years to become one of the top-rated golfers in the world. Not only that, Montgomerie Jnr would return to Switzerland to record the twelfth tournament victory of his professional career. The Canon European Masters would also be the tournament in which he would play his lowest ever round, a dazzling ten-under-par score of 61.

One golfer who has a lot to smile about: Colin Montgomerie.

Colin Stuart Montgomerie was born in Glasgow on 23 June 1963. Public school educated, he grew up in a well-heeled, middle-class family who lived no more than short-iron distance from the clubhouse at Royal Troon. Despite having the Club Secretary as his dad, he was restricted from playing the championship links until he was 16. Instead, he spent his early teenage years honing his game on Troon's less well known Portland course nearby.

A promising amateur, his career was boosted by three years on a golf scholarship to the Baptist University in Houston. As well as leading to a degree in Business Management, the spell overseas also helped fine-tune his competitive instincts. After winning both the Scottish Amateur and Stroke Play Championships, Monty signed off as an amateur by competing in his second successive Walker Cup match at Sunningdale in 1987. Playing off an impressive handicap of plus 3, he beat rising American star, Billy Andrade, 3 & 2 in the singles, then turned professional later the same year.

Surprisingly, success in the paid ranks did not come all that quickly for the ambitious Montgomerie. Struggling throughout his curtailed first season his official prize money earnings amounted to a paltry £2,051 for 164th place in the Order of Merit! Yet, despite experiences like those at the Swiss Open in Crans-sur-Sierre, he came back even stronger and more determined the following year. Moving up to 52nd place in 1988, he boosted his earnings up to a highly respectable £60,095. Picking up Rookie of the Year for his efforts, he then made his tournament breakthrough the following season by winning the Portuguese Open. This victory included a course record 63 (nine under par) to finish a massive eleven strokes ahead of the field. Colin Montgomerie, it seemed, had finally arrived.

By the end of the 1989 season, he had played well enough to better his previous position by another 27 places, to finish 25th. Establishing a pattern of year-by-year improvement, it is a record which he has taken great pride in sustaining. After finishing 14th in 1990, despite not having won a tournament, Montgomerie got into the top five (fourth) for the first time in 1991. His playing record since then is not only a testimony to the brilliance of his golf but also his remarkable consistency.

After finishing third in 1992 behind winner Nick Faldo and second place Bernhard Langer, Montgomerie came out the next season determined to go two places better. No doubt helped by Faldo's decision to play more tournaments in the United States, the big Scot won both the Dutch Open and Volvo Masters en route to capturing his first European Order of Merit. Then, just in case anyone thought it might have been a fluke, Monty did it again in 1994, and 1995, and 1996, and 1997! Breaking the long-standing record of Peter Oosterhuis this makes him the most dominant British golfer of any era.

In terms of pure golf, his greatest ever season was probably 1996. Shedding over 30 pounds in weight during the winter through a strenuous fitness programme, a more streamlined Monty appeared in time for the early season Dubai Desert Classic. Showing he had lost little of his competitive edge, or indeed nerve, he came to the 72nd hole needing a birdie to win. The second shot on this tough par-5 is played over water to a narrow green, and Monty hit a magnificent driver off the fairway to within a few feet to record his first victory of the year. A wonderful effort, it won him the Canon 'Shot of the Year' Award.

In an intriguing year-long battle with Welshman Ian Woosnam, Montgomerie finished runner-up in both the Deutsche Bank and Alamo English Opens before winning the Murphy's Irish Open at Druids Glen. Then, with competition for Europe's number one spot becoming an increasingly strong feature of the season, Woosnam took full advantage of his rival's absence from the Volvo German Open to go back to the top. As for Monty, he had been forced to withdraw from the tournament in Stuttgart because of a sudden illness suffered by his father.

Obviously a difficult and emotional time for Colin personally, his decision to enter the One-to-One British Masters the week later was only made after seeing some improvement in his father's condition. Finishing a highly creditable ninth at Collingtree Park, his efforts helped keep him in touch with Woosnam who finished four places higher to increase his overall lead in the standings. Then, no doubt encouraged by his dad, his decision to play in the Canon European Masters at Crans-sur-Sierre also proved to be the right one.

With Woosnam surprisingly absent from the Swiss resort, Montgomerie needed a top-two finish to leapfrog the Welshman back to the top of the Money List. But after two rounds, his fellow Scot Sam Torrance led the field by six strokes. Now sitting eight shots back, Monty knew he needed a drastic improvement on his two opening scores of 65 and 71 if he were going to win. It was then his whole season turned around. Pulling himself into contention, his third round score of 61 (ten under par) has been described as one of the finest rounds ever played on the European Tour. And not surprisingly, it is the personal choice of Colin Montgomerie for the 'Round of My Life'.

Even in the rarefied atmosphere of the Swiss Alps where the ball can fly up to twenty per cent further than normal, it was a remarkable 18 holes of golf. The fireworks started with an opening birdie four, on the 536-yard 1st. Pars on the next two were then followed by an incredible sequence of eight birdies in the next 11 holes. With Montgomerie in imperious form, even a bogey on the 208-yard par-3 11th failed to dent his charge to become the first player to break the magic 60 barrier on the European Tour. Ten birdies in the first 14 holes had put him right on target. Then, with a comparatively easy stretch of finishing holes ahead, including the eminently reachable 520-yard par-5 15th, the birdie trail suddenly dried up.

I needed two more birdies but then the wind started to get up. It got quite severe and difficult. At 18 my second with a sand-wedge was blown right over the back and I felt unfortunate not to have birdied at least one of the last four. I didn't mis-hit a shot but the wind was gusting alarmingly and the greens were drying out fast.

One stroke behind leader Sam Torrance going into the final round, Montgomerie followed up his 61 with a brilliant 63 in the final round to take the title. A new European Tour record for 36 holes, his weekend brilliance relegated his Dunhill Cup team-mate to runner-up spot, despite Torrance being the only player in the field to break 70 in all four rounds. But Sam only had praise for his younger rival, 'I have nothing but admiration for Colin,' he said. 'He's a fabulous golfer. When you lead by so many shots at the halfway stage, and then shoot two 68s, you do not expect to lose.'

Catapulting himself back up to the top of the Order of Merit, Monty's victory greatly contributed to his fourth consecutive number one spot in Europe. The first prize of £127,950 took him almost £60,000 ahead of the absent Woosnam. Yet, on reflection, he knows the round of his life could have been even better. Describing his efforts after the final round Montgomerie said,

> I've never played better in my life. If I'd finished yesterday like I did today, I'd have shot 58, never mind 59. It's certainly the best I've ever driven the ball. I've never felt so relaxed. Winning for a third time this year to go back to the top of the rankings was always my goal and it's got me up for finishing number one again.

A perfectionist at heart, even occasionally to the point of petulant frustration, Montgomerie exhibits an indomitable confidence in his own ability.

Six weeks later Colin Montgomerie would get his wish. With Ian Woosnam a long way back in second, Colin eventually finished the season in pole position with over £1 million in official prize money. As for his glorious round at Crans-sur-Sierre, the lowest round in his career so far, he commented,

> I had the opportunity to shoot 59 and it proves that it's on and I'm capable of doing it. It's the best round of golf I've ever played in Europe and ranks with the 65 in the last round of the 1995 US PGA Championship at the Riviera Club when I tied with Steve Elkington.

By any standard, his remarkable 61, and lengthy reign as European number one, are feats of which he is justifiably proud. Yet behind the statistics and course

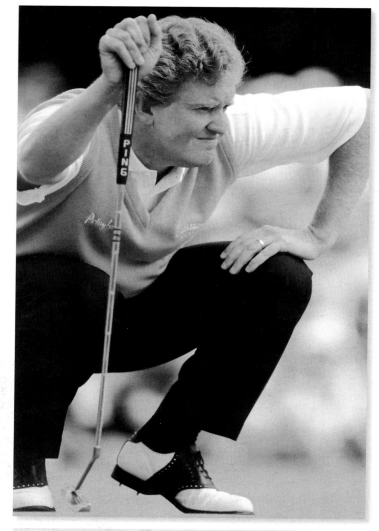

Colin Montgomerie lining up a putt during the 1996 Masters at Augusta.

records, there is a hint of disquiet in the Montgomerie camp. 'I am still probably the most consistent player in the world,' he has often said in typically honest fashion. 'I have a swing that always makes money. It buys me nice homes and cars. But I know I have to start winning on the big occasions. To finish close is not good enough.' And for 'big occasions' read majors.

Increasingly frustrated at not having captured one of golf's glittering prizes, Montgomerie, probably more than any player alive, knows the true value of a major win. Not in terms of financial security, he had that long ago, but the longer term historic perspective. Coming from Scotland, a country steeped in golfing tradition, he knows the only lasting testimony to a golfer's skill is having his name engraved on a major trophy. Other professional tournaments, no matter how prestigious they may currently be, will always come and go. But the four major championships will be around as long as golf is played, and Monty knows it.

Perhaps this explains why his performances in the Open Championship have been so woeful. Likewise, when he competes in Scotland, the weight of expectation is such that he often tries too hard. Witness the anguish when Australian Peter O'Malley beat him into second place in the 1992 Scottish Open at Gleneagles after finishing eagle-birdie-birdie-birdie-eagle. Equally his success in the 1995 Dunhill Cup at St Andrews was owed in no small part to having team-mates Sam Torrance and Andrew Coltart around to share the pressure – and the blame should things have gone wrong.

An intelligent but highly complex individual, Montgomerie's attitude is best summed up when he says that, 'I hate losing more than I like winning.' One of the top-rated golfers in the world, his many strengths currently outweigh any technical weaknesses he may have. An intriguing mixture of opposites, he is probably the best middle distance putter in the world, yet sadly lacks the same delicate touch around the greens when it comes to chipping.

Montgomerie has often said how the United States Open realistically offers his best chance of winning a major, despite having lost out to Steve Elkington in a play-off for the US PGA Championship at Riviera in 1995. Played in the more temperate weather of June, rather than steamy August, he knows how much the conditions for the Open are likely to suit his long game. He is an accurate driver of the ball, and US Opens are usually played on courses with tight, tree-lined fairways and penalising rough (an advantage less obvious on the wide open fairways of

Augusta or the windswept links of the Open Championship). But, having come close on three occasions, with each perhaps more brutal than the last in terms of competitive pressure, Monty knows how hard it can be to come so near to winning.

At Pebble Beach in 1992, a superb final round of 70 in windswept conditions had taken him to the top of the leader board. Even Jack Nicklaus himself had congratulated Montgomerie on becoming 'our national champion'. Then, after sitting on a winning aggregate score of 288, with only a few others left on the course, an inspired Tom Kite came in with 70 and beat him by two. Then, as if adding salt to the wound, Jeff Sluman pushed the Scot back into third with another last round 70.

Two years later at Oakmont, it was a similar story. After tying the lead with rounds of 71, 65, 73 and 70, Montgomerie lost out in the 18-hole play-off with Ernie Els and Loren Roberts. After tied scores of 74, the South African eventually beat Roberts on the second hole of sudden death. Monty, drained by his efforts of the previous four days, was left nursing his wounds in the clubhouse after a tired round of 78.

Blessed with a languid and rhythmical swing which launches the ball both long and accurately, Monty also has a short-fuse temperament which can result in him being distracted during the crucial final stages of a tournament. That was the case at the US Open at Congressional Country Club near Washington in 1997. With Els once more the bogey man, the two players were battling it down the stretch on the final day when the South African struck a championship-winning approach to 12 feet on the penultimate hole. Montgomerie, in reply, missed the green with his second, chipped poorly from deep rough, complained to the marshals, then dropped the shot which effectively lost him the tournament.

Ernie Els later described his second to the 17th hole as 'the greatest shot of my life'. He also made the right noises in the post-tournament press interviews about Montgomerie being a future major winner. But for the tearful Scot, it was not much consolation. No doubt heartily tired of being labelled with the-best-player-never-to-win-a-major tag, his decision in late 1997 to stay in Europe rather than play full time in the United States came as a surprise. But, like always, Colin Montgomerie will do it his way or not at all. And for that alone, there is not a fan of European golf who does not wish him well.

However, when and if it does happen, it will neither make him any better, or worse as a golfer than he is today. All it will do is settle any niggling doubts Monty has about his own ability to win the big one.

Jack

Nicklaus

65 in the final round of the US Masters at Augusta National, Georgia, 11–14 April 1986.

At the age of 46, Jack Nicklaus rolled back the years to win the US Masters a record sixth time in 1986. Perhaps the greatest player in the history of the game, he had been written off before the tournament as too old. Yet on the final day he burst through the field with one of the greatest last round charges ever seen at Augusta National – including a remarkable six-under-par 30 on the back nine. Leaving younger players like Seve Ballesteros and Greg Norman in his wake, Jack entered the record books by becoming the oldest golfer to win a major championship since Tom Morris Snr in 1864.

It was somehow destined that Jack Nicklaus should win his sixth Masters title at Augusta in 1986. Possibly the greatest golfer in the history of the game, winner of 18 major championships since turning professional in 1961, his legendary career had been in steep decline. His last major victory had been six years before in the 1980 United States Open at Baltusrol, and even winning his own Memorial Tournament three years later had done little to persuade his critics that his best years were not over.

Aged 46 and plagued by persistent back problems, Nicklaus' critics had become more vocal in recent years. Like Arnold Palmer before him they cited his many off-course business interests as the reason for his lack of competitive edge. Coming into the Masters some were even more abrasive in their comments. One journalist writing for the *Atlanta Journal* had made his feelings perfectly clear. Among other things he suggested that Jack Nicklaus, father of five, was now an aging colossus who was all washed up. When would he finally go, went out the call? The era of the 'Golden Bear' was long gone and like many others, the writer wanted to remember Nicklaus as the imperious force he once was. After all, nobody enjoyed watching the great man struggle just to make the cut tournament after tournament.

Somewhat ominously, Jack's recent playing record seemed to echo this lack of commitment. Starting his twenty-fifth season as a professional, he had finished tied

60th in the 1986 Phoenix Open before missing the cut in two of his next three events. Then came even worse news. Only weeks before the action was due to get underway at Augusta National he had been forced to withdraw from the Tournament Players' Championship at Sawgrass with bad back pains. Once again rumours began to circulate about his impending retirement but, while angered by the press speculation, Jack Nicklaus continued to keep his own counsel.

When he finally did make it to the Masters in April it was the same old story. Now ranked a lowly 160th on the United States Money List, even his old rival and newly installed CBS commentator, Ken Venturi, suggested on air that he should consider bowing out. For Nicklaus there was no escape, yet the whole affair did offer one positive aspect. When he took up residence at the Augusta home he had rented for the week, he found that a close pal had pinned one particularly critical article on the fridge door. Jack to his credit read it but left it there for the week. For this immensely proud man it was to prove an important reminder of what he was trying to achieve.

Despite his difficulties, Nicklaus still believed he had at least one major championship left in him. The problem was nobody else did. So, when the right opportunity came along, he grabbed it with both hands. Not only that, it also gave him the chance to answer his critics in the most emphatic way possible. Written off before the tournament began, he would put together one of the greatest final rounds in US Masters history to win a record sixth green jacket! Charging through the quality field on Sunday with a magnificent seven-under-par 65, his message to all those who had doubted him came through loud and clear, 'I will go when I am ready and not before.'

Not surprisingly this round would also be the one he would select as the 'Round of My Life'.

Long-time rivals: Jack Nicklaus and Tom Watson.

> Obviously, the '86 Masters has to stand out as the most memorable. It was at a point in my career when nobody expected me to win. Other people were just too polite to say it to me. Most of my career at Augusta, people expected me to win whether it was the media, the fans, other players, or myself. And I don't think anybody did in '86. It was very special, probably the most special win I've ever had.

Son of a small town pharmacist, Jack William Nicklaus was born 21 January 1940 in Columbus, Ohio. When aged only ten, he took his first golf lesson with his life-long teacher, Jack Grout. A prolifically long hitter from a young age, he made meteoric progress throughout his teenage years. Breaking 80 at 12 years of age, he broke 70 at 13, won his State Open title at 16 and his first United States Amateur Championship at 19.

Blessed with a strong physique, he almost became the youngest winner in United States Open history when he finished runner-up to Arnold Palmer at Cherry Hills in 1960. Still only 20, he then proceeded to humble the legendary Merion with rounds of 66, 67, 68 and 68 en route to winning the individual prize in the World Amateur Team Championship. On possibly the most testing championship course in America, his record-breaking total of 269 gave him a thirteen-stroke winning margin. The lowest score ever posted in the event, it was a remarkable eighteen strokes fewer than Ben Hogan needed to win the US Open there in 1950! (Jack has often speculated that the best golf of his life was played at Merion that summer.)

By the time he turned professional in late 1961, there was very little the American golfing public did not know about Jack Nicklaus. He was already being compared to players like Bobby Jones and Ben Hogan. The only question that remained was just how long it would take him to win his first major. The answer to that came less than a year later.

After making his professional debut in the early season Los Angeles Open at Rancho Municipal where he finished tied for 15th, Nicklaus won the 1962 United States Open at Oakmont. Barrel-chested and sporting a harsh Marine-style haircut, he won the tournament in the play-off having shot 71. Yet considering his youth and the dramatic style of his victory, his success was not a popular one with the majority of American golf fans – not least because he had beaten the most beloved golfer of his day, Arnold Palmer.

Despite having come through with a gutsy final round 69, Nicklaus was perceived as cold and lacking in emotion. Palmer, in stark contrast, was one of golf's most celebrated figures. Highly charismatic, he played with seemingly wild abandon. Smiling at every great shot, grimacing at every poor one, Palmer was a golfer who wore his heart on his sleeve and sports fans everywhere loved him for it. This differed greatly from the calculating way his younger rival plotted his way around the course. Indeed, while Palmer won both the Masters and the Open Championship at Troon that year, it was his loss to Nicklaus in the US Open which most people remembered.

Over the next six years, Nicklaus would catch, then surpass, Arnold Palmer as the game's number one. Winning both his first US Masters and first PGA Championship in 1963, he then became the only golfer since Gene Sarazen to capture all four major titles after winning the Open at Muirfield in 1966. At 26, he was the dominant player in the world but his popularity with the American golfing public still suffered. At tournaments which he and Palmer attended, it was not uncommon for fans to hold up signs which read, 'Hit it over here Jack!' and point to the rough. His large physique also brought comments in his early years, with nicknames like 'Fat Jack' not uncommon.

After beginning his career in the paid ranks so well, the next few years proved to be barren ones as far as majors were concerned. From the 1967 US Open at Baltusrol, until his play-off win against Doug Sanders in the 1970 Open at St Andrews, his victories had been restricted to little more than the occasional United States Tour event. And while he was still actively challenging for major championships during this time, doubts even began to be voiced about his competitive nerve. Thankfully for Nicklaus all that changed after Sanders missed his now legendary four-foot putt on the final green at St Andrews.

A year later Nicklaus picked up his second United States PGA Championship at Palm Beach Gardens, Florida. He then became known throughout the next decade as the man to beat. Dominating the majors, his was a reputation bolstered by his uncanny ability to charge through the field with a spectacular final round. Even when he was not winning in the seventies, something he did eight times in total, he was rarely outside the top five of a major championship. Challengers to his crown, like Johnny Miller and Hale Irwin, came and went but when the dust finally settled there was Nicklaus still on top.

The mid to late seventies also saw a change in the public's attitude to the newly titled Golden Bear. With Palmer now mostly out of the reckoning, the fans warmed to the softer image Nicklaus now portrayed when winning. Instead of all the triumphant fist clenching of earlier times, he reacted to victory and defeat with great sportsmanship. He started the 1970 season by losing twenty pounds in weight and growing his hair longer, a change in image that was universally welcomed by the American golfing public. Gone was the hard-edged youth of the sixties. In his place was a seemingly less arrogant individual who competed as hard as possible, but was also a gracious loser when the need arrived.

Nicklaus in turn handled his new-found popularity well. A welcome visitor to Britain, he, like Arnold Palmer, had chosen to play in the Open Championship when many of his fellow Americans shunned the event for more lucrative tournaments at home. After finishing a creditable third on his debut at Royal Lytham in 1963, his lasting affection for the tournament saw him compete in every championship of the seventies and eighties.

Of course, he could always afford to do so. Among the highest-paid sportsmen in the world, his financial affairs have been shrewdly handled since his earliest years as a professional, first under the umbrella of his manager, Mark McCormack, then as head of his own organisation. With off-course business interests including equipment, clothing and golf course design, his annual income in the mid-seventies was estimated at around $3 million of which only a small percentage was prize money. Today, it is over ten times that figure.

On the playing side, his career floundered once more in the early eighties. Like the previous slump, it came almost without warning. After winning two consecutive majors in 1980, the US Open at Baltusrol then the PGA at Oakhill, Nicklaus looked set to carry his reign into the new decade. Indeed, though without a big win, 1981 had been among his best ever seasons with a second in the Masters, sixth in the US Open at Merion and fourth in the PGA Championship at Atlanta Athletic Club. In the Open at Royal St George's, he had bounced back brilliantly for 23rd place after starting the tournament with his worst ever opening round of 83. Yet the signs of decline were already there.

Forced to withdraw from the 1983 Masters after the opening round because of persistent back problems, the writing was on the wall for Jack as far as majors were concerned. To his credit, Nicklaus returned later in the season to finish runner-up in the PGA Championship at Pacific Palisades but the epitaphs were already being written. The following year saw little improvement. Taking the decision to cut back on his playing schedule, Nicklaus finished no better than 18th in any of the four majors. His young rival from the late seventies, Tom Watson, was now the dominant player in world golf and rumours about his impending retirement continued to circulate. He was also accused of letting his many off-course interests affect his form, especially his interest in the flourishing Muirfield Village Golf Club complex in his home town of Columbus.

After finishing joint sixth in the US Masters behind Bernhard Langer in 1985, the old Jack Nicklaus looked to have returned. Sadly it was only a temporary respite. Rounds of 76 and 73 in the US Open at Oakland Hills gave him his first missed cut in the tournament since 1963. A few weeks later, he missed the cut in the Open at Royal St George's after opening rounds of 77 and 75. In pure golfing terms it had been his worst ever season.

For Nicklaus, the 1986 season looked to have opened up in the same unhappy manner. Finishing 60th in the early season Phoenix Open, he followed this up with missed cuts in the AT&T Pro-Am at Pebble Beach and the Honda Classic at Eagle Trace, Florida. However, there were some important changes being made before the Masters in April.

His caddie at Augusta would be his son Jackie. A low handicap golfer himself, Jackie knew his father's game inside out and was often able to offer some useful tips along the way. But it would take more than a good caddie to win the Masters. No doubt stung by the criticism of his early season performances, Jack had spent long hours on the practice range fine-tuning his game. Working on his long game away from the prying eyes of golf journalists, he had made some good progress in the weeks immediately before the tournament. Returning home one night he told his wife, Barbara, 'I think I might have found the fellow out there I once knew – me.'

He had also found some inspiration in that scathing article by Tom McCollister of the *Atlanta Journal*. Writing in his autobiography *Jack Nicklaus: My Story* he described how he felt reading the item,

> According to this piece I was finished, washed-up, kaput, the clubs were rusted out, the Bear was off hibernating somewhere, it was all over and done with, forget it, hang 'em up and go design golf courses whatever. Similar sentiments had been expressed enough times during my career for me to invariably shrug them off, but, coinciding as it did with my upbeat attitude about my game, this one struck a nerve. 'Finished, huh?' I said to myself. 'All washed up am I? Well we'll see about that this week.' I insisted on leaving the clipping on the door. I had never needed external stimuli to spark my competitive drive, but maybe the arrival of this one was fortuitous, perhaps even an omen.

Making steady but unspectacular progress in the opening two rounds, his scores of 74 and 71 left him just above the cut line. On the third day, most of the attention was focused on the leading groups which included Greg Norman, Tom Kite, and the charismatic young Spaniard, Seve Ballesteros. While Jack's round of 69 gently nudged him up the leader board, his effort was considered little more than a pleasant sideshow to the main event. After 54 holes he stood at two under par for the tournament, four strokes behind the leader, Norman. Yet while he had some quality players ahead of him including Watson and Langer, there were only seven in total between him and the lead. And for Jack Nicklaus that was an important consideration going into the final day.

> The natural tendency when trailing going into the final round of a tournament is to focus mostly, or entirely on stroke deficit in evaluating one's chances and deciding strategy. I'd learnt a long time ago that an equally important factor is the number of players needing to be overtaken. That evening, weighing how I was by now and putting against the number of golfers ahead of me, I felt good about my chances.

Resting before the final round, Nicklaus had taken a phone call from his second son, Steve. Replying to his son's question about what score it would take to win, he had considered his answer carefully, 'I told him I believed 66 would earn me a tie and 65 would win.' For someone not known for making predictions it was a highly prophetic moment.

The opening few holes yielded little in the way of success for Nicklaus. Like most of the field, he recorded a predictable birdie on the par-5 2nd, but gave the shot back almost immediately by three-putting the 4th green. Still only level par for the round, a drilled approach shot to the 9th offered a reasonable chance of birdie from around 12 feet. Minutes later, as Nicklaus prepared to strike his treacherous downhill putt, a huge roar came echoing through the pines from the 8th green.

Soon the news filtered back that Kite had holed a spectacular wedge shot for an eagle three. Stepping away, Jack then calmly resumed his familiar crouching style over the ball. Then just as he was about to putt, an even greater roar came from the same arena. This time it was Ballesteros who had chipped in for eagle.

'Ballesteros and Kite both holing wedges while I was on the 9th green was a shock. I said "Boy! they made a lot of noise." So I turned around to the gallery and said, "Maybe we can get something started and make some noise of our own right here." '

The turning point: the moment when Nicklaus holed his putt across the 17th green in the final round.

The crowd laughed sympathetically but their thoughts, like his, were probably on the hole behind. Taking his stance for the third time, Jack set the ball rolling down the lightning-fast green and straight into the hole for a birdie three of his own. As the ball hit the back of the cup, the roar which greeted his birdie was certainly genuine enough. But perhaps it might have been even louder if they had known what a key turning point it would be.

Another birdie on the long par-4 10th heralded perhaps the greatest nine holes of golf in Masters history. Now four under par, the scoreboard to the right of the 18th fairway showed there were now only six players between him and the lead. Arriving at Amen Corner, the notorious stretch of holes from the 11th to the 13th, both Jack and his son knew what was needed. Sizing up the approach to the 11th green, Jackie handed his father an 8-iron. Moments later, the ball thudded down to within 20 feet of the hole. This time there were no distractions and, snapping up his second consecutive birdie, Nicklaus moved to five under par. Now there were only two men ahead of him, Norman and Ballesteros. Roars of encouragement were now replaced by a tangible feeling of excitement, even expectation.

> As I walked onto the 12th tee, I received an incredible ovation from the thousands of people gathered in the wooded area that forms the peak of Amen Corner. Few of them, I imagined, had expected this rally by the old guy, but it was clear how much they appreciated it and wanted it to continue.

A missed short iron to the left of the 12th green, followed by a tentative chip, resulted in a dropped shot. Under any other circumstances it could have been a disaster but for Nicklaus it had the opposite effect. Now three shots behind, it cleared his mind of all negative thoughts. Caution was no longer an option and the only chance he had of overhauling the leaders was to attack. At the par-5 13th, a solid 3-wood down the tight line left him with a fairly straightforward approach into the green. Having given himself a relatively flat lie, a solid 3-iron was enough to carry Rae's Creek and put him within easy two-putt birdie range, a task he completed without too much effort. Now back at five under par, Nicklaus was in the hunt once more.

A chip-and-putt par from the back of the 14th green was followed by a huge drive down the par-5 15th. Measuring just under 300 yards, the shot was a real throwback to the golden days of his youth when such drives were commonplace. Now, as they stood in the middle of the fairway, father and son speculated what an eagle would do for his chances. Handing over a 4-iron, Jackie said quietly, 'Let's see.'

Hardly deviating an inch off line, the ball homed in on the flag. After pitching within a couple of feet, it had run on to finish a disappointing 15 feet above the hole. The chance for a dramatic eagle was still there but it had looked so much better from back down the fairway. Walking towards the green, Nicklaus glanced up at the scoreboard once more. Seve Ballesteros had eagled the 13th and taken a firm stranglehold on the tournament. Once again, Jack knew what he had to do.

Like on the 9th, Nicklaus backed away from his putt when cheers broke out round the adjacent 16th green. Taking up his stance once again, he stared down the line from his sideways-on position and set the ball rolling down the slope towards the water. Anxiously watching as his putt almost gathered speed at the end, the 46-year-old golfer leapt into the air as it dropped in for the eagle he wanted so badly. The huge roar which went around the 15th green, and continued on until he had reached the 16th tee, gave notice to everyone else in the field – Jack was back.

> Glancing at the scoreboard to the right of the 15th green as I headed to the 16th tee, I saw that he [Seve] was the only player ahead of me, and by only two strokes. The thought that went through my mind was, 'Well, he still has some golf ahead of him.'

Time would prove just how right he was. With the normally sedate Augusta crowds excitedly flocking to the Nicklaus pairing, Jack prepared to tee off on the par-3 hole. Even with the flag tucked in its traditional final day position of back left, he knew this was not the time to play safe. With a 172-yard carry across water to the hole, Jackie handed his father a 6-iron with orders to hit it solid. His father duly obliged and with the ball coming to rest only feet away, yet another great roar echoed around Augusta National. The putt for another birdie was a mere formality.

But for Nicklaus, the possibility of winning the Masters only dawned on him walking towards the 17th tee. Cheered on by the crowds, this deeply emotional man blinked back the tears which threatened to engulf him. Walking ahead of his father, Jackie dared not look back in case it set both of them off. 'Now, for the first time, I was absolutely certain I could win myself a sixth Masters,' he said later. 'As we walked to the 17th tee, I told Jackie, "Hey, I haven't had this much fun in six years."'

For Ballesteros, preparing to hit his second to the par-5 15th, it was a pivotal moment. Even with Nicklaus performing heroics ahead he was still in control of the tournament. Now after a booming drive, he stood in the middle of the fairway with his caddie, his brother Vincente, pondering his options. With the green well within range, the Spaniard needed just a birdie effectively to close out the rest of the field.

Perhaps disturbed by the cheers which greeted Nicklaus at the 16th, the two brothers had held a long discussion over which club to use, a hard 5-iron or an easy 4. In typical style, Seve decided upon the finesse shot. It was to prove a fatal mistake.

Going with the 4-iron, his lazy second was badly underhit and disappeared into the lake guarding the front of the green. Minutes later, the dazed Spaniard walked off the green with a bogey. And while not completely disastrous in terms of his score, the effect on his game was devastating. The unshakeable belief in his own ability to win at Augusta vanished along with his ball at the 15th. Then as the leader board registered the change in Seve's score, Augusta suddenly became a hive of excited whispers. Not only was Jack burning up the back nine but now he could actually win.

Reminding himself that the tournament was still there to be won or lost, Nicklaus' solid tee shot on 17 was followed by a short-iron approach to within 12 feet that, however, left him with a twisting downhill putt. It took all his legendary concentration just to work out the line. Crouching over the ball for what seemed an age, he set it rolling with little more than a gentle brush of the putter face. As it wandered towards the hole, he brandished his putter like a sword urging the ball on and on down the slope. Finally it reached the edge of the hole, halted for a moment, then dropped in out of sheer exhaustion.

> At nine under par I now led the 1986 Masters. From my birdie at the 9th, to the one I'd just made to get in that position, I had played the most aggressive golf of my career in a major championship since my make-or-break final round at the 1972 British Open.

Now approaching the 72nd hole, Nicklaus required a birdie at the last for an incredible inward half of 29. More importantly, it looked like he needed a regulation par to win the Masters. After Jack had driven his ball up the centre of the fairway with his 3-wood, Jackie instinctively embraced his father. No matter what the final result, they had shared some glorious moments together that day. Indeed, the experience of watching this former golfing giant restored to his proper place at the pinnacle of the game would have been an honour whether they were related or not.

The second shot, like the first, was greeted with huge cheers when it was delivered safely into the centre of the green. Jack began the short walk up the final fairway, applauded every step of the way. Having rolled back the years, he now stood on the threshold of the most popular victory in decades. Throughout the entire final day, he had held both his emotions and nerves in check. Now two putts looked to be good enough to make him the oldest winner in Masters history.

> I will never forget the ovation we received on our walk up to the green that day. It was deafening, stunning, unbelievable in every way. Tears kept coming to my eyes and I had to tell myself a number of times to hold back on the emotions, that I still had some golf to play. But, as at Muirfield in 1972 and St Andrews in 1978 and Baltusrol in 1980, it was awfully hard to do.

In typical Nicklaus style, two putts on the 18th were duly accomplished with the minimum of fuss. Walking off the final green, he hugged his son before acknowledging the loud and persistent cheers with a modest wave of the hand. Afterwards in the press tent, Jack was full of praise for the part his son had played in his long awaited victory.

It was just a wonderful experience to have one of the people I care most deeply about share by far the most fulfilling achievement of my career. And what made it even more wonderful was that Jackie also enjoyed it so much.

While the tournament had not been won yet, the huge crowds knew who their true champion was. As he had hoped the night before, Jack had scored a final round 65. But whether it would be good enough to win now depended on whether Norman, Kite or Ballesteros could catch him. Yet, like most fairy tales, it had to have a happy ending. And while Nicklaus waited in the nearby Bobby Jones cabin watching the drama unfold on television, the other leading players seemed to go out of their way to make it happen.

Like Tom Kite, Seve Ballesteros had come to the 17th one stroke behind Nicklaus with two holes to play. Still smarting from his mistake on the 15th, he three-putted for bogey and effectively took himself out of the running. In contrast to the excitable European, the rock-steady Kite came to the last needing a birdie. It failed to materialise and the stage was left to the Australian, Greg Norman.

Stepping onto the 16th tee, Norman found himself two behind Nicklaus. A birdie two on the hole then halved the deficit to just one stroke. Despite being blocked out from the green by a wayward drive at the 17th, he conjured up another birdie that made them level at nine under. Having put together four consecutive birdies from the 14th, Norman needed just one more to make him Masters champion. But as in previous times, Norman found it impossible to take full advantage of a championship-winning opportunity. After an uncharacteristically safe 3-wood on the difficult dog-leg final hole, it was odds-on a play-off.

Left with a long second Norman selected a 4-iron but a shortened backswing resulted in a nervy push into the gallery on the right. Now, needing a miraculous chip into the hole to win the Masters, the Australian sensibly settled his mind on getting down in two just to force a tie with Nicklaus. To his credit, he negotiated the shot with consummate skill bringing it to a halt 15 feet away. Then, just as some of the crowd headed off towards the 10th tee to await the play-off, he missed the putt. Adding yet another sorry chapter to his saga of near misses in major championships, the shell-shocked Norman headed off towards the scorer's tent.

Then slowly it dawned on everyone. Jack Nicklaus had won the 1986 Masters!

For Nicklaus it was a dream come true. In his article in the *New Yorker* magazine, the venerated golf writer Herbert Warren Wind described Jack's victory as, 'nothing less than the most important accomplishment in golf since Bobby Jones' Grand Slam in 1930.' That was high praise indeed but the facts bear it out. At 46 years of age, Nicklaus had won his sixth Masters title. Not only that, he had negotiated the last ten holes at Augusta National in birdie, birdie, birdie, bogey, birdie, par, eagle, birdie, birdie, par.

I don't think I've had ten holes of golf that were any better. Seven under with a bogey wasn't bad. But I've never had trouble bringing back my skills when I'm on a roll. My attention span gets more acute.

Possibly the greatest sustained run in the history of championship golf, the legendary Golden Bear is justifiably proud of his golf that day. That was over ten years ago. And while it will almost certainly turn out to be the last major of his remarkable career, who would bet against him doing it again should he ever put himself in contention? Certainly not Seve Ballesteros or Greg Norman for sure.

José-María

Olazábal

61 in the first round of the World Series of Golf at Firestone Country Club, Akron, Ohio, 23–26 August 1990.

In one of the game's truly great rounds, José-María Olazábal made one of the toughest courses on the US Tour look almost simple. Stretching well over 7,000 yards, the South Course at Firestone Country Club had been described as a monster by a number of top professionals in previous years. But the young Spaniard showed it scant respect in the first round of the 1990 World Series. Opening up a four-stroke lead he dominated the tournament from start to finish. Following up his remarkable nine-under-par round of 61 with three consecutive 67s, he went on to win by a record margin of twelve shots. Still only 24, his unexpected victory over one of the strongest fields outside of a major helped establish him as one of the finest young players in world golf.

The history of golf is littered with great individual rounds: Bobby Jones' 'perfect' 66 at Sunningdale in 1930, Ben Hogan's last round 68 at Carnoustie in the Open of 1951, and who can forget Tom Watson's epic 65 against Jack Nicklaus in the final round of the 1977 Open Championship at Turnberry? Each one stands out for different reasons, whether it was the drama of the occasion or the individual brilliance of the round. But if you took a straw-poll of top professionals and asked them to nominate the round of somebody else's life, the answer would be a lot clearer. For sheer golfing excellence, José-María Olazábal's 61 in the opening round of the 1990 World Series of Golf would be hard to beat.

Played over the exacting South Course at Firestone Country Club in Akron, Ohio, it was a stunning exhibition of skill and control from a golfer renowned for his bursts of low scoring. A new course record, it confounded those who said Denis Watson's 62 of 1984 would never be beaten. Six years later in the same event, the hugely talented Spaniard would prove them wrong. One of only three players able to break par that week, his four-day total of eighteen under par set a new tourna-

José-María Olazábal concentrating on a chip shot during the 1991 Epson Grand Prix.

ment record and established Olazábal as a new force in world golf.

'That's awfully low,' said runner-up Lanny Wadkins, whose own 72-hole record of thirteen under par had lasted since 1977. 'I mean, thirteen under, nobody ever scared that record for thirteen years, and now it gets shattered. I figured that record would be around for a while, and I'd be long gone before anybody broke it. I sure didn't think I'd be here to finish second to it. I wish I could've played with him, just to see how he was playing.'

Those who did witness Olazábal bring this monster 7,148-yard course to its knees in the opening round, now speak about it in awed terms. Not only for the (nine under par) score of 61 – which many had thought impossible – but also the seemingly casual way in which it was attained. Past US PGA champion Paul Azinger described how Olazábal had taken the game 'to a different level' that day. Whatever the truth, the young Spaniard would at least pick up a lasting nickname. From that day on, he has been known in the United States as the 'Firestone Killer'. Not surprisingly, the round would also be his personal choice for the 'Round of My Life'.

José-María Olazábal Manterola was born on 5 February 1966 in Fuenterrabia, Spain. The son, and grandson, of a greenkeeper, his early childhood was spent literally in the middle of a golf course. Brought up in the Basque country at the Royal San Sebastian Golf Club, 'Chema', as he is known locally, picked up his first club shortly before his second birthday. A gift from one of the members, it was cut down by his father for use around their modest house. Four years later, he had learnt the basics of the golf swing, having taken advantage of free coaching lessons given by the club at the weekend. Within the year, he had won his first junior competition.

'I don't know what my score was but I was seven and I won the category for the under-nines. That was no real surprise because I spent almost all my time with a golf club in my hands. Simply there was nothing else for me to do. There were no other children around to play normal children's games with, so all I had to do was play golf.'

It proved to be time well spent. Coming as he did from a poor working-class background, as a teenage prodigy he relied on help from the Spanish Golf Federation to further his amateur career. Yet despite this, his progress was nothing short of meteoric. When he was 15, he travelled to Scotland to represent the Rest of Europe in an international match against Britain at Gullane. Staying on to compete in the British Boys' Championship, Olazábal got to the semi-finals where he lost at the second extra hole.

For the determined young Basque, it was to prove the start of a sparkling amateur career. In 1983, he won the British Boys' Championship at Glenbervie. He quickly followed it up with victories in both the Spanish and Italian Amateur Championships. A year later, he made it to the final of the British Amateur Championship at Formby where he faced his future Ryder Cup team-mate and long-time rival Colin Montgomerie and eventually ran out the winner by the margin of 5 & 4.

In 1985, the same year Olazábal would turn professional, he completed the hat-trick of major amateur titles by winning the British Youths' Championship at Ganton. Then almost for good measure, he picked up the silver medal for finishing top amateur in the Open Championship at Royal St George's. Not surprisingly, the R&A sought to commemorate his remarkable achievements by presenting him with a silver quaich that today holds pride of place in the Olazábal trophy cabinet alongside his many other trophies.

José-María Olazábal described his first professional win in the 1986 European

Masters/Swiss Open at Crans-sur-Sierre as like 'breaking down a wall'. Removing any lingering doubts he may have had about making it in the paid ranks, it catapulted him on to further success. Later the same year, he followed his debut win with another victory in the Sanyo Open on his way to finishing runner-up in the Order of Merit to winner Seve Ballesteros. With official prize money earnings of £155,263, it also made him a cast-iron certainty for Rookie of the Year. As for Ballesteros, the two Spaniards would later become close friends as well as forming one of the most successful partnerships in Ryder Cup history.

Since then Olazábal has maintained a remarkable consistency in his tournament play. Apart from his enforced absence in 1995-96, he has averaged at least two victories every year since he turned professional. Never out of the top twenty in the European Money List, he has rarely finished outside the top half dozen. A five-time Ryder Cup professional since 1987, he played a vital role in the 14–13 victory over the United States at Valderrama in 1997. Playing on his home soil of Spain, it was a special moment indeed for the proud young golfer.

> Playing in the Ryder Cup at Valderrama was very special for me. Having qualified for the team after being out of the game for eighteen months was a dream come true. Like my victory at Las Palomas [in the 1997 Turespaña Masters] it was very emotional. All those memories of my time away would come back. Even though I was not able to beat Lee Janzen in the singles, the overall experience was very satisfying. It meant a lot to me especially with Seve as captain.

The two played so much competitive golf together, it was somehow natural that Olazábal would be compared to the great Seve Ballesteros throughout his early career. Yet compared with Seve's three Opens and two Masters titles, José-María's record is little more than adequate in terms of majors. Back in the late eighties, Ballesteros felt the low, piercing way his younger rival hit the ball would suit the type of windswept links courses used in the Open Championship. But in typical style, Olazábal went out of his way to prove him wrong by winning the 1994 US Masters at that most American of golf courses, Augusta National. Indeed it was Seve who pinned a note to his locker on the final day which read, 'You are the best. Go out and win.'

Surprisingly, Olazábal's first, and so far only, major win came after one of the most self-reflective periods in his young life. This was the result of losing out to Ian Woosnam in the climax to the 1993 Masters when he bogeyed the final hole to finish runner-up. Described by others, including Seve, as the best player in the world, the 27-year-old professional was having a difficult time proving it. With the game becoming increasingly hard work, this often charming but occasionally melancholic individual seemed content to stalk about the golf course under his own private black cloud.

Throughout the early part of 1994, even his close friend and mentor Sergio Gomez described his attitude as more suited to the 'slaughterhouse' than the golf course. Often threatening to quit the game unless things improved, matters came to a head at the Mediterranean Open. 'He was struggling and he couldn't cope,' said the amiable Gomez. 'Well, one day I lost my patience as well and told him, "Okay, go ahead, quit, throw it all away." '

Perhaps the shock of being read the Riot Act by someone who is more of a father to him than a manager did the trick. After coming through to win the tournament, José-María had time to reflect on the value of his friendship with Gomez. 'Sergio is a good friend and very important to me,' said Olazábal, underlining the bond of mutual respect between the two men. 'Our relationship is very special. He

Spanish Ryder Cup star Olazábal helping the European team retain the trophy at The Belfry in 1989.

works only with me and no one else, and that is very important.'

In the weeks that followed, José-María knuckled down to some hard work. Having decided to team up with his old teacher, John Jacobs, he made swing changes over the long winter break that soon started to bear fruit. Renewing a relationship which dated back to his early teenage years when 'Dr Golf' was coach to the Spanish Golf Federation, the destructive hook which had plagued him over the past few seasons was all but eliminated. Better performances followed. The black cloud lifted.

A few weeks later, José-María Olazábal beat Tom Lehman into second by two strokes to win the 1994 US Masters. Even with seven Americans in the top ten at Augusta, the Spaniard looked set to conquer the golfing world like Ballesteros before him. Yet sadly it was not going to be. The career-threatening illness which would steal almost two years out of his life had already started to become a problem. If 1994 had given him the golfing success he craved, the next two years brought little more than pain and frustration.

After a seemingly routine operation to shorten his big toe, further complications had set in which made it increasingly difficult for Olazábal to walk. Throughout 1995 he was only able to compete in eight tournaments in Europe and, inevitably, was forced to pull out of the Ryder Cup side for Oakhill in September. Then, in 1996, José-María was absent for the entire season suffering from what looked like a severe case of rheumatoid arthritis. With rumours constantly circulating about the severity of his condition, it was even suggested that he might spend the rest of his life in a wheelchair.

In September the same year, his luck finally changed for the better. A consultation with a top homeopathic specialist from Munich finally diagnosed the root cause of his illness as a back hernia. Beginning treatment immediately José-María started a series of exercises aimed at building up tissue and muscle in the metatarsal area of his feet. The treatment was frustratingly slow and difficult, but by February 1997, he was back competing in the Dubai Desert Classic.

> Obviously, there was a chance that I might not play again, but I never said to myself that I would give up that chance. I always kept some hope within myself that some day the situation would change and I would be able to play golf again.

Following a highly creditable twelfth in Dubai, including a third round 65, his emotional victory at the Turespaña Masters in March set the stage for a triumphant return to the Ryder Cup in September. As before, José-María Olazábal ended the season by returning to his home in San Sebastian. There, away from the high pressure world of professional golf, he would spend time relaxing with his family, including his grandmother who always lit a candle in the window each time he left for a golf tournament.

No longer plagued by injury, he is able to look forward to the future with renewed enthusiasm. So, in a career noticeable for its incredible highs and terrible lows, which round does José-María Olazábal consider to be the 'Round of My Life'?

> Obviously my Masters victory in 1994 was special to me. But when I consider what is the greatest single round of my life it does not come to my mind. I've been fortunate to play some great rounds – 62 at Gleneagles in the 1987 Scottish Open, and 63 in the 1992 Open de Tenerife – but the best has to be my 61 at Firestone in 1990. In golfing terms alone it would stand out as my best ball-striking round ever. Not only that, it was my first win in America and to win by twelve shots in any tournament is always very good.

Olazábal dominated the World Series event almost from the start. Opening with a remarkable nine-under-par 61, he literally blasted the field apart and, from that point on, never really looked back. Watching the fireworks on day one, his playing partner, John Huston, agreed. 'He played great,' he later said. 'I sort of thought the way he was going, the tournament was pretty much through the first day.'

Amazingly, not long before the World Series had begun Olazábal had been struggling badly with his putting. Less than two weeks earlier, at the United States PGA Championship at Shoal Creek, Alabama, he despaired of making a consistent stroke at the ball until two close friends had spotted the fault. A minor alteration to the forward press he made before putting worked wonders, and it went on to pay handsome rewards at Akron.

With scant roll on the heavy fairways, the South Course at Firestone Country Club was playing its full length. In a round which would go down in golf history as one of the very best, Olazábal made a blistering start shooting five consecutive 3s from the 1st (birdie, eagle, birdie, birdie, par). The best of these was his eagle at the 497-yard par-5 2nd hole. Courtesy of a glorious 3-wood second which pitched no more than 20 feet from the pin, his putt never looked like missing. It was the same story over the next few holes, though his habit of striking arrow-straight iron shots to within a few feet of the cup made putting almost irrelevant. For example, at the difficult par-4 4th, he covered the 458-yard hole with a drive and 5-iron for yet another tap-in birdie.

Never the greatest driver of a ball, Olazábal set about using his 1-iron off the tee to great strategic effect. This, along with the accuracy of his mid- and short-iron approaches, meant he could literally take the course apart. 'If you are as natural a straight iron player as Olazábal is,' Lanny Wadkins pointed out, 'you can fire for the pin time after time.'

Olazábal made his first mistake of the day on the 219-yard par-3 7th. But after dropping a shot by missing the green from the tee, he immediately came back with another birdie on the 8th. Then the

Olazábal at the 1990 World Series in Akron, before the injury that threatened his career.

José-María Olazábal

fireworks really started. At the short par-4 11th he almost sank a full 9-iron approach before tapping in his birdie putt.

Inspired to greater feats of brilliance, he then birdied the next three holes to go a remarkable eight under par after 14 holes! Then with the chance of breaking 60 a real possibility, he struck a superb 2-iron to within a few feet of the hole at the 221-yard par-3 15th. With the crowds at Akron getting larger and more voluble every minute, his missed putt was a real blow. But Olazábal remained undaunted, 'I remember saying to myself, "You're not going to hole every putt so don't worry." '

Two holes later he did it again. After hitting a superb 8-iron approach to within five feet at the 17th, he inexplicably missed the putt and ended any possibility of breaking the magical 60 barrier for the first time in his career. Amazingly, José-María had never even considered the possibility until near the end, 'I didn't realise it could have been a 59 until my caddie [Dave Renwick] told me at 17 – I was thinking par was 72.'

After making par at the last for 61, the Spaniard credited his score to a combination of wonderful long-iron play and putting.

> I hit all my irons very well, but I managed to put the ball even closer with my long clubs. I've played this good before, tee to green, but I've never putted this well.

So how close had he come to breaking 60? 'He had a very good chance to shoot in the 50s,' said John Huston in the press conference afterwards. Asked if he said anything to Olazábal during the later stages of the round to encourage him, Huston replied, 'No but I said, "nice birdie" a lot.'

The reaction to Olazábal's incredible round was not long in coming, and not all of it was good. After a first round 66 of his own, past US Masters winner Larry Mize had asked, '61? Where did he play?' It was the same reaction from Payne Stewart who became increasingly agitated after being told his first round 65 had left him four strokes behind the leader going into day two. Even a local radio hack, who consistently emphasised the María in Olazábal's name, suggested the only reason he had shot 61 was that he played off the women's tees!

Getting in on the act, some Akron locals even had the bad grace to mention the large number of trees lost through Dutch Elm disease in recent years. Dropping large hints about the course not being as tough as it once was, they failed to recognise that unless the missing elms had been planted in the middle of the fairway, they would not have bothered Olazábal in the least.

No doubt surprised by the amount of criticism which had followed his opening round, Olazábal went on to break a host of records that week, including the tournament record. Following up his 61 with three excellent rounds of 67, his massive twelve-stroke winning margin was the best ever in the World Series event. Demolishing a world-class field, it put him fourth behind Bobby Locke, Byron Nelson and Ben Hogan on the list of record winning margins in United States PGA Tour history.

Having proved his remarkable first round score had been no fluke, Olazábal's playing partner, Lanny Wadkins, had bowed in mock homage as they walked off the 18th green on the final day. Now with a fit José-María Olazábal back chasing golf's glittering prizes, who can say more of his rivals will not be doing the same in the years to come.

Arnold

Palmer

65 in the final round of the US Open Championship at Cherry Hills Golf Club, Denver, Colorado, 18–21 June 1960.

With 18 holes remaining, Arnold Palmer found himself seven strokes behind tournament leader Mike Souchak. Ignoring those who said he was too far back to win, he drove the green at the 346-yard 1st hole for the first of his six birdies on the front nine. A 35 coming home gave Palmer a 65 and a winning score of 280, two shots ahead of the highly rated amateur Jack Nicklaus. Having already won the US Masters at Augusta in April, it gave Palmer the second leg in a potential Grand Slam.

At his peak, Arnold Palmer was probably the most famous sportsman in the world. The first golfing superstar, he was the very personification of the American Dream. Son of a greenkeeper from the hard-edged steel town of Latrobe, Pennsylvania, he rose from humble beginnings to dominate the world of professional golf in the early sixties. Able to count kings and presidents among his close friends he was also considered the people's champion. Charismatic and genuine, it used to be said that, when Arnie hitched up his pants before going for the big one, golfers all over the world held their breath.

For millions of golf fans Palmer was the man who made the game exciting. Indeed, for many American sports fans, he *was* golf. In a career which coincided with the new and exciting era of televised sport, audiences thrilled to his special brand of hell-for-leather golf. Coming hard on the heels of the Hogan era, Palmer played his golf to a simple maxim. Hit it hard, go find it, hit it hard again.

Of course, success brought rich rewards. Able to boast all the trappings associated with a millionaire sportsman, Palmer was almost certainly the first golf professional in history to make more money off the course than on it. The outstanding sports personality of his day, he went on to build a highly successful business empire which at one point included five highly paid lawyers working for him

Arnold Palmer: the people's champion.

exclusively. But ever mindful of his growing band of adoring fans, the legendary Arnie's Army, two full-time secretaries were also employed just to answer his mail.

Known throughout the early part of his career as the 'Charger', Palmer built up an awesome reputation as a fearless competitor. Accompanied by shouts of 'Go for it Arnie!' the athletic golfer, with his boyish good looks, could often be counted on to provide a thrilling finish to a tournament. Time and again, he would race out of the pack with a barn-storming finish, to pick up first prize. And while he would later come to regret the tournaments, especially the United States Opens, that slipped from his grasp, his career record of four Masters, two Open Championships and one US Open certainly stands the test of time.

Perhaps his most dramatic victory came in the 1960 United States Open at Cherry Hills, Denver. Trailing tournament leader Mike Souchak by a massive seven strokes going into the final round, Palmer had been written off as a possible winner. Yet after blasting through the field with a sensational 65, including 30 on the front nine, he made many of those who had doubted him eat their words. Certainly one of the most famous individual rounds in the championship's long history, it would also be Arnold Palmer's personal selection for the 'Round of My Life'.

I have been very fortunate to play some great rounds in my career. But the one that springs to mind most is the final round at Cherry Hills in 1960. Talking about my chances in the locker room beforehand with golf writers Bob Rosburg and Bob Drum, then going out and shooting such a low score to win was very satisfying. That is why I consider it the greatest round of my life.

Born on 10 September 1929 Arnold Daniel Palmer was given his first golf club by his father when he was four. By the time he was eight, he was competing with some of the older boys who worked as caddies at the nine-hole course at Latrobe. 'I couldn't wait to get out of school and on the golf course,' said Palmer. 'I hated to study but nobody had to force me to work on my golf. I loved every minute of it.'

Aged around 11, the young Arnie took up caddying and found himself serving directly under his father Milfred. Known as 'Deac' Palmer, dad had originally been employed at the club as greenkeeper before moving up to the post of professional and caddie master. An authoritarian figure who Palmer later admitted he argued with 'like cat and dog', he was to prove a lasting influence on his son's career.

Later working in his father's pro shop, where he learnt all the rudiments of club-making and repair, Arnold played in his first National Junior Championship in 1946. Fitting in long hours of practice between his other duties, his first taste of major competition was not a great success. But despite finishing a long way behind his future rival in the paid ranks, Bob Rosburg, it failed to dim any enthusiasm he had for the game.

As a young adult, Arnold Palmer enrolled at nearby Wake Forest College. In an unsettled period of his life, he quit halfway through his senior year after his closest friend, Bud Worsham, was killed in a tragic car accident. Almost on impulse he signed up for three years in the US Coast Guard. He hardly picked up a club for his first few months, but was then transferred to Cleveland, where his interest in golf began to return. Boosted by new friends who played every week whatever the weather, his passion for the game returned – and this time for good.

Palmer was still only 24 when he left the Coast Guard. Another spell at Wake Forest to finish his education also ended prematurely when, in his own words, 'I just couldn't apply myself.' Returning to Cleveland after just one term, he began work as a manufacturer's agent. Continuing to play golf with little thought of a professional career, he was the surprise winner of the 1954 United States Amateur Championship at the Country Club of Detroit.

Beating Robert Sweeny one-up in the final proved to be a major turning point in his life in more than one way. Weeks later, he was invited to play in a tournament at Shawnee in Delaware where he met his later bride-to-be, Winnie Walzer. Proposing within the week, the still happily married couple planned to arrange their honeymoon around the groom's debut in the Walker Cup at St Andrews. It was not to be. With the pressure on to earn a living, Arnold Palmer turned professional on 19 November 1954. After first seeking advice from his father, he signed his first club sponsorship deal and then married Winnie at Christmas.

Starting out on a shoestring budget, Palmer's early career was hampered by the PGA rule that no rookie could accept money from official events until he had served a six-month probationary period. Undeterred, Palmer picked up almost $2,000 in two unofficial tournaments which he immediately invested in an old caravan. He then joined the Tour on the Pacific Coast, with the caravan serving as home for the first few months of married life.

Having won enough prize money in non-sanctioned events, Palmer was in a good position by the time his six-month trial period was over. Building on this successful start to his professional career he became leading money winner in 1958 with $42,607. With the battered old caravan now a distant memory, Palmer now had enough to build a white ranch-house overlooking Latrobe Country Club for himself, Winnie and his two young daughters.

Only three years after turning professional, big paydays were becoming a matter of course. Yet it was not until 1960 that Palmer first caught the imagination of the golfing public. He had already won the Masters two years earlier at Augusta National, but on this second occasion he made the first of his legendary Palmer charges. Needing two birdies in the last two holes to tie tournament leader Ken Venturi, he got both in spectacular style. While Venturi was in the clubhouse practically trying on his green jacket, Palmer holed from 25 feet on the 17th for birdie, before drilling his approach to the final green to within five feet. Dropping his half-smoked cigarette on the green before setting up to putt, Palmer calmly stroked the ball into the back of the hole. His victory in the play-off magnified his new found reputation as a miracle worker.

The first of many such miracles in his career, Palmer made the late comeback his trademark. At Augusta, his long-time Masters caddie, Nathanial 'Iron Man' Avery, described his boss's attitude on such occasions. 'It's all or nothing,' he said some years ago. 'This man don't know what it is to play safe. He tugs at his glove, jerks on his trousers and starts walking fast. And then he turns to me and says, "The game is on." '

After winning the 1960 Masters, the ambitious Arnie Palmer said,

> I won't be content until I score a professional Grand Slam. My ambition is to win the Masters, the US and British Opens and the PGA all in a single year. I think it would be a greater achievement than Bobby Jones' Grand Slam in 1930.

If Palmer had not been aged 31 at the time, it could have been the bravado of youth talking. But as he approached the second leg, the United States Open at Cherry Hills, he was playing possibly the best golf of his career. It would be a tournament which further added to the Palmer legend. It would also be the tournament where he would play the one round in his career of which he was most proud.

With the Open being held in Denver for only the second time in its history, Palmer came into the tournament on a real hot streak. After the Masters, he finished second in Houston, fifth in the Tournament of Champions, 22nd at the Colonial and fifth in Oklahoma. With the second major of the season scheduled for the following week, it was during practice in Oklahoma City that a friend flew Palmer and Dow Finsterwald out to Cherry Hills.

With the event being played 5,000 feet above sea level, both players were concerned about the effects of high altitude on the flight of the ball. Estimating the average travelling distance of a drive at about seven per cent further, Palmer felt confident he could at least drive the green at the 346-yard 1st hole. While he would fail in each of the first three attempts, his fourth in the final round would go into golfing legend as one of the finest drives ever hit.

In the tournament itself, the relatively unknown Mike Souchak made a blistering start with opening rounds of 68, 67 and 73. With the last two rounds both played on the final day, Palmer had drifted seven shots behind after the morning round. Worse still, one glance at the leader board during the brief lunch break showed fourteen players between him and Souchak. 'I didn't know how I was going to win,' said Palmer, 'but I knew something had to give. I shot 72, 71 and 72 and I couldn't believe I had played so well without having any more to show for it.'

In a locker room conversation which is now part of golfing folklore, Palmer discussed his chances with a small group of golf journalists including Pittsburgh golf writer and good friend, Bob Drum. Arnie had asked whether he still had any chance of winning.

'No, you're too far back,' came back the answer from Drum.

'What if I shoot 65?' suggested Palmer as he prepared for his afternoon round. 'Doesn't 280 always win the Open?'

'Yeah, when Hogan shoots it,' came back the withering reply from another writer Dan Jenkins.

Standing on the elevated tee at the 341-yard par-4 1st, the situation had looked impossible. But, accompanied by shouts of 'Go Arnie, go' from his army of adoring fans looking for a Masters-style fight-back, Palmer responded in magnificent fashion. After his three previous failures, this time he drove the green, finishing no more than 20 feet away from the hole. Cheered all the way, he reached the green and surveyed his putt for eagle. Two putts later he collected his first birdie and was off and running.

Perhaps inspired by his own brilliance at the opening hole Palmer set about the opening nine at Cherry Hills in tigerish mood. At the 410-yard 2nd he holed a 30-foot chip from off the green for another birdie; another superb wedge approach to the 3rd to within one foot of the flag, birdie again; 20-foot putt on the 4th, birdie once more. In fact the only real surprise of the round came at the par-5 5th, a hole he would expect to birdie but failed. Perhaps it resulted from having spotted Drum and Jenkins walking down the fairway. Palmer's comment at the time was, 'I wondered how long it would take you two to get out here.'

Picking up the pace with yet another birdie at the 6th, he followed it up with a fine wedge approach to six feet from the pin at the 411-yard 7th. At this stage in the round, Palmer had played seven holes and birdied six. Then at the testing 230-yard par-3 8th, he dropped his first shot after failing to get up and down from a green-side bunker. After starting so well, the 9th also proved a bit of a struggle. No doubt still thinking about the hole before, Arnie went through the back of the green with his 6-iron approach. Then with a real crisis looming, he bravely holed from eight feet for his par and an incredible first nine of just 30 strokes.

Yet despite equalling the US Open record for nine holes, Arnie was not a happy man. 'I wanted that 29, damn it!' he said to Drum. 'But you've just taken the lead in the Open!' replied the surprised journalist.

Palmer got the message and after cadging a cigarette off Jenkins to calm his nerves, he set about making the tournament his. But, standing on the 10th tee, even he could not imagine that it would only take a level par 35 on the back nine

to win. One by one his closest rivals challenged then fell back. The record books show that third round leader, Mike Souchak, slumped over the closing holes for a 73 and a 283 aggregate, three strokes back.

Palmer putting with his familiar knock-kneed style during the 1967 Piccadilly World Matchplay at Wentworth.

Of the remaining players out on the course, the highly rated amateur Jack Nicklaus had his own shot at the title before three putts at the 13th and 14th saw him fall back into second place. Eventually finishing two strokes behind Palmer, his 283 total was the best ever score by an amateur in the history of the event.

It was the same story for the legendary 'Hawk', Ben Hogan. Looking for his fifth US Open title, he had been in contention throughout the final round until he gambled everything on a risky pitch over water on the 71st hole. Feeling his injured legs might not carry him through an eighteen-hole play-off the following day, it was one gamble too many for the legendary Texan. Catching the water with that approach, he then suffered the humiliation of more dropped shots by running up a triple-bogey seven on the final hole. But as the dust settled, there was only one champion and that was Arnold Palmer.

Acknowledged as one of the finest rounds ever played in championship golf, Palmer's 65 only added to his growing legend. Showing a remarkable ability to snatch victory from the jaws of defeat, he had captured the hearts and imagination of America's sports fans. After the tournament, congratulations poured in from all over the world, including one from his great golfing buddy, past US President Dwight D. Eisenhower.

Nothing, it seemed, could dim the widespread admiration felt for the charismatic golfer from Latrobe, Pennsylvania. Even when his dreams of a Grand Slam were cruelly dashed a few weeks later in the Centenary Open Championship at St Andrews, the legend lived on. Finishing runner-up to Australian Kel Nagle by a stroke, Palmer was making another spectacular charge when a heavy rain-storm forced postponement of the final round.

Back in the United States, he led the first round of the PGA at Firestone, Akron, but fell away leaving the title to Jay Herbert. Along with Ben Hogan, who won the Masters, United States and British Opens in 1953, Palmer had come within a whisker of achieving the impossible. But sadly his dream of Grand Slam glory would remain just that, a dream.

Indeed, that remarkable victory at Cherry Hills was his only US Open title, though he twice made the play-off, in 1962 when he lost out to Jack Nicklaus 74 to 71, and 1963 when he finished third behind Julius Boros and runner-up Jacky Cupit. That said, Palmer became the dominant player in world golf for almost five years after his glory year of 1960. Adding another six major titles to his name, his remains a record of which he is justifiably proud. Yet, looking back, did the aggressive style which won him those great championships ultimately act against him?

'People always accused me of purposely getting behind so I can pull out of a hole,' he said about the cost of pulling off such remarkable golfing comebacks. 'That's ridiculous. On those tight finishes, I bleed a little bit myself. If I had my way, I would win every tournament by twelve strokes.'

Unlike his greatest rivals, Jack Nicklaus and Gary Player, Palmer would never win the United States PGA Championship. And while he would accumulate over 70 tournament victories worldwide, including success in his Senior career, he failed to achieve even the alternate Grand Slam of all four Majors in different years.

Offered the chance to play one shot over again, the great man said, 'That question applies to too many shots. There was the [United States] Open in 1966, Augusta in 1961, the British Open in 1960, the PGA at Firestone in 1961. I could go through a few PGAs, at Columbus [1964], at San Antonio [1968], where a shot made the difference between winning and losing.'

Though hardly any of his millions of fans ever noticed, Palmer started running into mini-slumps as early as 1964. In April that year, he captured his fourth US Masters title and five weeks later won the Oklahoma City Open. Then without warning, he went through a tournament-winning drought lasting almost a year. Failing to make any showing in the majors, his string of second and third place finishes throughout the season only added to his frustration. He would eventually finish $81 behind Money List winner Jack Nicklaus.

Hogan always contended that putting was the first thing to go for the majority of pro golfers. Certainly Palmer suffered spells in his career when the hole just was not big enough. 'I haven't putted well since 1960,' he said during a poor patch in 1963. 'My game is better than ever it was from tee to green. I simply can't get the ball in the hole.'

In the mid-sixties, major championships began slipping away. In 1965 Palmer suffered a big disappointment when his younger rival, Dave Marr, came through to win the PGA Championship over Palmer's home course of Laurel Valley. Desperate to put on a good show before thousands of his supporters, the previously invincible Arnie struggled throughout the entire week. He finished with rounds of 74 and 73, leaving him a lamentable 14 strokes behind Marr, and the obituaries were not long in coming.

Most golfing pundits put his apparent decline down to his huge off-course business interests. Mostly generated by his close association with his manager and trusted friend, Mark McCormack, Palmer certainly had his fair share of commercial deals. In the sixties he endorsed items ranging from cigarettes to luxury cars. In the quiet winter season, he acted in movies, cut instructional records, and was paid small fortunes for occasional walk-on roles on television. The hottest property in American sport, he had even produced and starred in his own show called *Challenge Golf*.

Independently wealthy by the time he was 30, Palmer's own desire for golfing glory was undiminished. Yet having set such high standards over the previous few years, his loyal army of fans looked for any excuse for their hero's decline. But by the end of 1965, the knives were out. At the Ryder Cup at Royal Birkdale, he was criticised in sections of the golfing press for his overall performance – this despite winning 4 out of a possible 6 points! The next decade would be spent attempting to capture a small taste of the glory he once had.

Thankfully he no longer has to prove anything. Still adored by his fans, as shown by his emotional walk up the final fairway at St Andrews in his last Open in 1995, his appearances are a high point for any tournament. Many years after his famous handshake contract with McCormack, Palmer still tailors his off-course interests to suit his golfing commitments. He is still independently wealthy. He still plays his golf with the passion of a teenager. And while his tally of seven majors will no doubt be surpassed by lesser players, the greatness of Arnold Palmer lives on.

Coming from an era when golf professionals were actively discouraged from entering the clubhouse in many US states, he grabbed the game by the scruff of the neck and turned it upside down. Through his genius he made golf seem both exciting and accessible to the man in the street. Indeed, his role in introducing people from all walks of life to the game cannot be overstated. That, if anything, is the true legend of Arnold Palmer

Independently wealthy by the time he was 30, Palmer's desire for golfing glory remained undiminished in later life.

Gary

Player

64 in the final round of the US Masters at Augusta National, Georgia, 9–12 April 1978.

Despite having won seven majors, South African great Gary Player was seen as a spent force coming into the 1978 Masters. Turned 40, he had not won a US Tour event for the previous four years and was not expected to make any showing against the new crop of young up-and-coming players. Paired with the 21-year-old Spaniard, Seve Ballesteros, he was still five strokes behind Tom Watson with nine holes to play in the final round. Confounding his critics, Player came back in just 30 strokes (six under par) to win his third green jacket and the ninth major of his career.

If faith can move mountains then winning golf tournaments must have proved a fairly simple matter for Gary Player. One of the most dedicated professionals ever to grace the game, his career record of nine major championships is quite remarkable. Especially when you consider just how many thousands of miles he travelled from his homeland in South Africa to compete in them. His tally of three Opens, two PGA Championships, three Masters and one US Open makes him one of only four golfers in the history of the game to have achieved the modern Grand Slam. Is it any wonder then that the 'man in black' is considered among the greats of golf?

Possibly the most travelled competitor in the world of professional sport, Gary Player has dedicated most of his adult life to the science of competition. A tournament golfer since he was 18, this fitness fanatic has been challenging for the game's glittering prizes for four decades. Since his first Open victory at Muirfield in 1959, he has globe-trotted his way to over 130 wins worldwide. Now in his early sixties he shows little sign of slowing up as he plunders some of the richest prizes on the United States Senior Tour. And all this for someone who was once told by a well-known British professional, 'Go home young man, and get yourself an honest job.'

As the record books show, Gary Player ignored the advice preferring the other option of practice, practice and even more practice. Now as he reflects on his remarkable career, just what is Gary Player's choice for the 'Round of My Life'?

That is a tough question to answer. I consider myself very fortunate to have played many wonderful rounds in my life. After all, how do you rank one great round above another great round. It's almost impossible. I think if you were to ask me about the 'tournament of my life' it would be a lot simpler. Winning the Open for the first time in '59 at Muirfield was very special. My first major championship, it meant a great deal to me at the time. Then I would certainly consider being the first foreigner to win the Masters at Augusta in 1961 – battling against the king of US golf, Arnold Palmer, and beating him. At the time I thought that would be hard to top. But then in '78 I had a final round of 64 to win my third green jacket. I came back in 30 that day to win by a shot. Can you imagine it? I also had three lip-outs for birdies. If they had gone in, I would have shot 27 for the last nine holes! If that had happened I don't think Augusta would have invited me back, do you?

Gary Player was born on 1 November 1935, at Lyndhurst near Johannesburg. The youngest of three children, his mother Muriel died of cancer when he was eight and the demands placed upon him by his authoritarian father Harry, who spent most of his life working in the gold mines, have been given as reasons for his incredible will to win. He excelled at King Edward VII school in all sports including rugby, cricket, swimming and athletics. He also played golf from an early age at nearby Virginia Park. In this time of boyhood dreams of golfing glory he even had his own heroes.

The three players who captured my imagination when I first took up golf were Bobby Jones, Byron Nelson and Ben Hogan. All are legendary figures in the game and I used to get a big kick reading about their exploits.

Gary Player turned professional in 1953 at the age of just 16. Taught as a youngster, never give up, never quit and always compete as hard as you can, determination was something that would stay with him for the rest of his life. Some years later, a friend who shared a room with Player during their first years on Tour remembers waking up one night to find him staring at the mirror repeating over and over again, 'I'm going to be the greatest golfer in the world. I'm going to be the greatest golfer in the world.'

With money borrowed from his father to help get started, Player soon made enough to finance his own efforts on the fledgling South Africa Tour. Two years later in 1955 he won his first official tournament and so impressed the members at Killarney Golf Club in Johannesburg, where he was assistant, that enough money was raised to send him abroad for the first time. Now on his way, he not only won tournaments in South Africa, Egypt and Australia, but finished

Gary Player with his daughter and son.

fourth behind Peter Thompson in the Open Championship at Hoylake in 1956.

On the basis of a glowing letter written by his father to Clifford Roberts, Chairman of Augusta National, outlining his son's many achievements, Gary received a surprise invitation to play in the 1957 Masters. Still only 21, the young South African made little impact that week but did gain invaluable experience playing in a major championship abroad, experience which would prove crucial four years later when he recorded his first Masters victory in 1961.

This success, coming only two short years after he had won his first major championship in the 1959 Open at Muirfield, made Gary Player the most highly rated non-American golfer in the world. Making rapid progress, he made it three majors by winning the United States PGA at Aronomink in 1962. The ambitious South African achieved his lifelong ambition of capturing all four majors in 1965, beating Australian Kel Nagle in a play-off for the US Open at Bellerive, St Louis. It was something that meant a great deal to him at the time.

> Up until my victory in the 1978 Masters, the win at Bellerive was probably my most memorable. I remember it was played in tremendous heat and humidity and I kept myself going by eating lots of honey. Probably what made it so important was that no overseas player had won the title for forty-five years, and what made it particularly significant for me, is after beating Kel Nagle in the play-off it made me only the third golfer in history to complete the Grand Slam – Ben Hogan and Gene Sarazen being the other two. I also had the satisfaction of donating the cheque of $25,000 to cancer research and to promote junior golf. For me, the title and the Grand Slam were more than enough reward.

Shortly after his first US Open triumph, Gary Player decided to follow the example of his rivals, Arnold Palmer and Jack Nicklaus, and place his career in the hands of Mark McCormack. It was that decision as much as anything else which contributed to his reputation as one of the 'big three' in the late sixties and seventies.

Probably better known outside the United States than either Nicklaus or Palmer, Gary Player was marketed as an international superstar whose image as a tough, never-say-die competitor was more than matched by his ability. Yet despite being a tireless practiser and student of the golf swing, Player himself was privately riddled with doubts about his own technique. Back in 1973 he decided to ring the legendary Ben Hogan at his home in Fort Worth, Texas. Speaking from Brazil, Player requested Hogan's advice about his swing but the terse Hogan had replied, 'Who do you work for?' When the answer came back, 'Dunlops,' Hogan suggested if Player ever wanted tips on the golf swing again, he should 'call Mr Dunlop,' and put the phone down.

While the humour of the situation was probably lost on the serious-minded Player, his equipment sponsors Dunlop thought it was a marketing godsend and immediately began using Hogan's comments in their advertising. But in truth, Player had very little need for Hogan's advice. By 1974 he was probably the best golfer in the world, recording both his second Masters and Open wins that same year, along with top-ten finishes in the US Open and PGA Championship.

Yet it was not all plain sailing for Gary Player in the United States in the early seventies. Forthright in his opinions about various subjects, including race, he was the subject of death threats when it was thought he had expressed tacit support for the apartheid system in South Africa.

On one notorious occasion in 1969 he was attacked during the US PGA Championship held at the National Cash Register Club in Dayton, Ohio. After the

Gary Player explodes from a bunker during the final round at Augusta.

event had been picketed by civil rights activists on the opening two days, matters came to a head in the third round when spectators began barracking him when he was about to putt on the 9th green. Then, walking to the next tee, someone hurled a cup of ice cubes in his face. It was an ugly moment which Player handled with dignity. Turning to the man he asked, 'What have I ever done to you, sir, that you would want to do this to me?'

With the death threats considered serious enough, Player was given an armed guard during the final round of the tournament. Perhaps not surprisingly, he made very little showing that year. Sadly little had changed by 1970 or 1971. With tournament organisers forced to assign him guards throughout his first eleven tournaments, matters came to a head at the 1971 United States Open at Merion. With a tip-off given about a serious attempt on his life, police protection was even extended to the house he rented for the week of the championship.

Later describing it as 'a frightening experience', Player resolutely refused to quit any event the protesters attended. Showing unshakeable self-belief throughout the whole controversy, he continued to champion his right to free speech and even

Player celebrates as his winning putt hits the back of the hole on 18.

questioned why Nicklaus and Palmer had not been similarly vilified over the United States policy in Vietnam.

Thankfully, though, the controversy blew itself out and he was soon left to get on with winning golf tournaments.

Reflecting on his two major victories in 1974, American golf writer Herb Warren Wind suggested it was perhaps time for Player's critics to revise their opinion of his ability. Then almost as soon as the ink was dry on the typewriter, Gary Player forgot how to win for the next few years. As if, on reaching the peak of his career, he lost the ability to push himself that final mile when a tournament came down to the wire. While there would always be the occasional triumph somewhere in the world, generally his form was never quite good enough going into a major.

Nicklaus put it down to tinkering constantly with his swing in an effort to get more distance off the tee. Player, the supreme optimist, disagreed completely. Despite being described as 'washed up' by the American media, he never gave up on winning another major. Then in the 1978 Masters at Augusta, his dream finally came true.

Going into the Masters, the South African had been playing solidly enough but after three rounds lay a massive seven strokes behind leader Hubert Green. Perhaps more importantly, he was several strokes behind two-times Open champion, Tom Watson, who rarely, if ever, failed to mount a solid last day challenge. Paired with the young Spanish maestro, Severiano Ballesteros, Player suggested to a friend the night before the final round that it would probably take a 65 to win. The friend, not surprisingly, remained unconvinced. Yet, walking to the first tee the next day, Player was reminded of a prayer which he would repeat to himself throughout the round, 'I can do all things through Jesus Christ which strengthen me.'

Gaining inspiration from his faith, Player's attitude was in direct contrast to Seve's. Seve thought that, from seven shots back, he had left his challenge 'too late'. Player had other ideas.

Teeing off over forty minutes ahead of the leaders, Player made a solid if not spectacular start. A birdie-three on the uphill 9th took him to five under par. Now five strokes behind Green and three adrift of Watson and the unknown Rod Funseth, Player needed something special to happen. It was not too long in coming.

A twisting long-range putt on the long par-4 10th for a birdie three took Player to six under par. Roared on by a crowd obviously delighted to see him back in the thick of the action, he struck a fine short iron over Rae's Creek to the 12th green and holed the putt for yet another birdie: seven under. A great approach at the dog-leg par-5 13th gave up another birdie and now the chase was really on.

With Hubert Green, Tom Watson and Funseth playing in the groups just behind, what followed was one of the most absorbing battles of will in the history of championship golf.

Coming up the 11th, leader Hubert Green looked disturbed as he listened to the shouts which greeted yet another superb mid-iron approach by Player to a few feet at the par-4 14th. Moments later, a wayward approach of his own would drop him back to nine under in joint lead with Funseth. Watson and Player, who missed his short putt on 14, were now tied third at eight under.

Another birdie by Player at the par-5 15th lifted him into a share of the lead at nine under. Now aged 42, the South African miner's son looked unstoppable as CBS television researchers anxiously trawled through the record books to find the oldest winner of the Masters. But, just as commentator Jack Whitaker was about to give out the information, Watson rammed home a 25-foot putt for an eagle on the par-5 13th. It seemed the tournament would go the way everyone expected after all.

Player responded by drilling his tee shot over the lake at 16 to within 12 feet, then holed the putt for a birdie two. The leaders were trading blows back and forth like a bare-knuckle boxing match, for Player was joined moments later on ten under by Green and Funseth, who both birdied the 13th. With holes beginning to run out, it was Tom Watson who faltered first. Needing just a short putt on the 14th green for his par, the normally reliable putter inexplicably missed to register his first bogey of the back nine. Despite managing to claw the stroke back on the next hole, and a share of the lead at ten under, the miss had shaken Watson and offered encouragement to his rivals.

Arriving on the final green, Player instinctively knew he would have to hole his slick downhill putt from 15 feet to have any chance of winning. Ballesteros, who by now had little interest in his own round, urged the putt on as it sped towards the hole. As it dropped in the centre, Player punched the air in delight. Embraced by a tearful Seve, he had negotiated one of the most testing nine-hole stretches of golf in 30 strokes: six under par.

Most legendary victories, and Player's 1978 Masters victory was certainly that, usually require some assistance from the fates. With Funseth faltering under the pressure, Watson came to the 18th needing a birdie to win. Sadly, a bogey on 17 had dropped him back to eleven under and tied with Player. Momentum lost, there would be further heartbreak at the last for the Kansas-born professional. A wayward drive saw him struggle onto the green in three strokes. Moments later, he would miss his par from 12 feet and his chance had gone. Watching the action from the back of the green, Player was still in the hunt.

Hubert Green's was perhaps a more tragic story as he came to the 18th needing a birdie three to tie. Three putts at 16 had taken him out of the lead, but a magnificent approach to three feet at the last looked to have restored the damage. It was not an easy putt and the large crowd became uneasy as Green appeared to take much longer over his deliberations than normal. Settling over the ball, he caught the muffled voice of a radio reporter relaying the action back to his studio. Green pulled away before once more taking up his familiar crouched position over the ball. Inevitably, the putt was poorly struck and never looked like threatening the hole.

Gary Player was the champion at last. At the advanced age of 42 he had won his third Masters title and the ninth major championship of his career. Receiving his green jacket from the hands of past champion Tom Watson, his broad smile showed just how good it felt to win again.

Nick

Price

70 in the final round of the US PGA
Championship at Bellerive Country Club, St
Louis, Missouri, 13–16 August 1992.

Going into that final round, Nick Price was level with Jeff Maggert and two behind the relatively unknown Gene Sauers from Georgia. Having suffered a string of disappointing finishes in past major championships, including dropping three shots in the final five holes of the 1982 Open at Royal Troon to hand the title to Tom Watson, question marks hung over Price's ability to handle the pressure and win. A final round 70 at Bellerive would answer those questions. The first major success of Price's career, it gave the talented Zimbabwean the confidence to go on and win others, most notably the 1994 Open Championship at Turnberry.

The game of golf is littered with highly talented players who made their fortune but ultimately failed to capture one of the four major championships. Invented by the American media back in the seventies, the unenviable title of best-golfer-never-to-win-a-major gets passed around from player to player until it finally settles like the proverbial albatross on the shoulders of one poor unfortunate. Unfortunately for Zimbabwean professional Nick Price, in the early nineties he was next in line and, until the final round of the 1992 United States PGA Championship, it rather looked like he would have to live with it.

Long recognised as one of the best ball-strikers in the game, Nicholas Raymond Leige Price is probably the most 'international' golfer playing today. Born in South Africa, brought up in Rhodesia (now Zimbabwe), he travels the world on a British passport courtesy of his English mother. A contemporary of Faldo, Langer, Woosnam, Ballesteros and Lyle, he joined the European Tour in 1978. Fulfilling his early promise as World Junior Amateur champion, his most notable opening successes came in the 1980 Swiss Open and 1981 Italian Open. Returning home the following year, he topped the South African Money List but always felt he was playing catch-up with his closest rivals because of his two years' National Service in the Rhodesian Air Force.

> At the time I regretted losing two years out of my career. When Seve
> won the Open at Lytham in 1979 and the Masters in 1980, I felt I was
> lagging behind. On the other hand, I look back now and think two years
> was nothing.

Winning his player's card on the United States PGA Tour in 1981 was one major turning point for Nick Price, as was his chance meeting with the then little-known golf coach, David Leadbetter, a short time later. Realising he needed some radical help with his lightning-quick swing, Price put his faith in the English-born, Zimbabwe-raised teacher but the early results were mixed. In the 1982 Open Championship at Royal Troon, he handed the trophy to Tom Watson on a silver plate after being three shots up with six holes to play in the final round. It had been a bruising experience but Price remained undeterred.

> I had been to see David four months earlier, and if I hadn't there's no
> way I'd have been in a position to win at Troon. My game wasn't good
> enough when I went to him. I'd never seen my swing before, and when I
> saw it on video for the first time I knew I had some serious work to do.

Yet it was not long before the partnership between the two started to bear rich fruit. In 1983, a final round 67 in the prestigious World Series event at Akron gave Nick Price his first victory on American soil, along with an invaluable ten-year exemption from having to qualify. With his professional career now all but secure, Price was delighted with his rapid progress. Speaking shortly after, he was quoted as saying, 'I wanted to prove that I hadn't choked in the Open. I wanted to prove I could stand the pressure, so maybe now I can relax.'

Unfortunately for the highly talented young professional, he did relax, possibly too much. After his early progress with David Leadbetter, it was thought only a matter of time before major trophies adorned the Nick Price cabinet. But for the next five years, the only thing golf proved to be was a major struggle! While regular prize money continued to roll in, tournament victories all but dried up with his only win coming in the Trophée Lancôme in France in 1985. Price would not actually win again on the US Tour until 1991 when he captured both the Byron Nelson Classic and Canadian Open.

At Augusta National in 1986 Price grabbed the US Masters by the throat after shooting a course-record 63 in the third round. Then, almost as quickly, he stepped aside to allow 46-year-old Jack Nicklaus to win his sixth green jacket. Picking up the silver medal for runner-up was little consolation but, two years later, he began to see some real improvement. Competing in the Open Championship at Royal Lytham in 1988, he led going into the final round. Then, after locking horns with the inspired Seve Ballesteros, he settled for second once more despite putting together a 69 in the tense final round.

Finishing two strokes back, he reflected on how his nine-under-par aggregate would have been good enough to win most majors. Once again the light at the end of the tunnel had proved to be an oncoming train. Yet he took defeat in a positive manner.

Nick Price with the Wanamaker trophy.

At that stage in my career it was the most exciting thing that had ever happened to me. We just kept hitting good shot after good shot. The way I look back on 1988 is that it was a great experience and one I shall never forget. I played awfully well for four days but did not win, in the same way Jesper Parnevik played really well for four days at the Turnberry Open [1994] and did not win.

....

Forever the optimist, Price felt a major was closer than ever but, once again, it would prove a long and often frustrating wait. Continuing to play most of his golf in the United States, he was now in his mid-thirties and question marks were beginning to be raised over his competitive temperament. He was a nice guy but could he stand the heat? Perhaps he needed to be a bit tougher? He was gifted but did he lack the killer instinct it took to win a major?

In the final major of the 1992 season, the United States PGA Championship, Price would give the doubters his answer. Played at Bellerive Country Club in St Louis, Missouri, his golf that week left no one in doubt that he was made of the 'right stuff'.

Following other notable first-time major winners in 1992 – Fred Couples (Masters) and Tom Kite (US Open) – Price went into the final round knowing what he needed to do to win. Building on his past experiences, he formulated a game plan which would give him the victory he craved and, in most people's opinion, richly deserved. Making no mistakes, he would attack only when necessary. It was an unusual strategy but one that worked. Dropping only one shot to par all day, he stood back as others took the lead then tossed it away. In the end his final round of 70 would be enough.

Not only that, it would catapult him to even more major success in the coming years. Having finally broken through, he astonished even himself by winning a pair in 1994, the Open at Turnberry and the PGA at Southern Hills. He is now among the most prolific tournament winners of modern times, but is it any wonder that Nick Price finally settled on the last round at Bellerive that started it all as the 'Round of My Life'?

I think the most obvious answer would be the last eighteen holes at Turnberry in 1994, but I wouldn't say that was the round of my life. Certainly it would be one of the most memorable rounds of my career but at Turnberry only the last nine holes were really any good. It was undoubtedly the best nine holes I have ever played in my life and included three exceptional holes, the 16th, 17th and 18th, but nine holes is not a round so it does not really count.

My lowest ever competitive round is 61. I've shot that twice. Rounds like that are always fun but they are not what I would consider great rounds. Maybe I would feel different if it was a 59. Obviously that would have more significance. There were also a few great ball-striking rounds like my course-record 63 at Augusta, but they all came in the second and third rounds of a tournament with very little pressure on.

Of course there are others like my last round at Lytham in 1988 to consider. But, on reflection, I would pick the final round in the US PGA Championship at Bellerive mainly because it was my first major win. All the factors that were missing during my other major championship opportunities were there when I won in '92. It all seemed to come together for me. The discipline was there. The strategy and the style in which I could play was all there. I played an almost risk-free round when

I needed to. I let the opportunity come to me. I didn't try to create or force the opportunities like I had done in the past. I'm sure that was the key to the whole round.

Moving into the final round of that fateful PGA Championship, Price found himself level with Jeff Maggert and two behind Gene Sauers from Georgia. Drawing inspiration from players like Nicklaus, Floyd and Kite, who had all won majors in their forties, the 35-year-old Price felt confident and set about making the title his.

I had a theory about what it would take to win a major under such circumstances. I followed that theory that day and it paid off. The key was patience. Not playing too aggressively when you don't need to and not trying to force the issue. A lot of guys when they get to the last nine of a major feel like they have to do something superhuman to win – I know I did for many years. Invariably a lot of the time if you just play a good solid round shooting 69 or 70 – one or two under par – more often than not that can win it for you. It was this element of my victory I am probably most proud of, because knowing these things and doing them are a million miles apart.

Price went into the final round at Bellerive knowing what he would have to do to win.

With both Sauers (75) and Maggert (74) falling back in the later stages of the round, perhaps the most worrying sight for Price was Nick Faldo climbing steadily up the leader board. Another Leadbetter pupil, Faldo had challenged strongly initially with opening rounds of 68 and 70. Then, without warning, he had fallen back on Saturday with an uncharacteristic score of 76. (His pregnant wife Gill had been rushed to the local hospital earlier in the week suffering from severe migraines.)

Price and Faldo were paired together in the penultimate group, and it soon became obvious that the championship lay between them. Cheered on by the enthusiastic St Louis crowd, neither man made any mistakes but Faldo was making birdies. A massive six strokes behind Price going into the final round, by the time they played the 15th, Faldo had closed the gap to just three. Yet even after the Zimbabwean dropped his only shot of the day there, it was never going to be good enough. With holes running out fast and Price in full control of his game, Faldo's

67 left him in a four-way tie for second place with Jim Gallagher Jnr, John Cook and the hapless Gene Sauers.

Coming down the last there was only ever going to be one winner. A 70 would be good enough to give Price victory by two clear shots but, in truth, it seemed a lot easier than that. While it would be an emotional victory for the amiable professional and his now famous caddie, Jeff 'Squeaky' Medlen, Price still had the odd demon to face going down the closing stretch.

> By not taking any risks, on the back nine for example, I made only one bogey, and that was because I picked the wrong club on the 15th. Other than that it was pretty darn flawless for 18 holes. But having been close on so many other occasions then losing out, I started having the craziest thoughts. I had to try and block them out and not to think about them during the round. But in many ways you cannot help but think about them. I thought back to the '88 Open at Lytham against Seve and the '82 Open at Troon against Watson. Thankfully it all worked out OK in the end.

Not long after, Nick Price held the huge Wanamaker trophy aloft and pocketed a record cheque for $280,000. Having come so far, he seemed determined to enjoy his moment in the sun. In typically generous style, he granted every interview request and even had time to star in a television trailer for *Inside the PGA Tour*. A popular winner, it was only later that someone pointed out who the champion was the last time a major had been held at Bellerive. That was back in 1965 at the US Open, and it was another man from southern Africa, Gary Player!

Looking back on his most memorable major win, Price is convinced more than ever that he owes almost all of his success of the past few years to his final round at Bellerive.

> One thing I am also certain of is that, if I hadn't won that day, I don't think I would have been able to go on and win my other major championships. This is a serious point. Ask any top professional playing today about what it means to win their first major. The first one is always tough, perhaps the toughest. The second one is also hard, but the third is definitely not as tough as the other two. It's like the hurdle is twenty feet high. Then once you've won your first major it's like six inches and you feel you can just hop over the thing. That's maybe why experienced players, major winners for example, find they have an advantage coming down the stretch of any tournament. They know what it takes to win and that is something you cannot buy.

1989

Ronan

Rafferty

71 in the final round of the Volvo Masters at
Valderrama Golf Club, Sotogrande,
27–30 October 1989.

In a remarkable climax to the 1989 European season, Ronan Rafferty came to the 72nd hole of the Volvo Masters at Valderrama looking to become the first Irish professional since Christy O'Connor Snr in 1962 to win the Order of Merit. Having challenged strongly for the number one spot throughout the year, the 25-year-old professional from Newry came to the final green faced with the ultimate pressure putt. Just over three feet, the last putt, on the last hole, of the last event of the year, both the Volvo Masters title and the Order of Merit depended on its outcome. With Nick Faldo in the clubhouse awaiting a possible play-off, the young Irish professional stepped up and bravely holed it under the most testing of circumstances. Having come through to win, it confirmed much of the rich promise he had shown in the late eighties.

Eight years before Valderrama Golf Club in Spain staged the dramatic 1997 Ryder Cup encounter between Europe and the United States, it witnessed one of the most sensational finishes to a professional tournament ever seen.

In the final tournament of the 1989 season Ronan Rafferty needed a short putt on the final green to win the prestigious Volvo Masters tournament. If that was not pressure enough, he knew that, should he hole it, he would also top the European Order of Merit for the first time in his career. That success would open doors to invitations all over the world, including the American majors, and he knew it was not an opportunity that would come along every day. Also, having battled for the number one spot with José-María Olazábal throughout most of the season, it was not a chance he intended to waste.

Looking increasingly tense as he viewed the line of the putt, the possibility of failure was etched into his face. Having come so far and with so much at stake, how could he possibly let it slip now? Rarely one to dwell on any shot, Rafferty addressed his putt from around four feet with seemingly undue haste. Then, with barely a final glance at the hole, he sent the ball on its way. It was certainly not the best putt he had ever hit but moments later it hardly mattered. Accompanied by a huge cheer from the crowd around the green, it drifted round the side of the hole before falling in almost apologetically.

As the dust settled over Valderrama, the talented 25-year-old could reflect on his dual triumph. The record books show that his winning total of 282 (six under par) had been enough to win the Volvo Masters by a single stroke from Nick Faldo. His final round of 71, including a wonderful four-under-par 32 on the back nine, was enough to make him the first Irish golfer since Christy O'Connor Snr in 1962 to win the Order of Merit. Taking his season's earnings fractionally over the £400,000 mark, it left José-María Olazábal in second place and Nick Faldo in fourth. It had been a triumphant day all around.

Though it set off a night of celebration at his home club of Warrenpoint, Ronan Rafferty would have to delay his own party until he returned to Northern Ireland a few weeks later. Within minutes of his victory, he was on a plane out of Gibraltar Airport heading for yet another tournament in Japan. Perhaps, in hindsight, he should have delayed his journey and savoured the moment a little longer. But, like most young men, he probably thought having done it once, he would do it again. Sadly it was not to be.

Having achieved many of his golfing ambitions that day, he has never quite scaled the heights of 1989 again. Slipping back to fifth in the Money List the following season, then 35th, his desire for top honours seemed to diminish as the years went by. No longer challenging for golf's most glittering prizes, his last professional win on the European Tour came in 1993 at the Höhe Brücke Open in Austria. Only his fourth victory since the glory days of 1989, it seems scant return for one of the most naturally gifted players around.

Today, with a new career in television punditry beckoning, his playing career is spent in comfortable anonymity. Intelligent and thoughtful, Ronan will no doubt make a great success of his new profession. Yet many will remember those seemingly far-off days at Valderrama when he took on Europe's best and won in the round which, not surprisingly, he would select as the most memorable one of his career.

> I think it was the 'Round of My Life' for a number of reasons. First of all it had been a fight out between myself and José-María for the Order of Merit for much of the season. Then to be paired together in the final round at Valderrama, in the final tournament of the season, made it even more special. There are very few times when matters are so well defined in golf, and to come through and win on the last putt made it very memorable for me personally.

Ronan Patrick Rafferty was born on 13 January 1964 in Newry, Northern Ireland. Having picked up his first club at nine years of age, he enjoyed a successful amateur career which included winning the British Boys' Championship in 1979 and the English Strokeplay in 1980. A year later, he became the youngest golfer to play in the Walker Cup and turned professional soon after. Then, with great things predicted for him, he suffered the setback of failing to win his player's card at the PGA Qualifying School. Spectacular success followed by unexpected disappointment would be a pattern which would continue to haunt him throughout his career.

Having qualified for the European Tour via success on the Safari Circuit later in 1981, the enigmatic Ulsterman spent the next few years looking to establish himself. Moving up the rankings from a respectable 48th in 1982, he improved each year until he finally got a top-ten spot (9th) four years later in 1986. Then, just as before, Rafferty went backwards finishing 15th in 1987 before regaining his former position the following season with earnings of £236,241.

Yet, despite his ability to accumulate generous amounts of prize money, his first tournament win in Europe continued to elude him. A frustrating omission, it was certainly not for the lack of tournament-winning experience. Along with being a member of the three-man Irish team which had won the Dunhill Cup at St Andrews in 1988 he had a number of overseas victories including the Venezuelan Open, New Zealand Open and the Australian Matchplay.

In the end, it was probably down to self belief. A complex individual prone to occasional bouts of harsh introspection, Rafferty always had the ability to compete with the best, and in 1989 he proved it. Having turned professional at the tender age of 17, by now he was an experienced campaigner and instinctively felt this might be his year. He was right. Following on from his minor success in the short-lived Equity and Law Challenge at Royal Mid Surrey the year before, he

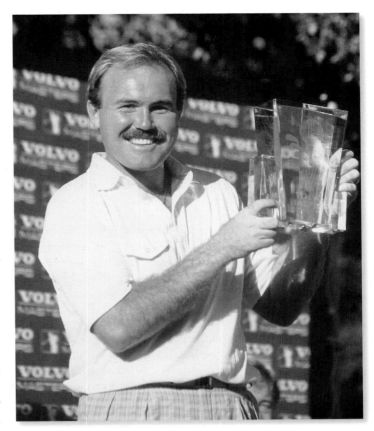

Ronan Rafferty holding the Volvo Masters trophy following his victory in 1989.

kick-started his best-ever season by winning the Lancia Italian Open at Monticello in May.

His first 72-hole victory in Europe after eight years of trying, it opened the floodgates to further success. Perhaps realising that winning a tournament was not as hard as he once thought, Ronan quickly followed it up with his second triumph in the Scandinavian Enterprise Open. Still only 25, he was now in the special position of challenging for the European number one spot going into the second half of the season. 'To win the Order of Merit,' he had commented back in May, 'I'd need to be playing seriously well.' By the time the Tour reached Valderrama in southern Spain for the final event of the 1989 season, he had done just that and was in a great position to win.

Long before the golfing year stretched well into winter and beyond, the Volvo Masters was considered the last hurrah of a long season. Open to all Europe's top golfers, it usually decided the final placings in the Order of Merit, especially who would finish number one. With one of the largest prize funds of the year on offer, the standings were often in question until the final day and this year was no different. Going into the last round, both contenders for the title were challenging for the tournament, Ronan Rafferty and José-María Olazábal.

Having taken part in the recent Ryder Cup match against the United States at The Belfry, in which Rafferty had contributed an invaluable win in the singles against Mark Calcavecchia to earn his team a draw, each knew what the other was

Relief etched on his face, Rafferty celebrates his winning putt on the final green at Valderrama.

capable of. But while Rafferty had begun the season better, it was home favourite Olazábal who headed the Money List immediately prior to the Volvo Masters. Yet over the first three rounds the balance changed again and it was Rafferty who led going into the final round at Valderrama.

Looking to follow his idol, Seve Ballesteros, as the only Spaniard to win the prestigious Order of Merit, Olazábal was in good position nonetheless after three solid rounds of 69, 70 and 74. Now in second place, holding a one-stroke advantage over Nick Faldo in third, he trailed Rafferty by two shots going into the last day. Despite this, it was probably Olly who had more reason to feel confident about their forthcoming battle, paired together on the last day.

The Irish golfer had suffered a play-off defeat at the hands of Olazábal only a few weeks earlier in the Dutch Open. A major blow to his Order of Merit aspirations, it had come in devastating fashion at the ninth extra hole! Indeed, it showed enormous courage when Rafferty bounced back the following week with closing rounds of 64 and 65 to win the Scandinavian Masters at Drottningholms. Now, as the two young professionals prepared to go head-to-head in the last round of the Volvo Masters, just who would come out on top? Or as one golf journalist humorously put it, 'Ronan or Olly – Who will reign in Spain?'

With so much at stake, opinion favoured the slightly more experienced Olazábal. But Ronan Rafferty had other ideas and set about contributing his own personal chapter to European Tour history. Played over a course which called for accuracy as well as length off the tee, both players struggled to find either in the opening nine holes. By the 10th hole, it seemed the Spaniard and Irishman were so intent on duplicating each other's mistakes that Faldo, playing in the group ahead, would win the tournament by default.

All three were level at the top of the leader board. Rafferty had dropped three shots to par with a stumbling 39; Olazábal had scored 37 and Faldo 36. Then, just as it seemed the pressure had got to him, the talented Irish professional demonstrated how much confidence he had gained from his victories earlier in the year.

I scrambled around the front nine totally but managed to hold it together. Even after I double-bogeyed the 8th, I never lost hope that I would come through in the end. That is what confidence does for you. I'm not sure I was even that nervous. Coming into the event I had been playing some of the best golf of my life and could do very little wrong.

I'd won my first tournament on the European Tour in Italy in May. I was beaten in a play-off for the Dutch title in July and then won the following week in Sweden. I had been runner-up to Nick [Faldo] at the British Masters, with both of us breaking the tournament record, and was playing at the peak of confidence going into the Volvo Masters. So even after blowing up on the front nine, I knew I could win.

....

Breaking away from the leading pack, Rafferty birdied the 10th, 12th and 15th to forge ahead. Olazábal, unable to sink a worthwhile putt over the closing nine holes, had nothing left by the time both players reached the 17th. Playing this now famous par-5, minus the water in those days, Rafferty holed yet another putt from 12 feet for birdie. Taking him to six under par for the tournament, it put him level with Faldo whose earlier birdie on the 16th had seen him take the lead.

The pressure was really on going down the stretch. Faldo was playing well and I had to birdie hole after hole just to keep up. I remember standing on the 15th tee after Faldo hit it into 15 feet and holed for birdie. I then followed him by hitting it into 20 feet and making birdie myself. It was the same story on the 17th. I drove it into the left rough, pitched out on the fairway, hit a 7-iron to 15 feet then holed for another birdie just to stay level. It was a tough few holes. Perhaps that is why it came as such a surprise when Faldo blew up on the last.

....

....

With a play-off looking the most likely result, it came as a shock to everyone when the 1987 Open Golf Champion faltered on the final par-4 hole. Clipping a tree with his approach, the normally reliable Faldo then failed to get down in two from a greenside bunker resulting in an unexpected bogey. With the door now wide open, Rafferty had been presented with a golden opportunity to complete a remarkable double. Needing just par to win the tournament (£66,600) and the Order of Merit (including a bonus of £65,000) the task could not have been more clearly defined.

Looking down the narrow avenue of cork trees which gave the hole an almost claustrophobic feel, Rafferty could have wished for an easier par-4 to play. With the hole turning gently from right to left and stretching well over 430 yards, it would require his most accurate drive to find the fairway. Thankfully the Irish professional kept his nerve and provided it. Then with all the hard work seemingly done, he followed it up with a poor second shot.

I had managed to drive it around the corner and felt that was really it. Then with my concentration not quite as sharp as it might have been under the circumstances, I underhit my 5-iron approach which did well to scramble its way onto the front fringe. But I knew Faldo had dropped a shot at the last and that made a big difference to my thinking. Perhaps if I had needed to birdie the hole I might have played it better.

....

With the front fringe cut short, Rafferty was able to take his putter for his third but, even then, it became a nervous putt up the green to around four feet. He not only holed the most important putt of his career, to put together four winning rounds of 72, 69, 70 and 71, but finished the eighties as the new European number one.

That was a great moment for me personally. Getting down in two from off the front fringe to win both the Volvo Masters and the European Order of Merit was a dream. Especially after putting together the best consecutive nine holes of golf I had played in my life. Sure, I felt a little apprehensive over the final putt, but I knew even if I missed, the worst thing that would happen was I would have to beat Nick in a play-off. That said, coming through under that sort of pressure was very satisfying.

As for the future, that seemed a long way off for the confident Ronan Rafferty. After reaching such heights so early in his career, he described his last round hero-ics as 'no big deal at the time'. Convinced that further success was just around the next dog-leg, the high standards he set himself back in 1989 were sadly never achieved again. Why this happened is uncertain; perhaps his priorities changed after having such success at the young age of 25. Then again perhaps it is more simple than that.

Rafferty is known as someone with a collector's passion for fine wines, an enthusiasm in which the pleasure often comes in the attaining of a rare vintage rather than drinking the wine itself. Having attained his own particular vintage in 1989, maybe the desire was never quite so strong second time around. For Rafferty, the intervening years have made him a little more reflective about his most famous tournament victory.

'Golf has those special moments every so often and you have to take them with a certain amount of grace. After all, they do not come along all that often.'

Whatever the truth, Ronan Rafferty remains a credit to his sport and, should he ever need a short putt to win the Open, only a fool would bet against him holing it.

Costantino

Rocca

69 in the final round of the Volvo PGA
Championship at the West Course,
Wentworth, 24–27 May 1996.

*Without a win on the European Tour for three years, Rocca went into the
final round of the Volvo PGA tied for the lead with Mark McNulty and
three strokes clear of Nick Faldo. With the result in doubt until the final
hole, the former factory worker from Bergamo held off the reigning US
Masters champion to win by two.*

For Costantino Rocca you could say that life began at 40. A landmark event for
most people, but for the barrel-chested pro from Bergamo in northern Italy, it
signalled a massive change in fortune. Not long before his December 1996
birthday, 'Costa' had stood on the 17th tee at Wentworth in the Volvo PGA
Championship. With just two holes to play in the final round, he was level with six-
time major winner Nick Faldo and challenging for the title. Needing something
special, he suddenly burst out clear, birdied both holes, and won by two clear shots.

A fearless exhibition of attacking golf under pressure, it finally put to rest any
lingering question marks over his competitive nerve. Yet it had been a struggle. A
year earlier, in the 1995 Open at St Andrews, he had arrived at the 72nd hole needing a birdie three to force an unlikely tie with clubhouse leader John Daly. In what
proved to be a real roller-coaster ride, the amiable Italian shocked everyone by
stubbing his chip for eagle but moments later he replaced the errant wedge with his
putter, and proceeded to hole out from over 60 feet, falling to the hallowed turf in
tearful delight.

After that the four-hole play-off was always going to be an anti-climax and so it
proved. The emotionally drained Rocca went through the motions but was never
really in it. The American holed his own long putt for birdie at the second and effectively cruised home. Daly picked up the Open trophy and Rocca returned to Italy with
a huge cheque for £100,000 by way of compensation. Yet, what would have been considered a triumph under any other circumstances was seen as a failure on Rocca's part.

The facts were simple. If Rocca had shot a level par round of 72, instead of 73 that day, European golf would have had a new Open champion. As things turned out, it had someone who had faltered badly under pressure and, for many, that was unforgivable. That is why his win at Wentworth was so important. Without a tournament win of any kind in the previous three years, the pressure was really on him to perform. But by capturing the flagship event of the season, Rocca finally proved he had what it took to win well. From that moment on, he has rarely looked back.

Having battled his way up the ladder of golfing success, from factory worker to top tournament player in less than ten years, his rise from obscurity is the stuff of fairy tales. Possibly the best mid-iron player in world golf, Costantino Rocca is now considered among the most consistent performers on the European PGA Tour. And is certainly one of the most popular if the crowds which follow him around are anything to go by. Yet, despite being a three-time Ryder Cup player, his fondest memory is of the Volvo PGA and his winning final round of 69.

> This was a great win for me, the best. After the Open Championship, this is the most important tournament in England. At Wentworth, I just tried to concentrate on each shot. Then to come through with two birdies at 17 and 18 for my 69 was very special. I was very nervous the whole day. I also had a lot of pressure on me, not having won for three years. Also beating Nick Faldo meant a lot to me personally. I remember reading a magazine interview with Nick Faldo in Italy where he said that if he lost a major to me he wouldn't mind. That was a great thing to say. This came into my mind when I saw Faldo was twelve under par in the last round. I tried to keep him second and did.

Costantino Rocca was born on 4 December 1956, the son of a poor quartz miner. His early adult years were spent working in a local plastics factory in his home town of Bergamo. A far cry from the luxurious surroundings of his present job, he would clock on each day from six o'clock in the evening to six the next morning. There he would stand at a machine press with cold water pouring over his hands as protection from the molten plastic. Having spent a mind boggling ten years of his working life at the factory, even today his large and powerful hands will revert arthritically to their former clenched position. Yet looking back, he remains typically relaxed about his life.

'I think I am lucky. For ten years I had to work twelve hours a day. It showed me just how hard life can be sometimes. But I learnt that nobody will give you any favours and if you do not work you have nothing. That is something I have never forgotten. But one thing I liked about the factory was the hours. It meant I could play golf in the morning.'

Like his hero Seve Ballesteros, Rocca's first taste of golf had come as a caddie. Aged just seven, he was sent out to work along with his brothers, in the hope they could contribute something to the family finances. But along with these duties Rocca found he had a real interest in the game. Not that playing the game in Italy was all that easy for a poor youngster when he first started. He recalls sneaking onto the L'Albenza course in the dark and having to listen for the sound of ball hitting tree, to find out whether he had hit a straight one or not. It was under such circumstances that this future Ryder Cup player learnt his golf.

'I worked as caddie because my family needed me to. I earned about 200 lira for a round. That was enough in those days to buy a kilo of bread. That was important. Each Monday the course was closed to the members and we caddies were allowed to play. I remember the very first tournament I ever played in was a caddie tournament. I was about 13 but did not win.'

Recognising his talent, L'Albenza Golf Club was instrumental in taking Costantino Rocca out of the plastics factory and into a part-time job working on reception. Now able to play almost every day, he was given the much sought after post as caddie master shortly after his 24th birthday. Then, despite still not having either a handicap or even his own set of clubs, the young Costantino was sent away to Rome in December 1981 to attend the Italian Federation's teaching school. It was to be a major turning point in his life.

It was while attending the teaching course that Rocca was persuaded by Australian golf coach, Tom Linskey, to try his luck on the tournament scene. Perhaps inspired by dreams of easy money, he immediately turned his back on a safe coaching career in his native Italy. Not surprisingly, his decision was viewed with some scepticism by those who knew him. 'It was like the American Dream for him,' said former Italian golf star, Sylvio Grappasonni. 'He was going on the Tour and would make millions. But it was a hard decision. In Italy you can make good money by teaching.'

At an age when some players are actually thinking about giving up the game, the 25-year-old Rocca turned professional off a not particularly impressive handicap of four. But, incredibly, he finished sixth at the PGA Tour Qualifying School in 1982, comfortably earning his card. Then, after a few false dawns, including losing his player's card three years running, he again qualified for the full PGA Tour via the back door route of the secondary Challenge Tour. Now married to wife Antonella, and almost a decade after starting out, Rocca finally broke through twice in 1993 to record his first PGA Tour victories at the Open V33 du Grand Lyon, then at the Peugeot French Open.

With success, and just over £450,000 in official prize money, came a place in the European Ryder Cup team to face the United States at The Belfry in September. The first Italian, and only the sixth non-British player to rise to such dizzy heights, it was not to prove the pleasant experience Rocca thought it would be. Losing out to Davis Love III in the singles after being one-up with two to play, the blame for his team's eventual 15 to 13 defeat was laid squarely on his shoulders. A deeply emotional character at the best of times, the criticism hit him hard.

'Costa' – Italian Ryder Cup favourite and one of the most popular golfers on the European Tour.

The newspapers wrote that I personally lost the Ryder Cup.
Sure, I missed a short putt on 17 to win, but so did many others that day.
But they put me on the front pages. It was amazing. I missed a little putt
and I became famous.

Fortunately his later Ryder Cup experiences would be far more enjoyable. In the 1995 match at Oak Hill, he played well enough to be picked for every foursome and four-ball match, contributing an invaluable three points from a possible five to his winning team. A spectacular ace on the par-3 6th during his foursome (partnered with Sam Torrance) against Davis Love III and Jeff Maggert also helped round off a good performance. And despite losing out again to Love in the singles, Rocca at least helped lay to rest some of the ghosts which had haunted him since The Belfry.

Yet some doubts still remained about Rocca in the minds of the golfing public. Certainly he was a good money earner. He eventually finished fifth on the 1995 Money List with almost £616,000 – but, without a tournament win of his own, how

Final green joy at Wentworth for Costantino Rocca.

good was he under pressure? In the 1996 Volvo PGA Championship at Wentworth, the answer would finally come. Going into the final round, he was tied for the lead with Mark McNulty. While the experienced pro from Zimbabwe was an obvious threat, one of the chasing pack was soon of more immediate concern. After solid opening rounds of 67, 69 and 72, the reigning US Masters champion, Nick Faldo, was sitting just three strokes behind in third.

In the strongest European field of the year outside the Open, Faldo had attracted most press attention over the first three days. It was his first tournament appearance in Europe since his dramatic last round victory over Greg Norman at Augusta and the Englishman was in good form. At eight under par going into the final round at Wentworth, he was in perfect position to do it all again.

With the final day scheduled for a Bank Holiday Monday, the crowds were understandably bigger than normal. It had already been a well-attended event and with the rain-sodden 'Burma Road' at Wentworth playing all of its 6,957 yards, the big-hitting Italian had put himself in ideal position to pick up the first prize of £166,660. Joint leader after three excellent rounds of 69, 67 and 69 (eleven under par) Rocca was naturally considered among the favourites to take the title.

In typical style, Faldo started the final round aggressively by making birdies at the 1st and 4th holes and going to the turn in 33. Rocca, out two groups behind with McNulty, maintained his impressive form by scoring 34. Then after a Faldo birdie at the par-4 11th had narrowed the gap to just one, Rocca pulled away once more by making four down the long par-5 12th. With any number of golfers falling in and out of contention, it was a typical roller-coaster ride for the Italian. McNulty matched his playing partner's birdie on the 12th, doggedly holding on to his share of the lead. Then, after failing to save par from a greenside bunker on the 13th, he three-putted the next two greens and dropped out of contention for good.

While others like Paul Lawrie and Jarmo Sandelin would threaten somewhat later in the round, the tournament really became a two horse race between Rocca and Faldo. Faldo dropped a shot at the 13th after three-putting, but unlike

McNulty, quickly made it back with a birdie on the narrow, tree-lined, par-4 15th. For Costantino Rocca, the same hole would bring his first major crisis. A badly carved drive off to the right had left him stymied for a shot to the green. With a chip out sideways the only option, he was forced to hit a 2-iron third to a severely sloping green. Working to salvage his bogey, Rocca must have swallowed hard when he found that Faldo had birdied the same hole only minutes earlier. A two-shot swing on one hole was not what he wanted at this stage of the tournament.

Tied for the lead with three holes remaining, Rocca knew that Faldo would set a stiff target for him to follow. Sure enough, the six-time major winner hit a huge drive down the 18th, leaving himself little more than a 6-iron to the green. Having failed to make his birdie 4 at the long 17th, Faldo felt he needed something special on the closing hole really to put pressure on. Going for the flag on the front left of the final green, Faldo came up a few yards short and finished in a bunker. Then he made the capital error of failing to get down in two for his birdie. Perhaps the effort expended only weeks earlier at the Masters had taken its toll, certainly some golfing pundits suggested it as a likely reason for his poor finish. Whatever the truth, the door was now well and truly open for Costantino Rocca.

Despite his birdie-free finish, Faldo's last round 68 set a tough clubhouse target of twelve under par. Minutes later, Paul Lawrie bravely birdied the last to match it. Everyone now asked if Rocca could birdie one of the last two holes to win. He could. In fact, he birdied them both.

Two solid blows down the 17th left him little more than a short pitch to the hole. With memories of his fluffed 20-yard chip to the final green at St Andrews still strong in everyone's mind, Rocca held his nerve and floated a pitch to around four feet. Holing out for his birdie four gave him the luxury of being able to play the last in comparative safety. But in typically Italian style he finished with a flourish, holing from 12 feet for his birdie and a wonderfully composed round of 69.

As the putt hit the back of the hole, Rocca's joy was there for everyone to see. Jumping up, he punched the air in delight before walking off the final green with a smile as wide as the Tiber. 'This is not a consolation for the Open,' he said afterwards in his best broken English.

> This is a big goal for me. One of my proudest moments. I thought it was good just to drop one shot at the 15th. This morning my blood pressure was 200 and at the last it was over 300. I had a lot of pressure not having won for three years. That is a long time.

It was a victory which transformed his career and gave him renewed confidence for the challenges to come. Challenges which would include beating the much heralded Tiger Woods 4 & 2 in the Ryder Cup singles at Valderrama in 1997. His most recent triumph, this will certainly not be his last. A far cry from the bad old days, the huge hug from captain Seve Ballesteros showed just how much he had meant to the European team's second consecutive victory.

Yet in a life which has seen its fair share of ups and downs, it is no understatement when Costantino Rocca says, 'For me just to play is like a miracle.'

1929

Gene

Sarazen

68 in the final round of the Agua Caliente $25,000 Open Tournament at Agua Caliente, 23–24 October 1929.

With turmoil going on in the world money markets, Sarazen went to Mexico to compete in the $25,000 Agua Caliente tournament hoping to stave off personal financial ruin. After a disastrous third round 79 things began to look desperate. Three strokes behind joint leaders Al Espinosa and Horton Smith, he received a long distance phone call from his stock-broker the night before the final round. The news was bad. With the market about to crash, Sarazen was told that unless he could wire $10,000 to New York within 24 hours, he would lose everything. Knowing the $10,000 first prize would cover that, he told the broker to hang on, he would get his money. Next day, Sarazen shot 68, won the tournament and paid off his debt. And while he would suffer like many others in the months that followed, it proved just enough to keep him afloat.

The son of an immigrant Italian carpenter, Gene Sarazen is a golfing legend. Now more than seven decades since he won the first of his seven major championships, the 1922 United States Open at Skokie, he has played against some of the greatest players in the history of the game. In the bygone days of hickory shafts, he competed in the British Open with golfers like Harry Vardon and James Braid. In the early twenties he carried on a fierce professional rivalry with the great Walter Hagen. In the thirties he played countless exhibitions with the immortal Grand Slammer, Bobby Jones. After World War II it was Snead and Hogan. Then as Palmer and Nicklaus shared the spotlight in the early sixties, Gene was still out there swinging. And to cap it all off, he made one of the first televised holes-in-one in the 1973 Open at Royal Troon!

The link between past and present golfing generations, Sarazen remains the long-time honorary starter at the US Masters. Dressed in his trademark knickerbockers and turtle-neck sweater, he steps onto the first tee at Augusta

National each spring and drives off. And while arthritis forced him to give up playing in 1993, he still enjoys making his annual pilgrimage to the scene of his famous victory in 1935. Accompanied by his fellow greats Sam Snead and Byron Nelson, his appearance is now a popular and eagerly anticipated part of Masters tradition. Yet how many of the hundreds of fans who gather around the tee each year really know who Sarazen is?

The record books show he remains, along with Hogan, Nicklaus and Player, one of the only professionals in the history of the game to have won all four major championships. He was also one of the most flamboyant and attacking golfers of his era. Bobby Jones once said about him, 'The boldness of his play leaves no middle ground. When he is in the right mood, he is probably the greatest scorer in the game, possibly that the game has ever seen.'

With seven major championships to his name, including two United States Opens, three PGAs, one Masters and one Open, his place in golf history is assured. So, having played so many important rounds in his life, his choice for 'Round of My Life' will surprise many. As well as being the first professional to win the United States Open and PGA in the same year, his name will also be forever linked to a single shot he hit in the Masters 1935. Later described as 'the shot that was heard around the world' he holed his second on the par-5 15th at Augusta for a spectacular albatross on his way to winning the Masters. Witnessed by Bobby Jones, it helped popularise the game in the United States and make him among the best known sportsmen in the world. That said, his selection is as unique as perhaps the man is himself.

Gene Sarazen at Augusta in 1994.

You know I think that I have had two greatest rounds in golf and neither of them had anything to do with winning the National Open at Skokie in 1922, or with that spoon shot. From a straight golfing standpoint, my greatest day in golf came in the National Open at Fresh Meadows in 1932. But if I had to choose the most memorable round it would be one I played in a little known tournament in Mexico. Coming a day or so before the stock market crash of 1929, my entire life savings were in danger and it was a tournament I just had to win.

Born on 27 February 1902 in Harrison, New York, Gene Sarazen came from a poor but hardworking immigrant Italian background. He was first introduced to the game after becoming a caddie at eight. He quit school at 15 before following his father into a local carpentry factory. At 16 he was taken ill with a near fatal dose of pneumonia, a side-effect of the 1918 flu epidemic. Advised by the hospital doctor to get a job in the fresh air he began practising at a public course in Bridgeport, Connecticut. Golf now became his life, much to the disgust of his father, who believed the only people to play the game were 'brokers and bankers'. But Sarazen, determined to make his living from the game, carried on despite never quite having his father's blessing.

The only time my father watched me play competitively in my entire career was at the 1923 PGA Championship in Pelham, New York. Close to where we lived, he watched me play the 10th from the highway. He would never come onto the grounds. I had a 40-foot putt and missed it. That night he said, 'You mean to say they pay you fellows to play that game and you couldn't put that thing in the hole?' All I could think of saying was, 'Did you ever try it?'

....

Having left the factory, Sarazen's early golfing efforts were encouraged by a local club pro, Al Ciuci. A year later, with Ciuci's help, he took up his first professional post as assistant to George Sparling at nearby Brooklawn. Now given enough time to practise, the diminutive Sarazen (5 feet 5 inches) began thinking about making his living as a tournament professional. So much so that he actually changed his name from the Italian sounding Eugene Saracini because, 'it was not a bad name for a violin player or school teacher but a rotten one for an athlete.' It would prove to be the right decision with carpentry's loss turning out to be golf's gain.

Surprisingly powerful, Sarazen's golf swing was simple and direct and altered little under pressure. But perhaps his two greatest assets were his natural aggression and indomitable confidence. Almost from the start, he gained the reputation of never backing off in the final stages of a tournament. Never afraid to 'go for it' he gave the impression of being unbeatable when things went his way. Of course, when they didn't, he rarely made the top thirty. For him there was seldom any middle ground.

Gene Sarazen walking down the first fairway with rival Billy Burke during the 1932 US Open at Fresh Meadows. Despite a good showing, reigning champion Burke could do little to stop Sarazen recording his second victory in the championship.

Still plagued by the occasional health problem, Gene headed off to the Winter Tour in Florida in late 1919. Looking to make his fortune, he bought a $15 steamship ticket from New York before settling in Sebring. There he worked part-time in a freight yard unloading bricks by night while practising hard during the day. Then, after months of scraping a living, he left the Sunshine State with his tail between his legs and took up a teaching post at Fort Wayne, Indiana. Close to giving up, it was from there he got his first taste of major competition.

Using money the members had given him, Sarazen played in the United States Open at Inverness in 1920. Ending up tied for 30th, sixteen strokes behind the eventual winner Ted Ray, his performance was seen as encouraging. For the ambitious young pro the experience only served to heighten his desire to win the event. Then in 1922 at Skokie Country Club, Illinois, he finally got his wish.

Having beaten Bobby Jones and the unknown John Black into joint second place, Sarazen became the golfing sensation of the time. Still only 20, he opened up with rounds of 72, 73 and 75 to trail Jones and 'Wild Bill' Mehlhorn by three. With the final two rounds played on the last day, Sarazen went into the afternoon needing something special to win. It was not long in arriving. Just under 2½ hours later he returned with a 66 including a birdie on the last to beat Jones and Black by a single stroke.

This first major win was quickly followed by his second only a short time later. Played at Oakmont, his 4 & 3 win over Emmet French in the final of the PGA Championship established him as the best young player in the game at the time. As for being the greatest of any age, that was still in doubt. Walter Hagen had decided not to defend his PGA title in favour of playing a lucrative series of exhibition matches and poured scorn on anyone who compared him with Sarazen.

Almost inevitably a 72-hole challenge was arranged later the same year. Hagen would lose but looked to get his revenge at the PGA the following year at Pelham Country Club, New York. There, after meeting in the final, Sarazen repeated the lesson by defeating the flamboyant showman on the 38th hole. Hagen, who took a great liking to the brash young professional, would ultimately get his revenge by winning the tournament for the next four years. But for the time being, the 21-year-old Sarazen could take great satisfaction in winning three major titles in the space of a year.

Considering how fast things had happened it was perhaps no surprise when his career tailed off for a time. A combination of unnecessary swing changes and cashing in on his fame with a lengthy series of exhibition tours, helped dull his competitive edge. Over the next decade he still won the occasional tournament, over 20 in the United States alone, but none of them were majors. He had come close, but something had to change if his form were to return.

Then, under the most bizarre circumstances imaginable, it did. Playing in a minor tournament in Mexico in late 1929, he found some of his old competitive spirit. Needing to find some money fast, he entered the 72-hole $25,000 Open Tournament at Agua Caliente, just across the border from San Diego. With the stock market crash just around the corner and the financial crisis threatening to wipe away his entire savings, it was there he would play the most memorable round of his life. Scheduled over two days, it would also prove the most pressurised.

I'm afraid I was a little over anxious and in the first round I could do no better than a 75. This was four strokes back of the 71 that Ed Dudley turned in. I was trailing such seasoned tournament players as MacDonald Smith, Al Watrous, Harry Cooper, Horton Smith, Al Espinosa, Bobby Cruickshank, George Von Elm and half a dozen others. I bettered my position a little in the second round with a 73, but I was still three strokes back of Al Espinosa's 145. I thought three strokes was not too much of a handicap to overcome and my hopes were high as the third round started.

That round was a nightmare. I would like to forget it. I started with a bogey five, followed with a buzzard six, and I was even fives for the first six holes played. What kind of golf was that for a man who needed that $10,000 like nobody's business? I took a six at the 8th, and only through getting a par three at the 9th did I round the turn in 43 strokes. I couldn't be that bad. I really gave myself a talk as we were walking to the 10th tee – and it paid off – for I played the second nine in 36, giving me a 79 for the 18 holes and a 54-hole total of 227. But others were having trouble and my total score was only three strokes back of the leaders,

Horton Smith and Al Espinosa.

I was disgusted, went to my room and lay down for a little while. Then I saw the afternoon papers. The market was falling so fast I was alarmed. The telephone rang. They said it was long distance from New York. Thoughts of my family raced through my head but when I got to the phone I found it was my broker. The news was bad. He told me that for his own protection he was going to have to sell me out – unless I could wire him $10,000 within 24 hours. I didn't beg for more time. I just cracked back at him that he'd have his ten thousand. There was just one way to get the money and that was to overtake the field in the final round and win that $10,000 first prize.

My first objective was to wipe out the three stroke lead. We all [Smith, Espinosa and Sarazen] had fours on the 1st hole but I picked up a stroke at the long and difficult 2nd with a birdie three. Horton and I parred the tricky par-3 3rd but Espinosa went one over. At the 445-yard 4th, Horton and I again got our pars but Espinosa went one over with a five – now he and I were exactly even. But Horton was tough. When I birdied the 6th, Horton rolled in a birdie too. But I picked up a stroke on him when I knocked in a fine four at the 550-yard 8th hole. We all parred the 9th. I had scored 32, Horton had 34, and Espinosa had a 36. I was still one stroke behind Horton but I was leading Espinosa by a shot.

We messed up the 10th – Horton and I each taking a six and Al pulling back to even terms with me with a five. Then Espinosa grabbed the only par at the 11th and he was again a stroke ahead of me and tied for the lead with Horton. The next three holes were played in par by all three but I dropped a deuce [two] at the 15th to pick up a stroke on Horton and two on Espinosa.

I followed with another birdie, getting my three at the 16th. When I birdied the 554-yard 17th, I was in, as all three of us had pars at the last hole. I had a 68, three strokes under the course record and my 295 led Horton and Espinosa who were tied for second two strokes back. I had won the $10,000. But what the world didn't know was that the money, delivered to me in silver dollars in a wheel barrow, had already been wired east to save Sarazen securities!

For Gene Sarazen the win in Mexico helped save the day. Though, like many, he would suffer in the aftermath of the crash, it gave him the confidence to go on and win the major tournaments he craved. Realising that his greatest resource was his own golfing skill, he set about putting his career to rights. Three years later, after a lot of hard work on the practice ground, Sarazen rolled back the years to win his first Open Championship at Princes in 1932. Aided by a new sand-wedge he had developed with an extended sole, it was his first major victory for almost a decade.

Returning to the United States after the Open, Sarazen once again turned his attention to winning his own National Open. Despite doubts still being voiced in the golfing press about his ability to win the big one Gene felt confident that this would be his tournament.

With the British Open title in my possession I made up my mind to make it a double and win the American Open again. The championship was scheduled over my home course and I was at the peak of my game. But after shooting 76 and 74 for the first two rounds it looked as if I didn't have a chance. But I didn't give up. I don't believe in it. I didn't even give up when I shot 39 for the first nine holes of the third round. Everybody had written me off but I came to life just when the pressure was greatest. I shot 100 for the last 28 holes of that championship including a last round of 66. I was twelve strokes under fours and won by three from Bobby Cruickshank and Phil Perkins who tied for second.

This comeback victory instilled a new confidence in Gene Sarazen. A year later, he won his third PGA title at Blue Mound, Wisconsin, beating the inexperienced Willie Goggin by 5 & 4 in the final. Then, perhaps unwisely, he returned to the exhibition circuit once more looking to cash in on his new-found fame. In fact, the only reason he missed the first Masters tournament at Augusta in 1934 was because he was away touring in South America.

Feeling guilty about having turned down a personal invitation from Bobby Jones to compete in the inaugural event, Sarazen made certain he was at Augusta National the following year. Despite not having the 'major' tag it does today the tournament was special to Gene Sarazen for many reasons, not least because he produced one of the most sensational shots in golf history.

Late in the fourth round, Sarazen stood in the middle of the par-5 15th fairway after a good drive. Requiring three birdies in the last four holes to tie clubhouse leader Craig Wood, he was given little hope of winning. Then with Hagen as his partner and Bobby Jones watching the action along with the crowd behind the green he selected his spoon (4-wood) and unleashed a massive blow towards the hole. Clearing the water, it bounced onto the green and then ran into the cup for an albatross!

Having wiped out Wood's lead with one shot, Sarazen went on to tie his score at the 18th, then inevitably beat his hapless fellow American in the play-off. Hailed as a sensational victory at the time, it certainly helped put the Augusta tournament on the golfing map. But for the 33-year-old Sarazen, it would be the last major victory of his illustrious career.

By the time he lost to Lawson Little in a play-off for the 1940 United States Open in Cleveland, he remained the only tournament player to wear plus-four trousers. Considered an old-timer even before World War II had begun, the competitive break which followed ended any tournament-winning aspirations he may have still had. His wonderful career which had spanned parts of four decades was now over.

After taking some time to accept he was no longer a threat to the younger professionals, Sarazen moved into a new career as a television pundit in the mid-sixties. Asked to commentate on the popular series, *Shell's Wonderful World of Golf*, he was at least able to put some of his vast experience and golfing knowledge to good use. Even today, from his home in Marcos Island, Florida, he enjoys reminiscing about the old days. His memory, as sharp as ever, recalls all his great matches and as you listen to him speak about Jones, Hagen, and even Vardon, it is difficult not to get swept away on a sea of nostalgia for the good old days.

Today, his place among the golfing greats is assured. As one golf writer has said, 'Too bad television wasn't around twenty years earlier. Can you imagine what that double-eagle would have done for the game if millions of people had seen it?'

What indeed.

Tom

Watson

65 in the final round of the Open

Championship at Turnberry, 6–9 July 1977.

Matched head-to-head against the greatest player in the history of the game, Tom Watson took on Jack Nicklaus in the final round of the Open at Turnberry. With both men playing some of the finest golf ever seen, they made identical scores up to the last day – 68, 70 and 65 – to be three strokes ahead of third place Ben Crenshaw. The last day took on a matchplay feel as the lead passed back and forth between the two great players. Over the closing few holes Watson finally took the lead before holing a birdie putt on the final green to win by one – 65 to Nicklaus' 66. It remains among the most talked about rounds in the championship's long history.

Few people ever get to dominate the majors the way Tom Watson did from 1975 to 1984. Not only did he win eight including five Opens, two Masters and one US Open, but he had a string of top-five finishes which hinted there could have been even more. Always a popular visitor to Britain, his Huckleberry Finn face with its gap-toothed smile became almost synonymous with the Open trophy. As one golf journalist put it after Watson's fifth win at Royal Birkdale in 1983, 'It's a bit like strawberries and cream – you sort of get used to seeing them together.'

The Watson era also produced one of the greatest rivalries the game has ever seen. Following on from other great rivalries of the past like Sarazen and Hagen, or Snead and Hogan, he and Jack Nicklaus raised the game to new levels of skill and sportsmanship. In the decade from 1975 to 1985, these two great players won thirteen major championships between them, often competing head-to-head in the final rounds. Their most memorable battle for top golfing honours came in the Open Championship at Turnberry in 1977.

Nothing could split them until the final round as their identical scores of 68, 70 and 65 took them away from the chasing pack. The final round was set up for a classic confrontation with only one player able to come out on top. Then, over an Ailsa links burnt dry by the previous year's drought, they provided some of the most unforgettable golf ever seen.

Before the final round, both had said how it was a little like a western movie with Nicklaus, the ageing gunslinger, up against Watson, the new kid looking to make his reputation. Indeed, Jack joked about how much he was looking forward to adding another notch to his gun! But Watson would prove an elusive target. Coming through with a magnificent 65 to beat Nicklaus by a single stroke it would be the Kansas-born golfer who would win the Open that day. Perhaps the greatest round in Open history, it is Tom Watson's choice for the 'Round of My Life'.

> For me the final round at Turnberry in 1977 was the most memorable round I have ever played. Mainly because of the competitor I was up against, Jack Nicklaus. After the third day when we both shot 65, the final round became kind of a defining moment for me. After winning the Masters earlier that year, to find myself battling it down the stretch with Nicklaus again was very special. Because for me Nicklaus was always the man to beat – the best in the game. And for any competitor, no matter what sport you play, you want to beat the best. There were other times we went head-to-head like the US Open at Pebble Beach in '82. But for sustained pressure the most rewarding was certainly the Open at Turnberry.

Born on 4 September 1949 in Kansas City, Missouri, Thomas Sturgess Watson was introduced to golf by his scratch handicap father aged just six. After a fairly average amateur career, he graduated in psychology from Stanford University, before turning professional in 1971. Picking up $1,065 from his first ever tournament, the Kaiser International, the 21-year-old seemed well on his way. Yet it would be another three years before he won his first US Tour event, the 1974 Western Open.

With rumours of a fragile nerve under pressure beginning to surface in the American golfing press, fuel was added to the fire after Watson lost winning positions in both the 1974 and 1975 US Open Championships. In 1974 at Winged Foot, he even led for three rounds before shooting 79 in the final round to lose to Hale Irwin. So for Watson, newly arrived in Scotland for the 1975 Open at Carnoustie, the pressure was well and truly on. But like most truly great players he was able to come through in a crunch.

By his own admission he came into that tournament playing well below his best. But, with the help of his experienced British caddie, Alfie Fyles, he came to the long par-4 final hole needing a birdie to put himself into a play-off with Jack Newton. After hitting his long-iron approach to around 20 feet, he then punched the air in triumph as he holed the putt. It was to prove a major turning point in his career. The following day, in often appalling conditions, he went out and beat the talented Australian 71 to 72 in the last 18-hole play-off in Open history. Watson had now put his first foot on the ladder to golfing greatness.

Tom Watson teeing off during the 1977 Open at Turnberry.

> At Carnoustie in 1975 I was a greenhorn. I wasn't really in the tournament until I made the putt on the 72nd. But I did have some advice from my friend, Byron Nelson. He said [shortly before the final round], 'Shoot 70, even one under par, and your field will come back to you.' That's exactly what happened.

While this victory failed to convince many of his American critics, it did prove the start of a lasting love affair with the event for Tom Watson. The first of his five Open Championship titles, he would come to dominate the tournament over the next nine years winning at Turnberry in 1977, Muirfield in 1980, Royal Troon in 1982 and Royal Birkdale in 1983. Also finishing a close runner-up to Seve Ballesteros at St Andrews in 1984, his record in the event is quite remarkable. Yet surprisingly, his affection for British-style links courses did not run as deep.

> My love affair with British Open golf really started in 1979 at Lytham St Annes. I made the cut, but I didn't play well, struggling the whole week. Up until that time, I didn't like links golf. I didn't like the bumps and the bounces and the so called 'bad-breaks'.
>
> At St Andrews in '78, I didn't like the shots it required you to make. I liked target golf. I like to hit the ball through the air and stop the ball. That's the way I tried to pattern myself when I was a youngster, hit the ball high and that's the way I won my first couple of Opens. Then I started to watch my friend Lee Trevino. You know I said, 'Well this guy can't hit it high, and he can't hook it', but the more I watched him, the more I knew he had other tools in his chest, other weapons in his arsenal. These are the kind of shots you just don't see much on TV or in American golf.
>
> In '79 I said to myself, 'I didn't play well this week, but I think I understand a little more about the game over here. This is not just a game of targets and through the air and yardages. This is a game of shot-making values. I found I liked coming to a place where it requires you to use other tools in your bag other than the through-the-air tool.

Following his 1975 Open win at Carnoustie with two solid, but unspectacular seasons on the US Tour, Watson's career really took off in 1977, as did his rivalry with the Golden Bear himself, Jack Nicklaus. Yet despite the two becoming close friends, their first high profile clash at the Masters that year was not without some controversy.

On the par-5 15th at Augusta in the final round, the title was still up for grabs and both Nicklaus and Watson were challenging. Yet Watson, who ultimately came out on top despite a magnificent last round 66 from Nicklaus, later accused his rival of gesturing 'animatedly' to him after holing his birdie putt. Hinting that it might have been a touch of gamesmanship, Watson later admitted how upset he had been and how the incident had helped spur him on to victory. Fortunately, he later apologised, realising any such accusation was totally outrageous.

With Watson's hard-earned victory at Augusta National came a new respect from the American public and press. After the false dawn of players like Johnny Miller and Jerry Pate, here finally was a player who could seemingly challenge the invincible Jack Nicklaus. And despite speculation in the American press, no bad feeling spilled over into the second major of the year, the US Open at Southern Hills, Tulsa. But in a tournament won by the unorthodox Hubert Green, neither Nicklaus nor Watson made a sustained challenge. So the ongoing battle for supremacy switched to Turnberry and the Open Championship.

In a tournament that was later described as the 'Duel in the Sun' the two great professionals appeared to bring the best out of each other that week. With the Masters incident all but forgotten, they were inevitably paired together for the final round, having shot identical scores over the opening three days. The last eighteen holes became a two-horse race, and Watson was confident about his chances.

I was playing well during that stretch of golf with the Open at Turnberry probably at the peak. I'd had a good run in the States before that, so I thought going into the Open I had a good chance to win that week. Even after playing with Jack and us both shooting 65s, I felt pretty good about things.

Nicklaus appeared to get the better of the early exchanges. Having made birdie on the 428-yard 2nd hole, to Watson's bogey, it set the tone for the early part of the round with Watson continually forced to play catch-up. By the time they reached the 5th tee, Jack had moved three shots clear of his younger rival.

In typical style, Watson then blasted back with three birdies in four holes to draw level. With the heavyweight contest now well and truly underway, the excited crowds began to spill over onto the playing area. Important fairway bunkers were no longer in view off the tee and both players refused to play until marshals had pushed the fans back. The delay seemed to unsettle Watson and he dropped a shot at the 9th to reach the turn one down. Then he struggled for par at both the 10th and 11th, having to make a chip and putt from off the green both times.

Nicklaus was seemingly beginning to assert his vast experience. On the 11th, Jack missed a birdie putt from 12 feet but holed one double the length on the next green to extend his lead. Holding a two-stroke advantage with only six holes remaining, it was obvious that Tom Watson would need something special over the last few holes to win.

Bouncing back with a birdie of his own on the 13th, Watson narrowed the gap to one. With Nicklaus famed for coming through to win in situations exactly like this, both men walked onto the tee of the difficult par-3 15th. Nicklaus found the front edge of the green with a long-iron, while Watson pulled his ball pin-high but off to the left. With Jack seemingly certain of his par, Watson then bolted an outrageous putt from yards off the green into the hole for birdie, bringing the two level once more.

The dominant golfer of his era, Tom Watson won the Open Championship in 1975, 1977, 1980, 1982 and 1983, the Masters in 1977 and 1981, and the US Open in 1982.

Watson knew the significance of that particular stroke.

> I knew, with Jack on the front edge, I had to get down in two to stay even. Having hit my tee shot 20 yards left of the pin, I was left with a slick downhill chip off an impossibly bare lie. Being past the bunker on the left, I decided to putt it. I then watched it race down the green and into the hole. I was sure glad the pin was in because it could have gone a long way past considering how fast it was travelling.

Good fortune also favoured Watson at the next when his approach to the par-4 16th clung precariously on the edge of a steep bank leading to the burn. Both men eventually made par, but for Nicklaus the strain was finally beginning to tell. After a solid drive, he failed to find the green at the par-5 17th, coming up short and right with his second. With Watson on the back of the green with a 20-foot downhill putt for eagle, the pressure for Nicklaus to get down in two was enormous. Never noted as the best pitcher of a ball, Nicklaus managed to manoeuvre the ball to around four feet for a good birdie chance. Slightly downhill, it was a putt he would miss.

Having failed to match Watson's two-putt birdie, Nicklaus found himself one stroke down playing the last. Looking for a desperate birdie on the final par-4 hole, his attempt to blast it within short-iron distance resulted in a carved drive well out to the right. Then, as he deliberated on his second from the edge of a bush, Watson lined up his 7-iron approach from the middle of the fairway.

Wasting no time, his crisply struck shot landed on the green to a deafening cheer, finishing less than two feet away. Even Nicklaus' heroic effort in making the green in two from the rough failed to dent the enthusiastic applause. The destination of the famous silver claret jug now looked settled in Tom Watson's favour. Then, like every good thriller, there was one last twist in the tail.

With Watson no doubt contemplating his second Open title, Nicklaus quietly lined up his putt from almost 45 feet before ramming it into the back of the hole for birdie! Then, typically of the great man, he raised his arms calling for silence while Watson took a look at his putt. Moments later, Watson tapped in for a winning birdie and a famous one-stroke victory.

> Sure I felt nervous [over that last putt]. Back in those days the short putts were a lot easier than they are today. The crowd were still cheering for Jack but it didn't matter. I was ready to putt and thankfully it went in.

Walking arm in arm off the final green, the respect between these two great professionals was obvious. The intense rivalry which had threatened to sour their relationship was long gone. They knew, like millions watching the final-round drama unfold on television, that this had been golf at its very best. And while Tom Watson, like Jack Nicklaus, would go on to win other majors in the coming years, none would mean more to him than the 1977 Open Championship at Turnberry. Having beaten his great rival 65 to 66, he later described it as 'not only the greatest round of my life, but the most enjoyable round of golf I have ever played.'

Perhaps one incident from the round itself sums up just why many people consider it the greatest championship round ever played. Amid all the drama and sportsmanship on show, Watson had turned to Nicklaus on the 13th tee in the heat of battle and said, 'This is what it is all about, isn't it Jack?'

Lee

Westwood

63 in the second round of the Turespaña
Masters at Campo de Golf, Maspalomas,
Gran Canaria, 20–23 March 1997.

Playing in only his fifth event of the 1997 European season, Westwood burst through the field in the second round with a remarkable ten-under-par 63. Clipping three strokes off the old course record, it alerted the golfing world to this hugely talented youngster from Worksop. Going on to finish third in the Order of Merit that year, including a win in the prestigious Volvo Masters at Montecastillo, he also made an invaluable contribution to Europe's Ryder Cup victory over the United States at Valderrama, also in Spain. He has been noted as a likely future European number one and possible major winner.

If someone asked you to list the ideal attributes of a top professional golfer you might have to think for a moment.

For a start they should have the same delicate touch on the greens as a surgeon has with a scalpel. This would be closely followed by the ability to drive the ball further than most people go on holiday. Add the competitive heart of Evander Holyfield then top it all off with the laid-back attitude of Bob Dylan and you have a potentially great champion. Or in simple golfing terms you might have a golfer named Lee Westwood.

The most talked-about young professional on the European PGA Tour, he finally broke through in a golden spell at the end of the 1997 season winning the Volvo Masters in Spain, the Australian Open and the Taiheiyo Masters in Japan, as well as making a remarkably successful debut in the Ryder Cup at Valderrama in September. With results like these the beefy young player from Worksop looks set to take his place among the game's elite. And all this after beginning his year in a lowly 80th place in the official world rankings!

Since then his worldwide success has seen him rise into the top 25 for the first time in his career. Described as the British 'lion' to counter the United States 'tiger', his name is now high on the list of those considered potential major winners of the future. As for his own personal goals, these are typically straightforward.

> I've always enjoyed playing, almost from the beginning. Now I just want to see how good I can be without worrying about the prize money I have to earn. It has never been the main consideration anyway, although it's nice to treat the people closest to you. I think now I am more concerned with playing golf at the highest level I possibly can. For me competing against the best is the main attraction.

Son of a school teacher, Lee John Westwood was born on 24 April 1973 in Worksop. Following a highly successful amateur career which included winning the British Youths' Championship in 1993, he surprised no one by earning his player's card at the first attempt later the same year, finishing fifth in the Qualifying School. He confirmed his rich potential by reaching 43rd in the 1994 Order of Merit with the help of top-five finishes in the French, Turespaña and Extremadura Opens.

The quality of his golf took a surprising downturn in 1995 as he slipped to 75th in the Money List with just £86,334. The sparkle returned in 1996 along with his bank balance. Finishing a highly creditable sixth with £449,960, the money also enabled Westwood to concentrate on the thing he enjoyed doing most, winning golf tournaments.

His breakthrough victory had come in August 1996 in the Scandinavian Masters at Forsgarden, Sweden. Still only 23, he was one of six players going into the final round at three under par. Trailing the overnight tournament leader Thomas Björn by two, Westwood's closing round of 68 took him into a three-man play-off with experienced Tour veterans Paul Broadhurst and Russell Claydon. Then having scrambled a par on the opening hole just to stay alive, Westwood holed a monstrous 40-foot putt for birdie to take the title. Obviously stunned, his only comment at the time was 'incredible!'

Victory in Sweden also proved a turning point. In his first ten outings on the European Tour, Westwood missed five cuts. In the weeks which followed he exploded with eleven top-12 finishes in his next eighteen starts, culminating in a highly creditable second place finish behind Mark McNulty in the end of season Volvo Masters at Valderrama in Spain.

Taking his skills to the Far East later the same year, his next win also came via a tense play-off in the Sumitomo Visa Taiheiyo Masters in Japan. It was there, competing against a top-class international field including past United States PGA winner, Jeff Sluman, that Lee defeated fellow European Costantino Rocca at the fourth extra hole. Playing in the shadow of Mount Fuji, it was to prove a significant victory in more ways than one. Not only would it bring him widespread recognition outside of his home tour, it also confirmed his earlier decision to drop his original coach in favour of the more experienced Peter Cowen. Westwood later commented how, 'Peter has helped me hit the ball harder and to become more aggressive on the golf course. That was the

Lee Westwood signs autographs for his fans at the 1997 Open.

key to my victory at Gotembru [Japan] and for the rest of the year . . .'

Returning to Europe the following season, he confirmed his growing stature by finishing three places higher (third) in the Order of Merit than his previous year. Following up a mature performance in his first Ryder Cup, where he partnered Nick Faldo to victory in both fourball and foursomes, he finished 1997 in style by winning the Volvo Masters at Montecastillo. (Rescheduled because of Valderrama's commitment to the Ryder Cup.) Yet despite having banked £518,718 in official prize money in Europe, his hunger for competitive success drove him on to even greater heights over the winter.

Looking forward to the future with a big smile.

Hard on the heels of his win in Spain, he began with a second place finish to Mark Calcavecchia in the Subaru Sarazen World Open at Château Elan in Atlanta. He then successfully defended his Taiheiyo Masters title in Japan before finishing tied 21st in the Dunlop Phoenix Open. If that was not enough Westwood really hit the headlines at the end of the year by defeating Greg Norman in a tense play-off for the Australian Open title.

Westwood had finally arrived in the big-time. The plaudits were not long in coming for a man who could rack up over $500,000 in a matter of weeks, including one from Norman himself. 'I was really impressed with Lee when I played with him at the Open at Troon [1997] and his great finish speaks volumes for the way he plays . . .'

Despite much of the publicity which now surrounds his tournament appearances, the obvious highlight of his career so far remains his first appearance in the Ryder Cup. Although he narrowly lost to Fred Couples and Brad Faxon in the opening fourballs, his pairing with Nick Faldo proved to be an inspired choice by team captain Seve Ballesteros. Bouncing back strongly in the afternoon foursomes, the so-called 'odd couple' registered their first point by defeating reigning Open champion Justin Leonard and Jeff Maggert by 3 and 2.

Finding further success on day two, Westwood contributed greatly to the defeat of the powerful American partnership, Tiger Woods and Mark O'Meara. His first match against the newly crowned Masters champion, Woods, Westwood acquitted himself brilliantly – even coming back early the following morning after a weather interruption to hole a tricky downhill putt from ten feet to take the match by 2 & 1! Understandably drained, he failed to find the same inspiration for his next two matches which included his final day singles against Jeff Maggert. That said, Ballesteros singled him out for special praise as Europe recorded its second consecutive victory over the United States, by the narrow margin of 14½–13½.

So with so much happening in his short career which round would Lee Westwood select as the 'Round of My Life' so far?

I think it may surprise some people but the round I have chosen has nothing to do with the Ryder Cup or my win in the Volvo Masters at Montecastillo. Not even beating Greg in the Australian Open. I had thought about my first win in the Taiheiyo Masters – the final round – because that showed me I was good enough to win over a top-class field. It was also nice to know I could perform on really fast greens. That was important to me. But the round I have picked as the round of my life is my second-round 63 in the 1997 Turespaña Masters at Campo de Golf in Gran Canaria. That was special because I did everything well that day: driving, iron play, putting, everything. After all, it's not often you score ten under par on any course! And even though I finished second to José-María [Olazábal] in the tournament that has to be the best golfing round of my career so far . . .

Even for a player known for his spectacular scoring bursts, Lee Westwood's ten-under-par round at Campo de Golf was indeed special. In only his fifth outing of the season, he came out in the second round determined to make his presence felt and simply overpowered the Spanish course with a mixture of awesome length and accuracy. Though it boasted a strong par of 73, the resort-style course at Maspalomas relied strongly on a degree of wind to provide any sort of test. Without it the course was defenceless, and in the bright sunshine which greeted the second round of the Turespaña Masters eighty players took full advantage with under par scores including Westwood.

Because of the two-tee start used to alleviate congestion at many European Tour events, Westwood had begun his round on the 10th. Starting the day five strokes behind a whole gaggle of players on six under, including past Ryder Cup golfers Jose Rivero and Peter Baker, he knew that a good round was essential just to make the cut. Just under five hours later, he duly delivered one of the most spectacular rounds ever seen in European Tour history.

I was partnered by Peter Mitchell and Gordon Brand Jnr, and there was only a small breeze around to make scoring tricky. I had been playing great leading up to the tournament and just wanted to keep it going. Then everything sort of clicked.

The fireworks came early in the second round for the big-hitting youngster. Chipping in for a spectacular eagle on the par-5 11th, he quickly made another birdie on the 12th to go three under par after just three holes played. He followed this with a run of five straight pars and then a birdie on the long par-5 18th took him to five under for the tournament and into a position challenging for the lead.

Then, just when things looked to have cooled down a little, three straight pars from the 1st (his 10th) were followed by an incredible closing burst of four birdies and an eagle in the last six holes!

The run began at the 488-yard par-5 4th (his 13th). Westwood found a greenside bunker with his 3-wood second, but from not a particularly good lie, he proceeded to splash out to less than four feet and

Having picked up his first club at 13, Lee Westwood was playing off scratch only three years later. Today, he is rated among the best young professionals in the world.

calmly tapped in the putt for another birdie. Then from the 5th hole onwards Westwood holed birdie putts of eight, five and 18 feet respectively. Now a remarkable eight under par for 16 holes played, he was well on course to match his previous best score of 64 (eight under) in the Linde German Masters the year before.

Yet despite his earlier brilliance the Englishman came to the final two holes needing another birdie to match the round of 64 made by Paolo Quirici earlier in the day. While beating the Swiss professional's new course record was not top of his agenda at the time, Westwood was determined to finish well and put himself in good position for the second half of the tournament.

On the difficult 209-yard par-3 8th (his 17th) a solid par three left him needing four up the last for a round of 65. He found the rough off the tee on the 393-yard par-4 hole, but was left with little more than a pitching-wedge to the flag. Lining it up from 138 yards out, even the confident Westwood could not have predicted what happened next. Bouncing on the front half of the green, the ball ran up to the hole and dropped in for a dramatic eagle two for a remarkable round of 63!

That was incredible to finish that way. It was the key shot in the whole round and it looked in all the way. I think what made it so special was even though it was ten under, it could have been even better. I missed a few short ones which could have taken the score even lower, perhaps down to 60 if everything had dropped.

A glorious end to what had been a wonderful round of golf, even his close friend and manager, Andrew Chandler, described his young charge as 'having caught fire' that day. And who would argue? What does seem certain is that there will be many more days like that to come for the highly talented and likeable young professional.

Joyce

Wethered

The afternoon round in the final of the
British Ladies' Amateur Championship at
St Andrews, 13–20 May 1929.

The most legendary women's golfing figure of the twenties, Joyce Wethered returned from her self-imposed retirement to compete against the rising star of American ladies' golf, Glenna Collett. Meeting in the 36-hole final of the British Ladies' at St Andrews, these two giants of the women's game faced each other with not only personal, but national pride at stake. The most eagerly awaited match of its time, over 5,000 highly partisan Scots were there to cheer on the home player. Out of competitive practice and always nervous on such big occasions, the 28-year-old Wethered eventually came through to win by 2 & 1. Competitively drained, she retired for a second time with nothing more left to prove.

Every generation believes its sporting heroes and heroines are better than those who came before and those who come after.

No doubt golfers of the not too distant future will argue the merits of Tiger Woods and Ernie Els. Or, for the women, Laura Davies, Nancy Lopez and Annika Sorenstam. But in Britain of the late twenties there was rarely much discussion as to who was the most gifted golfer of the age. Quite simply it came down to a choice of two: Bobby Jones for the men, and the stylish Joyce Wethered for the women. But the question of who was the best was far less obvious. But perhaps Jones himself provided the answer when he said, 'I could not help saying that I had never played golf with anyone, man or woman, amateur or professional, who made me feel so utterly outclassed.'

Interestingly, these two giants played together for the first time shortly before the 1930 British Amateur Championship at St Andrews. Over from America in search of what proved to be the first leg in his historic Grand Slam, Jones partnered Wethered during a practice round over the Old Course. The American was full of praise, saying about their game together, 'We played the Old Course from the very back, or the championship tees, and with a slight breeze blowing off the sea, she did not miss one shot. She did not even half miss one shot.'

A year later, past English Amateur Champion Robert Harris was equally impressed. Describing a 72 she made around the windswept links of Royal North Devon, he commented, 'It was the best round of golf I had ever seen played. She beat the better ball of two ex-champions and a scratch player. There was no fireworks produced, only faultless golf. Vardon, Duncan and Bobby Jones, when I played with them, were wont to produce fireworks. But this round of Miss Wethered was above that class.'

The outstanding golfer of her generation, stories detailing her skill and concentration are legion. One incident which has since gone down in golfing folklore was the 'What train?' story. Her opponent and long-time rival, Cecil Leitch, later described what had happened in their match together, 'A train went rattling by, but so unconscious was she that she afterwards admitted she never as much heard it pass.'

This ability to concentrate purely on her own game was perhaps her greatest gift. A matchplay genius, she learnt from an early age to ignore her opponent and play the course. This more than anything contributed to her lasting reputation as a cold, almost ruthless competitor. British Ladies' Champion Enid Wilson once wrote, 'Her seeming remoteness from all the stresses and strains that trouble ordinary people bewildered her opponents. Her indifference to what they did became almost nightmarish.'

Joyce Wethered, the dominant woman golfer of her era.

Born in 1901, Joyce Wethered played her first competition at 18, reaching the semi-finals of the Surrey Ladies. Apart from a single lesson from Tom Lyle, the professional at Bude in Cornwall, she had learnt the rudiments of the game watching brother Roger (who was runner-up in the 1921 Open) and putting in countless hours of solitary practice. Blessed with a rhythmical golf swing which generated enormous power, Wethered quickly established herself as the dominant woman golfer of the early twenties.

In a period where amateurs, not professionals, were considered the benchmark of excellence, she held the title of English Ladies' Champion for five consecutive years. Making her debut in the competition in 1920 at Sheringham as a tall, gangling youth, she had struggled to qualify for the matchplay rounds in a lowly 25th place. Then, hoping for little more than 'one good day's golf before being knocked out', she amazed everybody by making the final. And if making the final was a surprise, winning it proved an even greater one.

Matched against the great Cecil Leitch, Joyce quickly found herself two down before lunch in the 36-hole final. She then gave away the first two holes of the afternoon to fall even further behind. At that point, with seemingly little to lose, she started to assert her own game. Clawing her way back, she eventually ran out the winner by 2 & 1 pulling off in her own words, 'the biggest surprise that ladies' golf has ever had sprung upon it.'

It was to be the first of many such memorable encounters between Wethered and Leitch. In the premier event of the women's golfing calendar, the British Ladies' Championship, the two would share the spoils, with victories for Wethered in 1922, 1924, 1925 and 1929, against Leitch's successes in 1920, 1921 and 1926. But while the older woman thrived on the pressure of competition, Joyce tolerated it as a necessary evil. Away from the drama of competition, she was by nature a shy person. Often preferring to practise alone, she took little part in the social whirl which often accompanied such events.

Despite her seemingly aloof attitude, Joyce was universally well liked by her fellow competitors and the large crowds which invariably followed her golfing progress. But sadly, the strain of repeating such a high standard began to take its toll. Past American Ladies' champion, Glenna Collett, described Wethered's plight some years later: 'To the onlooker she is phlegmatic and cold. Yet after a strenuous week of championship golf, she is forced to rest and leave golf for a fortnight or more.'

In one rare moment of introspection, Joyce wrote in 1933 about the pressure

Marching to glory: Wethered during the final of the British Ladies' Championship at St Andrews in 1929.

she felt during a close match: 'I know the feeling of standing on a tee with real fear in my heart, the match slipping away and the club feeling strange and useless in my hands.'

After winning her fifth English Championship in 1925, she decided never to play in the event again. By the time she played in the British Ladies' later the same year, her mind was made up. She would retire from competitive golf completely. During the tournament, held at Royal Troon, she gave no hint of what she had in mind. For the Scottish crowds who came to cheer her on that week, it was the same matchless Joyce, wrapped in a cocoon of concentration and playing flawless golf. Making the final, Bernard Darwin described her progress in *The Times* as, 'A series of executions carried out with merciful swiftness.'

The final itself was a tense affair. Matched against her old rival, Cecil Leitch, Wethered eventually won on the first extra hole after losing a two-up lead with three holes to play. It had been the most difficult and draining match of her career and, within days of the final, she announced her decision to retire at the age of 24. Citing the pressure of competition as the reason for her sudden and unexpected departure, her decision was greeted with a certain scepticism from the golfing press but after four years away the move began to look permanent.

For Joyce the time was spent catching up with the everyday life she had missed out on. Returning to her childhood Scottish haunts at Dornoch, she would spend hours relaxing on the river bank fishing for salmon. But despite her decision to give up competitive golf, her lasting affection for the game still saw her practising and playing the occasional social game. Then, almost without warning, circumstances conspired to stir her into action once again. By 1929 the highly regarded Glenna Collett was setting the standards in the women's game. Earlier that year it had been announced in the press that the American had entered the British Ladies' Championship at St Andrews. For Wethered, the growing reputation of Collett and the lure of playing one last competition over her beloved Old Course proved too much to resist. Amid speculation about how rusty she would be after her long break away from the game, she entered her first major competition in four years.

As before, the crowds flocked in their thousands during the week long event, hoping to see her defeat the American invader over the famed Old Course. Somehow fate decreed they would meet in the 36-hole final with what seemed the whole golfing world looking on. Played on the Saturday in front of 5,000 highly partisan Scottish supporters, the match itself was a classic affair. Wethered clawed her way back in typically defiant fashion after being six down during the morning round, eventually to win by 2 & 1 in the afternoon. It was the most celebrated victory by a British golfer since the First World War and the local constabulary were needed to smooth her passage through the throng of excited well-wishers. It would be the pinnacle of her albeit short golfing career and perhaps not surprisingly would be her choice for the 'Round of My Life'.

> I have no doubt in saying my afternoon round against Glenna Collett at St Andrews in 1929 was the round of which I am most proud. Never did such an important match swing in such pendulum fashion and I was so glad to have taken some part in it.

Despite the nationalistic fervour which had greeted the home girl's progress to the final, it was Collett who was considered the strong favourite to win the championship. The younger woman by two years, she was a proven tournament winner in the United States and had shown some wonderful form in the previous six rounds. Wethered in contrast had struggled badly. In her opening match against Phyllis Lobbett she had been constantly disturbed by people running across the fairways trying to get a closer look. Yet the American had good reason to fear the former champion. When they had met in one of the early rounds at Royal Troon in 1925, Collett had been beaten by the humiliating margin of 4 & 3.

> At Troon the match anticipated between her and me was worked up to such a pitch beforehand that one of two things were bound to happen. Either we should rise to the occasion or one of us would fail under the strain of it. As events turned out for me, I played some of the best golf I had ever succeeded in producing. With the exception of two poorish putts I know that I have never played the rest of the game so accurately or so well before or since possibly with the exception of the final in 1929.

With St Andrews a virtual ghost town, the morning round of the final finished two-up in Collett's favour. Unable to find any consistency on the greens Wethered lost five of the opening nine holes and looked a certain loser before recovering somewhat on the back nine.

> Our best ball score in the morning was 71. Glenna's deluge of par figures and under consisted of nine fours, one three and a two. Then my turn of good luck began. From the 9th I took 73 for the next 18 holes and in the afternoon round actually stood four up at the 9th.

Having turned the match around so convincingly it looked from that point that Wethered would stroll to victory. But Collett came back with birdies at the 10th and 11th holes to cut the deficit to just two. Losing two holes in quick succession appeared to disturb the English girl and altered the whole complexion of the final.

> I must confess I found playing the remaining holes very trying indeed. I also had the memory of throwing away a lead at Troon in a previous year which did not tend to make the position any more comforting. The 15th finally decided the result. I had sliced my drive and was unable to reach the green in two. A poor run-up left me six yards from the hole with Glenna lying practically dead in three. It looked like being only one-up and in such a crisis with still three holes to go, anything might have happened. But then the most opportune putt I have ever made came to my rescue.

Modestly describing the moment her long putt for a half hit the back of the hole as a 'happy surprise', Wethered retained her two-up advantage with just three holes remaining. The match had swung back in her favour for there was now too little time for Collett to mount a comeback. A half in par on the par-4 16th was followed by a catalogue of errors by the American at the Road Hole but even then Wethered was careful about slipping up so close to victory.

> Glenna took four to reach the plateau of the green. All the same I shall not easily forget the anxiety of keeping the ball safely in play. It is the most trying of experiences to keep cool just on the brink of winning. So easy to lose control and spoil it all. It was also impossible to ignore the pent-up excitement of the crowd which was ready to break out as soon as the last putt was struck.

Moments later Joyce Wethered capped her glorious comeback by holing the winning putt that gave her a fourth British Ladies' Championship. Greeted by the enthusiastic cheers of the large crowd, both players were literally engulfed in the chaos which followed. With barely enough time to shake hands, Wethered was escorted by two burly policemen to the nearby Russacks Hotel while Collett escaped toward the clubhouse. The greatest victory of her career, it confirmed Wethered's place alongside the legends of the British game. Yet, almost within hours of receiving the trophy, her decision to retire for the second time had been made. The history books show she was still only 28.

> It was only when the prize-giving and the speeches were over that I

began to feel really free once more. Then came the awakening to the fact that the greatest ambition of my life had been realised after all – the winning of a championship at St Andrews. As a finale of ten years from my first championship it seemed altogether too good to be true.

While she would return for several smaller events including the inaugural Curtis Cup in 1932, in which she beat Glenna Collett in the singles, Wethered would never compete in the major women's events again. In later years she played in the occasional exhibition match including a lucrative tour of the United States in 1934. Three years after that she met and married Sir John Heathcote-Amory taking the title of Lady Heathcote-Amory. In 1975 she was inducted into the US LPGA Hall of Fame at Pinehurst, North Carolina, in recognition of her legendary golfing achievements.

Her last few years were spent living in quiet seclusion at her long-time home, Knightshayes House in Devon. Until her death in 1997 she would rarely miss televised golf and in her late eighties was flown to nearby St Mellion to meet with fellow legend Jack Nicklaus. Considered the greatest woman golfer of all time, she remained interested in all aspects of the game and welcomed any enquiries about her remarkable life.

Rivals Joyce Wethered and Glenna Collett before their epic final at St Andrews.

Tiger

Woods

69 in the final round of the US Masters at Augusta National, Georgia, 10–13 April 1997.

Playing his first major championship as a professional, Tiger Woods came into the final round of the Masters with a record-breaking nine-stroke lead. Having reduced the famed Augusta National to little more than drives and short-iron approaches, he decimated the top class field with three opening rounds of 70, 66 and 65. Yet with Greg Norman's spectacular collapse the previous year after holding a six-stroke lead going into the final day still fresh in the mind, the pressure was still on the 21-year-old to come through and win. But come through he did. Breaking nine long-standing Masters records along the way, he strolled to victory with a final round of 69. One of the youngest ever winners of a major, he confirmed his early promise by beating the lowest 72-hole aggregate in the Masters with his record four-total of 270.

Rarely can one golfer have made such an immediate impact on the game as Tiger Woods. Heralded as the future of the sport, he breezed into the cosy world of professional golf like a whirlwind. Winner of an unprecedented three consecutive US Amateur titles by the time he was just 20, his record since joining the paid ranks in August 1996 is simply remarkable. Needing to accumulate $140,000 in his first six weeks to avoid the embarrassment of facing Tour Qualifying School at the year end, he took just three tournaments to win his card. Five weeks later, he had won two of his first seven US Tour events and accumulated over $1 million in prize money.

Since then his graph of golfing success has been one long climb steeply upward. In a story which would not be out of place in a Hollywood film script, his first full year in the paid ranks saw him crowned top golfer on the United States PGA Tour, number-one ranked player in the world and Masters champion. Now, as we approach the new millennium, Tiger Woods remains the most talked about golfer on the planet.

Born on 30 December 1975, Eldrick 'Tiger' Woods spent his early years growing up in Cypress, California. Son of a black lieutenant colonel in the United States Army and a Thai mother, his background was not exactly custom-built for golfing greatness. Yet, after picking up his first club at just eleven months old, the game has been an ever-present in his life. As, to a certain extent, has been a measure of fame.

Aged just three, Tiger Woods scored a creditable 48 for nine holes at nearby Cypress Navy Golf Club. Picking up the story, CBS News did a profile of him which in turn led to a TV appearance on the popular *Mike Douglas Show*. On this programme he was shown putting against legendary comedian Bob Hope – and winning.

A year later, he was back on TV showing off his golfing skills on *That's Incredible*. By the time he was five, Tiger was spending most of his free time practising hard at the local golf course. Making even more TV appearances over the coming years, he was already a minor celebrity by the time he was 12. Yet, amid all the showbiz glamour, what comes through most strongly in these early shows is how novel it was back in the late seventies to have a black youngster playing golf.

The 'Tiger' phenomenon confirming his early promise in the 1997 Masters.

The nickname 'Tiger' was given to him by his father to commemorate a South Vietnamese army buddy, and stuck into his early teenage years and beyond. With his father vowing not to forget a colleague who had saved his life on more than one occasion, the jungle sobriquet was not the only thing Woods Snr instilled into his highly talented son.

Employing the tough discipline of his Green Beret background, Earl Woods developed his own unique training methods. When Tiger was just 12, Earl was retained by a top sports management company as 'junior golf consultant' to his own son. Investing a six-figure sum into this young golfing prodigy, they seemed happy to let his father continue with his unconventional training methods. 'I knew him and how much he could take,' Earl Woods has said. 'So I pulled every dirty, nasty, rumbustious trick on my son week after week.

'I dropped a bag of clubs at the point of impact of his swing. I imitated a crow's voice while he was stroking a putt. When he was ready to hit a shot I would toss a ball right in front of his vision. I would cough as he was taking the club back. I played with his mind, and don't forget he was not permitted to say a word. Sometimes he got angry with me and would stop his club inches before impact and grit his teeth. But he learned. He became mentally tough.'

By 1990, at the age of 14, Tiger Woods began fulfilling his boyhood potential by becoming the youngest ever semi-finalist in the history of the United States Junior Championships. Showing commendable determination after his defeat, he bounced back one year later to become the youngest ever winner of the event, winning with a bogey at the first extra hole after being three down after six in the 18-hole final.

It proved the starting point for one of the greatest ever runs in US amateur golf. From 1991 to 1996, Woods captured six consecutive USGA championships including three National junior titles in 1991, 1992 and 1993, and three United States Amateur titles in 1994, 1995 and 1996. By the time he played his last National Amateur final against Steve Scott at Pumpkin Ridge, the match was being covered live by golf channels eager to cash in on Woods' growing fame.

Played a week before he left Stanford University to turn pro, Tiger Woods once again found himself in familiar territory. Having been down in most of his six championship finals, often going into the last few holes, he found himself five down at lunch to Scott in the 36-hole final. For anybody else that would have been it. Go down quietly, pack away your clubs and wish for better luck the following year. But coming from behind in major finals was something Woods was used to.

In the 1994 final against Trip Kuehne, Woods had been five down with only twelve to play before coming back to win at the last. At lunch, his father Earl had been widely quoted as saying, 'Let the legend grow.' Two years later at Pumpkin Ridge, and without all the mystical overtones, Tiger got the message once again and battled back with birdies at 16 and 17. Holing pressure putts on both greens, plus another in the second extra hole of the play-off to win, Woods finished his amateur days on a championship-winning high. Earl Woods later commented how his son always 'makes most of his must-make putts'.

A few weeks later, Tiger Woods opened up his professional career with a 336-yard blast down the 1st fairway in the Milwaukee Open. It would prove an enormous change for the 21-year-old and one which took some adjusting to in his first year or so. Speaking at a press conference in Thailand in 1998 he revealed,

> I've played junior golf, collegiate golf, amateur golf, where you are isolated for three months – June, July and August. But now I have to play from January all the way through to the last week in October. And that is three times as long as I've had to sustain a competitive edge. It took its toll on me. I was okay for six months but after that I was pretty tired. I probably played too much, too early and didn't spread it out enough. It will probably take me another three or four years before I find the right schedule for me.

Cool, composed and invariably polite in the many meetings he has with the world's press, it was all a far cry from eighteen months before when he first announced he was turning professional. Back then most of the talk had been about the massive $40 million sponsorship deal he had just signed.

With much of the speculation relating to his huge appeal to racial minorities, Woods diplomatically described himself as 'just a golfer who happens to be both black and Asian'. Certainly his diverse cultural background had the marketing men rubbing their hands in glee, especially as he claimed to be, among other things, one eighth Chinese, one eighth Caucasian and one eighth native American Indian! In those chaotic first few weeks, Woods himself often shunned any debate about race or colour, but those guiding his career had few such reservations.

Only days after turning professional, Woods' arrival was proclaimed in a controversial advertising campaign which had him saying, 'There are still courses in the United States I am not allowed to play because of the colour of my skin. Hello World. I've heard I'm not ready for you. Are you ready for me?'

Released as part of his five-year deal with major sportswear company, Nike, it seemed the staid world of American golf was certainly not ready for such in-your-face comments. It was probably not the sort of publicity the seemingly level-headed Woods was looking for. And while the ensuing controversy threatened to sour his entry into the paid ranks, pundits stood in line to say how the majority of private golf clubs in America would welcome him with open arms.

Thankfully the fire-storm of controversy quickly abated after the advert was quietly dropped. Woods sensibly got on with his golf and after winning three out of his first eight tournaments, even the $40 million sponsorship deal was soon forgotten. Indeed, by the time he had won the first tournament of 1997, the prestigious Mercedes Championship in California, the figure was starting to look particularly good value compared with the astronomic fees paid to top basketball stars like Michael Jordan.

And by the time the US Masters was over in April, it was looking like the bargain of the century.

While a large part of Woods' appeal was his ability to attract minorities to the sport, golf fans all over America took the charismatic youngster to their hearts. Like Arnold Palmer in the sixties, his appearance at a particular tournament often doubled the attendance figures. Television viewing figures soared as he powered his way around most courses in typical ball-busting style.

With his spectacular play-off wins and dramatic shot making the game suddenly became more exciting. Even those who had little interest in golf switched on to see how the Tiger was doing. Becoming the fastest player to win over $1 million in prize money, even his fellow professionals were often lavish with their praise. World number one Greg Norman described him as 'A breath of fresh air'. Past US Open champion Payne Stewart said, 'Tiger is the greatest thing to happen to this tour for a very long time.' Even the great Jack Nicklaus himself commented, 'I do not think there is anything in this game he cannot do.' High praise indeed for someone who had yet to compete in his first major as a professional.

Not surprisingly, for Woods' first appearance in the Masters, race once again became a major topic of conversation. Like many of the top private clubs in the United States, Augusta National had been widely condemned for its lack of Afro-American members. While change had been painfully slow, the Georgia Golf Club had hoped that by admitting their first black member in 1989 the tide of criticism might be stemmed. It would prove a forlorn hope. Indeed, it had not gone unnoticed that no black professional was invited to compete in the Masters until Lee Elder's appearance in 1975.

Adding fuel to the flame, the week following the Masters also marked the 50th anniversary of Jackie Robinson breaking major league baseball's colour bar, a landmark occasion in American sporting history, which had been personally and very publicly highlighted by President Bill Clinton. Accordingly Tiger Woods' appearance in the Masters became the focus of intense press comment outside the sports pages even before the tournament got underway.

When Woods finally arrived at Augusta National late on Tuesday afternoon and decided to play the back nine, the normally sedate venue exploded with excitement. Flanked by a group of well-armed security men, laid on by the club, news of his appearance spread like wildfire around the course. Excited by the prospect of seeing this great young talent, the normally sedate Georgia crowds rushed toward the 10th green hoping to get just a glimpse.

Two days later the Augusta fans enjoyed an even bigger treat. In a remarkable bonus for the first-day crowd, the past champion Nick Faldo was chosen to play with Tiger Woods. Augusta, it seemed, had stuck to their usual system of pairing the immediate past champion with the winner of the United States Amateur who, in this particular case, just happened to be Woods. It was an intriguing game to follow. The first time they had ever been played together, it was watched by one of the largest crowds in Masters history.

Throughout much of the opening round, Woods continued to blast it past the Englishman off the tee. With Woods' drives in excess of 300 yards, it was almost embarrassing to see the difference in length between the two. Yet, surprisingly, both players started their round poorly with Woods and Faldo at four-over par and five-over respectively at the turn. The course was crossed by unseasonally strong winds, which made approach shots impossible to judge with the rock-hard greens becoming even faster as the breeze dried them out.

Tiger Woods powering a huge drive off the 3rd tee in the second round at Augusta.

It seemed like everyone was scoring badly including the much heralded Woods. Then, almost without warning, a blistering series of birdies on the back nine achieved with the help of some scintillating iron shots brought Tiger Woods back in an amazing 30 strokes, six under par. He later revealed it was his tee shot on the 10th hole which so dramatically changed his fortunes.

> I had taken 40 on the front nine and needed to turn my game around if I was going to get back to even par. A 3-wood might have found the bunker or gone through the fairway. I needed the right club to feel the correct position of my golf swing. I found it with that shot and tried to carry that feeling with me all week.

It was a remarkable display made even better by the scores already posted in the clubhouse. Matched against Woods' two-under-par 70, Greg Norman had 77, Seve Ballesteros an 81, Corey Pavin 76, Tom Lehman 75, and Ernie Els 73. Nick Faldo, perhaps Woods' greatest rival for the championship, continued to struggle and eventually finished with a 75. Proving one of the toughest opening days in Masters history, it was perhaps best summed up by past US Open winner, Lee Janzen, who described playing Augusta as 'like walking through rattlesnakes'.

Following up his 70 on Thursday with a 69 on Friday, Woods built himself a two-shot lead over the rest of the quality field including Italian Costantino Rocca in second place. As 'Tigermania' started to grip the crowds at Augusta, it began to dawn on everyone that he could actually win it.

Jack Nicklaus had said before the tournament, that Woods had the ability to win more Masters titles than he and Arnold Palmer put together. This sort of talk, even coming from the Golden Bear, had been dismissed as yet more Tiger Woods hype, but as the third round of the Masters got underway, no one was quite as sure.

Woods' playing partner for the third round was Europe's top golfer, the experienced Colin Montgomerie, who teed-off with his own hopes for his first major win still very much alive. Eighteen holes and just over four hours later and it was all back to square one. Humiliated by the longest driver of a golf ball the world has ever seen, Montgomerie could only look on in anguish as Woods literally overpowered Augusta in a record breaking round of 65.

Accumulating the lowest three-round total ever recorded in the Masters, it left the smiling Tiger with an almost unassailable nine-shot lead over the rest of the field. Echoing the comments of Bobby Jones over three decades earlier when discussing the up-and-coming Jack Nicklaus, Jack returned the compliment by saying of Woods' display, 'He plays a game with which I am not familiar.'

Just two strokes off the Augusta course record, Woods had taken 30 putts when a more typical round would be around 27 or 28. The sheer length of his driving was truly astonishing with no better example than at the 555-yard par-5 2nd. After hitting his tee shot 370 yards, he pitched over the back of the green with a 9-iron when others were playing 5- and 4-iron shots.

Never using more than a 7-iron approach to any par-4 all week, for Woods Augusta took on the feel of a pitch-and-putt course. The 435-yard par-4 9th was a drive and sand-wedge; the 485-yard par-4 10th was a 3-wood and 9-iron; the 455-yard par-4 11th was a drive and a 'little' 9-iron, and so on.

Coming off the 18th green after the third round, the contrast between the two golfers could not have been more stark. After struggling to a two-over-par 74, Montgomerie was practically inconsolable. Not only had the big Scot seen his dreams of winning the Masters splintered into little pieces, he had looked totally second-rate against the rampant Woods. Like his Ryder Cup partner, Nick Faldo, had found on the opening day, hunting the Tiger had proved to be a very bloody experience indeed.

While not widely publicised, the Masters offers a total prize fund of $2.7 million (£1.65 million). The newly crowned Masters champion will walk away with $275,000 come Sunday evening. Fractionally more than the winner of the Open. But while first prize would have made a big difference to the bank balance of Costantino Rocca then in second, for Woods such a figure would be mere small change. Yet, people thought the pressure of winning his first major from such a commanding position must have some effect. After all, Greg Norman had lost a six-shot lead only the year before, and he was a vastly experienced world number one!

Questions at the press conference following the third round had been predictable enough, but every reporter there instinctively knew that Woods would not waste his chance. In fact, it was left perversely to Colin Montgomerie to frame the words which Woods had refused to do only minutes before. Speaking with some annoyance in his voice Monty had said, 'There is no way he is going to blow it. Faldo's not lying second for a start and Greg Norman is not Tiger Woods.'

Despite the words of encouragement from the European number one, the Greg Norman collapse the previous year showed that anything was possible. Paired with Costantino Rocca, Tiger Woods stepped onto the first tee at Augusta for the final round knowing history would either judge him a genius or a failure.

People had predicted great things from him almost since childhood and now it was time to deliver. On the plane over to Augusta, he had told his close friend and fellow Tour professional, Mark O'Meara, that he was playing well enough to win. Indeed, in their last practice round together in Florida, Woods had birdied ten consecutive holes to shoot 59! But this was not a resort course in Florida, this was Augusta National and the final round of the Masters.

No doubt aware of the criticism which would inevitably follow any slip-up, Tiger had been ably prepared by his father Earl.

> The round of my life? I think Sunday at Augusta was very important and special to me because so many negative things could have come from that. My dad pulled me aside in the morning and said to me, 'Son, when you go out there today, it's probably going to be the toughest round of golf you will ever have to play in your life. But if you stay true to yourself it will be one of the most rewarding rounds of your life.' And that stuck with me the entire day.

Looking to become the youngest winner in Masters history in his first major as a professional, Woods opened with a solid par on the 1st. Followed by a birdie on the par-5 2nd, it gave him the start he was looking for. 'I came out trying not to make a bogey,' he said later, 'and to make birdies when I could.'

After Costantino Rocca had matched his birdie at the second, Woods found his first bunker of the week at the 5th. Dropping his first shot since the 3rd hole on Friday, he quickly lost another at the 7th. Averting what could have been the start of a spectacular collapse, he then fought back with a birdie on the 8th after making a superb recovery shot from the pine needles.

While every hole on the back nine at Augusta is justifiably famous, it is the run of three holes at the far end of the course which grabs most attention. Known throughout the golfing world as 'Amen Corner', so named because you need divine assistance to get through with your score intact, it begins at the 455-yard par-4 11th. Named 'White Dogwood' after one of the many varieties of plant life found

Tiger Woods on the 14th tee and strolling to victory with a final round of 69.

on the Augusta estate, Woods' drive and short-iron set up a magnificent birdie.

Having now extended his lead to a massive eleven shots over Tom Watson in second place, Woods stepped onto the tee at the 155-yard par-3 12th. Among the most treacherous short holes in golf, the pros play to a shallow, kidney-shaped green sitting behind the infamous Rae's Creek. With high pines sheltering the tee from any wind, the hole requires the golfer to hit a high, floating shot through a swirling breeze that is difficult to judge. Mistakes are common.

In 1980 Tom Weiskopf ran up an horrific 13 here after tangling with both the water and a greenside bunker. Looking to avoid a similar fate, Woods sensibly took the advice of his experienced caddie, 'Fluff' Cowan, and played to the middle of the green with an 8-iron. Two putts later and he walked off with an invaluable par.

The final hole in the loop is the 485-yard par-5 15th. Stunningly beautiful but inevitably lethal if you go off line, this hole is a real crowd pleaser with anything from an eagle three, to a quadruple-bogey nine the possible outcome. After another booming drive down this right-to-left dog-leg, Woods left himself with little more than a 7-iron to the green. With huge pines all the way down the left giving the illusion that the green is nearer than it actually is, Woods' approach was still good enough to guarantee his second birdie in three holes.

Two birdies in three holes at 'Amen Corner' followed by another one at 14, and Woods was practically home and dry. Now eighteen under par with only a handful of holes left, his lead was an incredible twelve strokes. Left with a relatively simple run-in back to the clubhouse, Woods still knew the importance of playing those holes well. At the press conference later he said,

I knew I had to get through Amen Corner with par at worst. I couldn't let up on my concentration or anything. After I got by what I call the 'water' holes on the back nine, after I hit the tee shot at 16, I knew it was pretty much over because I knew I could bogey in.

To his credit, Tiger Woods kept up his assault on Augusta National looking for one last record, the lowest winning four-round total in the history of the Masters previously held jointly by Jack Nicklaus and Ray Floyd. The 21-year-old stepped onto the final tee needing a par-4 on the final hole to beat it. Wearing his favoured 'power' red shirt – his mother Kultida had forecast many years ago that this was the colour his aura was best in tune with – Woods prepared to drive.

Looking for one last mighty blast up the fairway, the top of his backswing coincided with the unmistakable sound of a motor drive camera from the massed ranks of photographers gathered behind the tee. Unable to stop, Woods hooked his ball into the crowd on the left. After glaring at the errant snapper, he stormed off up the fairway knowing a par would still give him the record he craved. 'I was at the top of my swing,' he said, 'when a photographer took a picture, and then fired off two more on the way down. That was uncalled for.'

Unable to make the green in regulation, the roar which greeted Woods' third shot to the final green proved just the start of the celebrations. The realisation that he could take 13 putts from five feet and still win did little to dampen the enthusiastic cheering which greeted his arrival. By the time he lined up the putt which would give him the Masters title, and the lowest score in the event's long history, the only one left to put pressure on Woods was Woods himself.

Moments later, as the ball rattled into the back of the hole, Tiger Woods punched the air in delight. In the first three rounds, he had beaten his playing partners' scores with alarming ease: Faldo by five strokes, Paul Azinger by six and Colin Montgomerie by nine. Now, after beating Costantino Rocca 69 to 75, his first thoughts were to hug his mother and father at the back of the green. Afterwards he said,

> Winning the Masters is always something I have dreamed of. But I never dreamt I would win with a lead like this. It's not what you imagine. You imagine duelling it out with, I guess the likes of Nick Faldo, Nicklaus or Watson, someone who is awfully tough to beat along the stretch. When I came here I was pretty confident of my playing abilities but that doesn't mean a whole lot when you come to Augusta because you've still got to perform. And this golf course can take anybody who's confident and humble them very quickly.

Of the chasing pack, only four other players would beat Woods' final-round score of 69. Tommy Tolles hit a best-of-the-day 67 to finish third, while veteran Tom Kite rallied with a birdie-par finish to end runner-up – twelve strokes behind. At least Kite, 1997 US Ryder Cup captain, had the consolation of knowing Woods would be playing on his team that coming September.

For Tiger Woods, Sunday evening was spent as guest of honour at the champions' banquet at Augusta. The first black golfer to win the coveted green jacket, his performance had taken the golfing world by storm. Asked if the victory had special meaning because Augusta had taken such a long time to invite an Afro-American to the event, Tiger had replied, 'Yes. Lee Elder was the first. He was the one I looked up to, and Charlie [Sifford], all of them. Because of them I was able to play here. I was able to live my dream because of those guys.'

For Tiger Woods, that dream looks set to live on for many years to come. No one knows how many major championships he will win before he is through. Perhaps, like the great Jack Nicklaus, he will continue winning tournaments well into his forties and fifties. Or maybe he will emulate the legendary Bobby Jones and retire before he is 30, having won all he can. Only time will tell. Certainly, if confidence and will-to-win are anything to go by, he will be around for years. Typically, after selecting his final round in the 1997 Masters as the 'Round of My Life' he smiled and added the comment, 'so far'.

And after all, who would argue with a Tiger?

Ian

Woosnam

72 in the final round of the US Masters
at Augusta National, Georgia, 10–13
April 1991.

*Looking for his first major title, Woosnam went into the final round at
Augusta leading by one stroke from Tom Watson. Despite only matching
his opening-round score of 72, his worst score of the week, it was a typically gutsy display by a golfer known for his battling qualities under
pressure. Eventually winning by one stroke from Ryder Cup team-mate
José-María Olazábal, his victory was the seventh by a European professional in the event since 1980. It was one of six tournaments he would
win that year and would confirm his place among the game's elite.*

When Ian Woosnam first emerged from deepest Shropshire to take on Europe's
best in 1978 he was not an immediate success. Travelling around in a battered
caravan and living on a diet of baked beans and chips, his career was going
nowhere fast. With little funding behind him, three visits to the qualifying
school were the hard price he paid for failing to keep his player's card. Even by the
time he had spent four seasons on tour he had accumulated less than £7,000 in prize
money. Frustrated by his lack of success, any desire Woosnam had expressed to
become the greatest golfer in the world now seemed little more than a hollow
boast.

With money running increasingly short, the unwelcome prospect of taking a
club pro's job started to beckon if he failed once more. But in best rags-to-riches
style, the battling Woosnam simply refused to give in. It proved to be the right
decision. After winning his player's card again in 1982 he won the Swiss Open en
route to finishing a highly creditable eighth in the European Money List with earnings of £48,794. Having finally broken through it proved just the start of 'Woosie's'
rise to golfing stardom. Within a decade of turning professional, not only would
the tough and determined little Welshman have silenced his critics he would have
become one of the most prolific winners in world golf.

Now a Ryder Cup regular, past World Cup winner and two-time World Matchplay champion, he is known as one of the greatest ball strikers around. Exhibiting an ability to drive vast distances with seemingly little effort, his no-frills style of golf has made him a popular draw wherever he plays. Aggressive and hugely powerful for his size – he stands 5 feet 4½ inches – he now has over 35 tournament victories to his name with many more likely to follow.

Rated among the most gifted players of his generation, Woosnam remains, along with Nick Faldo, Bernhard Langer, Seve Ballesteros, José-María Olazábal and Sandy Lyle, part of the select band of Europeans to have won the US Masters. His win back in 1991 almost certainly represented the pinnacle of his golfing achievements. Holing a dramatic winning putt on the final green to beat Spaniard Olazábal into second place, his reaction

Ian Woosnam sharing his Masters triumph with his wife Glendryth and children Daniel and Rebecca.

summed up everything which has made him such a popular competitor. Down on his haunches urging the putt home with his fist clenched in rugged determination, this was a victory he desperately wanted and probably deserved. His first major, it made all the years of struggle suddenly worthwhile. So perhaps not surprisingly, the final round at Augusta is Ian Woosnam's choice for the 'Round of My Life'.

I've been lucky to have many great rounds on the European Tour including two ten-under-par scores [62 in the Benson and Hedges International in 1985 and 62 in the German Masters in 1990] and a few nine-unders [including 60 in the Monte Carlo Open in 1990]. But the last round at Augusta in 1991 probably has to be the most memorable round I've ever played in my life. It was certainly the toughest. And even though it wasn't my best score, or even the best golf I played that week, it was one put together under the most incredible pressure. Perhaps that's why it means so much to me – to know I could handle myself under the stress and be able to come through and win a major. That's why I would choose it as the 'Round of My Life'.

Ian Harold Woosnam MBE was born on 2 March 1958. The son of a Shropshire farmer, he was brought up near Oswestry on the Welsh border. Spending his teenage years fulfilling the physically-demanding tasks expected of any farmer's son, his early golf was played at nearby Llanymynech. And despite the course holding the unique distinction of having 15 holes in Wales and 3 in England, his own allegiance has never been in doubt. 'I'm a Taff to the core,' says Woosie.

Physically powerful from an early age, Ian became an occasional participant in holiday camp boxing tournaments as a youngster. Known to have displayed a fierce determination never to be beaten, he later applied this aspect of his personality to his chosen sport of golf. Reaching low single figures before his 14th birthday, he reached the final of the Shropshire and Hereford Boys' Championship at Market Drayton in 1971. There he would begin his long-standing rivalry with the other finalist that day, Sandy Lyle. On that particular day Woosnam would lose but, in typically defiant style, he turned to Lyle after the match and said, 'One day I'll beat you.' It proved to be a prophetic statement in more ways than one.

Born within a few miles of each other, Ian was the elder of the two by two months. They were never particularly close, and Sandy Lyle had all the advantages which Woosnam could only dream about. Born at Hawkstone Park Golf Club, son of the local club pro, Sandy greatly benefited from having lessons and practice facilities always close at hand. Ian Woosnam, in stark contrast, was mainly self-taught and forever struggling to get time away from the farm to practise.

Though their two glittering careers would ultimately parallel each other, Woosnam spent his teenage years playing catch-up with the more naturally gifted Lyle. Indeed it was the same story when they both turned professional a few years later, Ian Woosnam in 1976 and Sandy Lyle in 1977. While Lyle's career flourished in the paid ranks, Woosnam hardly broke even in his first four years on tour. But the competition between the two boyhood rivals rarely dimmed. Three years after the big-hitting Scot won his first professional title, the 1979 European Open, Woosnam won the 1982 Swiss Open.

Woosnam celebrates his winning putt on the final green at Augusta.

For Woosnam, this first victory on the European Tour acted like a catalyst to further success. Free from the restraint of having to make enough money just to survive, his career blossomed along with his rivalry with Lyle. Now established among the top players in Europe, the competition brought the very best out of each other. Two years after Lyle had topped the 1985 European Order of Merit with record earnings of £254,711, Woosnam took the number one spot with prize money of £439,075.

That year also saw their own personal battle for supremacy reach its climax – in the final of the 1987 Suntory World Matchplay at Wentworth. Unlike their other match at Market Drayton all those years before Woosnam came out the winner this time. Watched from the sidelines by his wife of four years, Glendryth, and his father, Harold, beating Lyle one-up on the final green proved an emotional victory for the down-to-earth golfer. Yet victory had come as no real surprise. Already in his best ever season, he would go on to take the number one spot in Europe, having previously won the Jersey Open, Madrid Open, Scottish Open and Trophée Lancôme. He would also go on to represent Europe in the Ryder Cup and win the World Cup individual prize for Wales.

In truth, winning the 1987 Order of Merit and his defeat of Lyle at Wentworth should have laid to rest many of the ghosts which had plagued Woosnam over the years. But as the following season dawned, it seemed there would always be one more step to go as far as Woosnam himself was concerned.

In reality the battling Welshman had little to prove. But with question marks being raised over his ability to win a major, there hardly seemed enough time to enjoy what he had won! Of course, the pressure had quietly been building since Sandy Lyle became the first British professional since Tony Jacklin to win the Open in 1985. Then, if that was not bad enough, Lyle had become the first European to win the US Masters in 1988. Perhaps understandably Woosnam reacted angrily to the criticism. Never one to ignore a challenge, he dismissed the premise that you had to win a major to be considered a truly great player.

Throughout the next few years, Woosnam continued to play well in Europe finishing fourth and sixth in 1988 and 1989. With Lyle and Ballesteros now playing the majority of their golf in the United States, he recaptured his number one position on the Money List in 1990 with record earnings of £737,978. Despite his success doubts still remained, but by the start of the nineties Woosnam himself was now thinking positively in terms of major success.

As the 1991 season got underway, his reasoning could not be faulted. Playing some of the best golf of his life, an early season victory at the Mediterranean Open boosted his confidence just weeks before the Masters in April. Not surprisingly, he felt this could be his tournament and was not afraid to say so. Speaking shortly before the tournament began he commented, 'Faldo, Langer, Ballesteros and Lyle have all had at least one each, so perhaps it's my turn.'

He was right but not before some scares along the way. An edgy level par opening round of 72 put him five shots behind first-round leader Lanny Wadkins, and four behind veteran Tom Watson in second. In typical style, Woosnam fought his way back with superb rounds of 66 and 67, to take a one-stroke lead into the final round of the tournament. Despite having won many events in Europe from a similar position, these were relatively uncharted waters for the 33-year-old Welshman. He was paired together on the Sunday with past Masters champion Watson who was made favourite to lift his third title. Thankfully for all his fans back in Britain it was not to be. In fact the greatest threat to Woosnam's bid for his first major title would come from his Ryder Cup team-mate, José-María Olazábal.

The final round was not particularly special in terms of dramatic content, until the very last hole that is.

With one eye on the leader board Woosnam had gone about his work efficiently, making few mistakes. A steady stream of pars on the front nine had been enough to keep Watson at bay while others like Steve Pate (65) and Ben Crenshaw (68) threatened to challenge but were never quite close enough at the finish. As for the leaders there were only ever going to be two players who could win the 1991 Masters. Watson fell away with 73 to finish in a four-way tie for third and so it was left to Europeans Woosnam and Olazábal to battle it out over the closing holes.

Olazábal, also hungry for his first major championship, had battled his way into contention as he walked up the 18th. Tied for the tournament lead, with Woosnam waiting back on the final tee, the Spaniard's drive found the nearer of the two bunkers on the left of the par-4 18th. Despite this, he knew a simple par would put enormous pressure on his fellow European and was prepared to risk everything to make the green. Using his 7-iron, he then went from fairway bunker to greenside bunker. Splashing out to around ten feet, he left himself a difficult putt just to save his par. When that slipped past the hole for bogey, Olazábal had missed his chance, leaving Woosnam needing just a par to win his first major title.

However, for someone like Woosnam, whose natural shot is a right-to-left draw, the final hole at Augusta National is not ideal. A left-to-right dog-leg, moving up a steep hill towards a well-protected green, this deceptively difficult hole suddenly became the cause of much discussion between Woosnam and his long-time caddie, Phil Mobley. Asking the yardage to Olazábal's bunker, Woosnam then asked his surprised caddie, 'How far is it to carry those bunkers?' After a second's calculation, the answer came back from 'Wobbly', 'It's 268 yards to get over the lot.' Then, in what had looked an act of sheer madness, Woosnam decided to override his calculated game plan with some unscientific brute force.

> I know that when I hit it as hard as I can, the ball will either go straight or draw. It's natural to my swing. So when I saw Ollie [up ahead] in the bunker and then my playing partner Tom Watson in the trees on the right, I decided to go as far left as I could. There's nothing over there except the members' practice area and the only possible problem would be if a spectator walked off with my ball.

Left with little more than a short-iron second if his plan did come off, Woosnam felt this was a risk worth taking. He calculated that with the members' practice ground considered in-bounds and crowded with thousands of eager spectators, the only real danger would be the possibility of the ball ending up in a bare lie or footprint. Looking back it was a brilliant piece of strategy. But to pull it off you need to be able to carry the ball almost 300 yards.

Back on the tee, Woosnam launched himself at the ball. Holding nothing back it seemed for a moment to be heading into the same trap as Olazábal only moments earlier. But even the experienced on-course marshals looked somewhat surprised as the drive pitched into the crowd behind them. With everything just a little chaotic they quickly moved into the area where the ball had landed. Unaware of the mayhem which his tee-shot had caused, Woosnam became increasingly frustrated at the delay in clearing a space through which he could play his second.

'They had no idea what they were doing,' he said about the Augusta National marshals. 'I had to join in, shout at people, which was the last thing I wanted to do in that situation.'

Despite the delay, Woosnam could not have been more pleased when he came to play his second. The ground where the ball had come to rest was well-trampled but the lie itself was fine – he would at least have a shot to the green. After some frantic reorganisation, the marshals finally managed to carve a thin channel through the crowd into which an increasingly tense Woosnam could play his approach. Left with no more than a solid 8-iron to the flag, the lack of any discernible target was his last real problem.

'I couldn't see the green,' said Woosnam. 'I couldn't even see the stands. I had to aim at a particular tree on the tree-line 100 yards past the green.'

Describing the approach shot as one he could normally play 'with my eyes shut' Woosnam struck it well but came up short on the front fringe. With Olazábal looking on from the scorer's tent, he was then faced with a tricky decision.

> I think the key shot to the hole was my third. I could have chipped it, but I could have duffed it quite easily being so nervous. It was always going to be simpler to putt it so I went with the easy option. Even then I only managed to get within eight feet of the hole. Thankfully it worked out all right in the end.

With eight feet of tightly-mown green between Woosnam and the major championship he craved the pressure was now really on. Hitting the putt a little firmer to take out the break, no one was more relieved than him to see the ball rattle into the back of the hole. Absolutely delighted, the tigerish Welshman went down on one knee pumping the air with his fist in triumph as the Augusta crowd cheered their approval.

'Holing that final putt was the highlight of my golfing life. It was the sort of thing I used to dream about.'

For Woosnam, a level par round of 72 was enough to win the 1991 Masters and secure his place in golf history. For Olazábal the disappointment was obvious. Finishing one stroke adrift in second place, the record books reveal he would have to wait another three years before he would finally win a green jacket for himself. But at the time he was inconsolable, commenting afterwards, 'It was worse that it happened at Augusta, the number one course for me in the world. The skill that every player has can be seen at Augusta. It demands all the shots. Nothing is taken away from you. If you have skill and imagination you can show it at Augusta.'

What better testimony to Woosnam's achievement could there possibly be?